A SHORT HISTORY OF MEXICO

JOHN PATRICK McHENRY is an American who has lived in Mexico for over ten years, working as a free-lance artist, a bookseller, and manager of the Librería Británica. An infantry soldier in the Pacific and an Air Corps radioman in World War II, he received a bachelor of science degree from Northwestern University in 1949, lived for a year in Paris, painting and writing and traveling in Europe. Mr. McHenry has taught at the American Institute of Cultural Relations in Mexico City and now represents the American Book Company in Mexico.

A SHORT HISTORY
OF MEXICO

J. PATRICK McHENRY

Dolphin Books
Doubleday & Company, Inc.
Garden City, New York

ACKNOWLEDGMENTS

Several people have helped, with their suggestions and advice, to write certain chapters of this book. I am especially indebted to Mr. Crispin Tickell for his valuable comments on the first three chapters covering ancient Mexico and the conquest; to Miguel Díaz, who contributed information on Iturbide and the post-revolutionary period; and to Professor José Mireles Malpica for his kindness in checking the manuscript. And last but not least, to my wife, whose assistance and encouragement was constant throughout.

Revised Dolphin Books edition: 1970

TO MY MOTHER AND FATHER

TABLE OF CONTENTS

MAPS

1325(?)–1426 Tezozomoc, Ruler of Atzcapotzalco
1426–1472 Nezahualcoyotl, Ruler of Texcoco
1472–1481 Axayacatl, Emperor of the Aztecs
1481–1486 Tizoc, Emperor of the Aztecs
1486–1502 Ahuizotl, Emperor of the Aztecs
1502–1520 Moctezuma, Emperor of the Aztecs
1520–1522 Cuauhtémoc, Emperor of the Aztecs
1522–1526 Hernando Cortés, conquistador, Captain General of New Spain
1526–1535 *Juez de Residencia*
          1st *Audiencia* (Nuño de Guzmán)
          2nd *Audiencia*
1535–1821 A succession of 61 Spanish viceroys beginning with Don Antonio de Mendoza and ending with Juan O'Donojú, two of the best being Bucareli (1771–79) and the Conde de Revilla Gigedo (1779–94).
1822–1823 Agustín de Iturbide, Emperor of Mexico
1824–1828 Gen. Guadalupe Victoria, President of Mexico
1829–1830 Gen. Vicente Guerrero, President of Mexico
1830–1832 Gen. Anastasio Bustamante, President of Mexico
1832–1833 Gen. Antonio López de Santa Anna, President-Elect. Gómez Farias, Acting President
1833–1836 Gen. Santa Anna, Military Dictator
1836–1840 Gen. Anastasio Bustamante, Military Dictator
1841–1844 Gen. Santa Anna, Military Dictator
1844–1846 Gen. Joaquin Herrera, Interim President
1846–1847 Gómez Farias, Acting President

1847–1848 Peña y Peña, Interim President
1848–1851 Gen. Joaquin Herrera, President-Elect
1851–1853 Gen. Mariano Ariste, President-Elect
1853–1855 Gen. Santa Anna, Military Dictator
1855–1856 Gen. Juan Alvarez, Military Dictator
1856–1858 Gen. Ignacio Comonfort, Military Dictator
1858–1860 Gen. Felix Zuloaga, Military Dictator (Conservative)
1858–1861 Benito Juárez, Constitutional President
1860–1861 Gen. Miguel Miramón, Military Dictator (Conservative)
1861–1862 Benito Juárez, Constitutional President
1862–1864 French military occupation
1864–1867 Archduke Maximilian of Austria, Emperor of Mexico
1867–1872 Benito Juárez, President-Elect
1872–1876 Lerdo de Tejada, President-Elect
1877–1880 Gen. Porfirio Díaz, President-Elect
1880–1884 Gen. Manuel González, President-Elect
1884–1911 Gen. Porfirio Díaz, "elected" President seven times. He ruled Mexico as a military dictator.
1911–1913 Francisco Indalecio Madero, President-Elect
1913–1914 Gen. Victoriano Huerta, Military Dictator
1914–1914 Gen. Venustiano Carranza, Military Dictator
1914–1915 Gen. Pancho Villa, Political arbiter
1916–1920 Gen. Venustiano Carranza, Dictator
1920–1924 Gen. Alvaro Obregón, President
1924–1928 Gen. Plutarco Elías Calles, President
1928–1929 Portes Gil, Interim President
1929–1932 Ortiz Rubio, President
1932–1934 Abelardo Rodríguez, Interim President
1934–1940 Lázaro Cárdenas, President
1940–1946 Avila Camacho, President
1946–1952 Miguel Alemán, President
1952–1958 Ruíz Cortines, President
1958–1964 Lopez Mateos, President
1964–1970 Diaz Ordaz, President

A SHORT GLOSSARY

CACIQUE—Originally an Indian word meaning the Indian chief of a village, it is now used by Mexican journalists to mean political bosses in rural areas who manipulate businesses for their own personal profit.

CAMPESINO—An agrarian; a country person.

CREOLE—The Spanish translation is *criollo*, which in Mexico means a Mexican of pure Spanish blood.

EJIDOS—In colonial times these were communal lands for threshing and grazing. Since the revolution this word has meant tracts of land given by the government to small farmers.

EJIDARIOS—Farmers who work the *ejidos*.

GACHUPINES—Derogatory nickname for Spaniards living in Mexico.

HACENDADO—The owner of a hacienda.

HACIENDA—Stems from the verb *hacer*, to make. They were places where refined sugar was made from sugar cane or pure metals were extracted from ores (gold and silver). Formerly they provided work for an entire Mexican village; today they are massive, moss-covered ruins, relics of past times.

MULATTO—A person with part Negro and part Spanish blood.

PENINSULARES—Spaniards.

PULQUE—A milky, intoxicating drink made from the sap of the maguey plant.

TAMANES—Indians who were professional carriers. In Pre-Columbian times they did the work of horses.

ZAMBOS—A person with part Negro and part Indian blood.

ZÓCALO—The principal plaza of a city or town where usually the main cathedral and municipal buildings are located.

A SHORT HISTORY OF MEXICO

CHAPTER ONE

10,000 B.C.–A.D. 1518

When Christopher Columbus first sighted land in the Caribbean, he was certain he had reached the East Indies. It was only logical then that the golden-skinned natives he found on the islands should be called "Indians." His logic was unquestionably sound, but his calculations were a whole hemisphere off. By the time he realized the colossal magnitude of his error, the name for natives in America had been irrevocably fixed and the misnomer "Indian" comes down to us as an example of how logic can lead to absurdities.

What Columbus discovered, of course, were islands of America where flourished a culture whose principal center was as large (and as beautiful) as Venice, whose philosophy and mathematics contained some precepts as profound as those of the Greeks, and whose knowledge of astronomy was as accurate as that of European scientists. It is not likely that members of this culture would admit that Columbus had "discovered" anything. How their culture began and grew, what their heritage was, what ancestry they had, or how, indeed, man came to be in America at all, is not known for certain, since no written history (as we understand history) of pre-Columbian cultures in America exists.

The history that does exist has been logically re-created from crumbling pyramids, fading murals, broken pots, and strange stone carvings. *La Historia Universal de las Cosas de Nueva España* (*The Universal History of the Things of New Spain*), a work by a sixteenth-century Spanish monk named Father Bernardino de Sahagún, is the most important record we have concerning ancient Mexico, but it is so full of fantastic myths and legends that one needs intuition as well as science to understand it. For nearly three centuries this invaluable work gathered dust in obscure places until, early in the nineteenth century, an Englishman named Lord Kingsborough brought it to light in propounding his theory that Mexico, like Egypt, had been a distant outpost of the long-sunk continent Atlantis. Though his theory caused no great stir in scientific circles, the mass of material he gathered to support it was eagerly received by young men pioneering in a new branch of science called archaeology. Since then, archaeologists, geologists, and ethnologists, picking over the ruins of ancient Indian cities, have produced a myriad of artifacts on which the pre-Columbian history of Mexico has been constructed. In general their findings corroborate or throw new light on the writings of that early Spanish monk.

The remarks in this chapter are a kind of synthesis of the latest theories accepted by archaeologists and historians. Although presented in a matter-of-fact way, the story told here is far from certain and is liable to change with new discoveries by archaeologists. Their finds are incomparably more valuable than theories, for theories derive from logic, and logic, as we have seen in the case of Columbus, can lead to hopeless confusion.

In 10,000 B.C. that part of the North American continent now known as Mexico was covered with dense jungles in the lowlands, forests and patches of grassy plains in the highlands, and, in the north, deserts. The central plateau was humid and rich in vegetation and was visited frequently by groups of long-haired mammoths seeking succulent plants. From the trees they were scolded by flocks of colorful parrots. On the windy plains grazed herds of large bison, and groups of bounding antelope were common. There were also elephants. In damp places giant armadillos scratched for food. In dry places roamed the haughty camel. A species of horse, now extinct, ran wild in the highlands. And the rarest sight of all was man.

For over a century it had been suspected that man had inhabited Mexico as early as 10,000 B.C., but it wasn't until 1945 that this was decisively proved. Workmen digging foundations for a hospital in Tepexpan, a tiny village on the road to Pachuca outside Mexico City, unearthed the remains of a giant-sized mammoth near whose skull was found a crudely made spearhead. The eminent geologist and archaeologist called in to appraise the discovery found (with more digging) a few yards away and in the same earth stratum—calculated at 8000–10,000 B.C. by carbon tests—a human skeleton. A careful examination of his skull revealed that he was not a Neanderthal or Java man, as paleontologists had hoped, but a Homo sapiens. Frederick Peterson states, "Alive, in modern clothes, and walking about the streets of Mexico City, he would excite no comment whatsoever."

His presence in Mexico can be explained by conjecture only. Northern Asiatic tribes, it is said, pursued herds of mammoths across the ice-covered Bering Strait and, lured by the abundance of game on this continent, continued down the west coast to Mexico. Very little is known about the period between 10,000 and 1200 B.C. except that man was a hunter using a stonehead spear. It can be presumed, however, that a genius appeared sometime around 1500 B.C., someone who observed that seeds falling on the earth produced three months later a new growth of corn. The importance of that observation cannot be too strongly emphasized. Because of it man in Mexico changed from a hunter to a farmer—from a destroyer to a creator. And the seeds of civilization took root.

Gradually primitive man gave up his hazardous occupation of hunting and gave more attention to the soil. Tricks were learned. Fertilizers were discovered, taller stalks were developed, storage bins were constructed, and cooking corn became a skill. Man, for the first time, had leisure. He had time for making pottery and weaving cloth. Communities formed, in which languages developed, styles in art evolved, and religious rites became elaborate ceremonies. On the gulf coast were the Olmecs, on the peninsula of Yucatán were the Mayas, in the middle country were the Zapotecs, and on the central plateau were the Nahuas. In the valley of Mexico, on the southeast shore of a long irregular lake (now greatly reduced) three separate clusters of reed huts appeared—Arbolillo, Tlatilco, and Zacatenco.

By 1000 B.C. the docile farming people of these villages showed signs of influence from a more advanced and vigorous culture, probably the Olmecs living in what is now the tropical state of Tabasco. The Olmecs were then called the "magicians" because of their use of drugs (derived from certain mushrooms and cacti) to produce hallucinations, their ritualistic worship of the jaguar—a fierce leopardlike beast of North and South America—and their "seers" who could forecast the weather. Sculpture in stone and terra cotta became a primary art. The Olmecs in Tabasco produced some extraordinarily fine works in stone of Buddha-like figures and bearded athletes shown at their exercise. The "magicians" in the valley of Mexico turned out exquisite figurines in terra cotta—nude maidens with hourglass figures wearing stand-out skirts that conceal nothing but their navels. Other works of theirs show an unhealthy interest in the abnormal—hunchbacks, dwarfs, and monsters.

650–150 B.C.

Within the last century archaeologists have ascribed various names to this cultural period—the Upper Preclassic, the Late Middle Culture, the Formative Period, and, most recently, the First Architects and Priests. Villages built in this period show for the first time a definite plan. Each had a stone pyramid before which was a large plaza surrounded by an orderly placement of reed huts. Cuicuilco, Atzcapotzalco, Cerro de la Estrella (Hill of the Star), and Teotihuacán—to mention only those in the valley of Mexico—were founded in this period. The pyramid suggests that religious ceremonies had already evolved into pageants presided over by a hierarchy of priests. Agriculture had probably by then been well developed, particularly in the south where farms produced enough to feed the large population of Monte Albán. The sun and moon were deified and their powers were invoked whenever an excess of rain or sun threatened to ruin the crops. There was also a god of the wind, of war, of the underworld, of fertility, and of death. In fact, any natural catastrophe such as an earthquake or a volcanic eruption was considered retribution for not having been more attentive to the gods. Religion was, therefore, materialistic and praying was essentially bartering with the gods for favors. The sculptured relief of this period looks grotesque, as though its creators were so tortured with fears and anxiety that they were, it seems, blind to the beauties of nature.

150 B.C.–A.D. 800 or 900

This period is the golden age of pre-Columbian Mexico. Archaeologists can trace its complete cycle and have detected four distinct stages of its development: the Transitional, the Classic, the Baroque, and the Terminal. Perhaps the highest form of an Indian civilization in Mexico was reached during the Classic and Baroque stages. Ruins of the magnificent cities built then (widely separated by great distances)— Monte Albán, Teotihuacán, Tajin, Palenque, Xochicalco, and Yaxchilan—reflect a highly organized society and a cultural level comparable to the Etruscans. Their grandeur is overwhelming. In most cases, whole mountaintops have been leveled off into terraces, one rising above another, joined by broad stairs. The sites of Monte Albán and Xochicalco seem to have been chosen for their commanding view of the surrounding country. Each city, primarily a ceremonial center, had one especially ornate and imposing pyramid situated majestically on the highest terrace; some had a ball court and most had a device for observing the movements of the stars and planets. All outlying fields must have been under cultivation, otherwise the large urban population could not have been fed. Government and religion were one. The high priests dominated society and were undoubtedly the inspired men who sparked cultural advancement. Inexplicably these great cities were abandoned during the eighth century. Within fifty years their great market places, once teeming with traffic, were deserted, and rank growth of the jungle inched forward to swallow them up eventually. No one knows the reason for this change. Perhaps there was a revolution against theocratic oppression, or an invasion by northern barbarians.

Another mystery which, until recently, has been undeserv-

ingly ignored is that surrounding the making of stone carvings
in America before A.D. 900. The knowledge of using metal
for tools was not known in Mexico before A.D. 950 or there-
abouts. How, then, were the hard stones of Xochicalco, Teotihuacán, and Monte Albán carved with such delicate accuracy? One theory recently put forward states that those
ancient people (not only in Mexico but in Egypt and Peru)
cultivated a flower which when crushed emitted a potent
juice capable, under special conditions, of "melting" stone.
When the stone was the consistency of putty, they drew on
it with wooden sticks. The theory would easily be proved if
such a flower were to be found today, but unfortunately
searches for it have not been, so far, successful. Nevertheless,
as a theory it is no less acceptable than the more logical one
that chisels were made of stone. Anyone who has tried pound-
ing stone on stone knows it is virtually impossible to make a
clean straight line.

A.D. 900

Of all the many legends contained in the books of Father
Sahagún none is more beautiful than that of Quetzalcoatl—
the plumed serpent—*quetzal* meaning "feathers" or "feathery"
and *coatl* meaning "snake." That two such extreme opposites
as a gorgeously feathered creature of the air and a snake could
be brought together within one name implies that the idea
of transcendentalism was not unknown in pre-Columbian
Mexico. The word "Quetzalcoatl" probably began as a symbol
for an elated state of consciousness and was later bestowed
like a title on any individual who evinced in his deportment
signs of having permanently attained that state (like a saint
or a sage). One such man, says Frederick Peterson, lived in
the tenth century when cultures were in upheaval, cities were
being abandoned, and nomad tribes from the north invaded
Teotihuacán.

According to the Toltec calendar, he was born on Ce Acatl
(represented by one reed on the calendar stone), probably in
947. His father, Mixcoatl, was the ruling chief of the Toltecs
when his jealous brother Ihuitmal usurped tribal leadership

by murdering him. His mother, Chimalma, to escape assassination by her brother-in-law, fled to Tepoztlán, where she died in childbirth. Before expiring, however, she confessed that the child had been divinely conceived when she swallowed a piece of blue-green jade. The boy, when born, was called Ce Acatl Topitzin, meaning "Our Prince Born on Ce Acatl."

His grandparents watched over him as a child and sent him to the religious school at Xochicalco, where he astonished the faculty with his great wisdom and piety. Despite his youth, the high priests conferred upon him the highest title in the land: Quetzalcoatl. When a young man, he went to the land of his parents, found the remains of his murdered father, and carried them to Tula where he had them buried, in defiance of his uncle, Ihuitmal, with ceremonies befitting a dead king. Later, the Toltec sense of justice was satisfied when he pushed his uncle into a sacrificial fire. So respected was he for this act, the Toltecs proclaimed him their new leader.

His subjects were, by all accounts, a barbarous lot—unskilled, unmannered, and devoted to their god of darkness, Texcatlipoca. Quetzalcoatl began his reign by importing Nonoalcos (deaf and dumb people), descendants of the highly refined people of Teotihuacán. They worked as his artisans and architects and under his tutelage produced the distinctive designs for which Tula is noted—serpent columns, square pillars ornamented with friezes, giant-sized statues of warriors which were probably temple columns. He also drastically changed religious beliefs by forbidding human sacrifice.

The practice of sacrifice was carried on by most nations of antiquity. It was based on the very sound reasoning that to get, one must give, or at least give up. Usually choice animals or the best crops were burned on sacrificial altars to protect the fields from drought or deluge. To explain why human sacrifice should have been practiced in Mexico would require a long disquisition on the psychology of primitive man (who was not a carefree nature lover as the romantics would have him, but was morbidly fatalistic and ridden with fears). But certainly a longer disquisition on the psychology of modern man would be required to explain to a present-day primitive living in the jungles of Chiapas why the atomic bomb was dropped on Hiroshima killing tens of thousands instantly and destroying an entire city. Stated in its simplest terms, both resulted from that diabolical scourge of mankind: war.

War in ancient Mexico was fought primarily to obtain victims for blood-lusting gods. After an all-day battle few if any slain warriors were left on the field, since the object of the skirmish was not to kill but to capture. Each side would seize as many of the enemy as they could and haul them back to their village where they would be imprisoned until the day of sacrifice. On that day, they were painted blue, taken to the top of a *teocalli* (sacrificial pyramid), and there stretched across a stone altar. A priest with long, trailing hair matted with gore, wearing a bizarre costume, and wielding a blunt, obsidian knife, would rip open the victim's chest, plunge his hand into the opening, and wrench out the heart which, still warm and pulsing, was tossed into a stone urn on the altar.

Not all victims, however, were prisoners of war. In the works of Father Sahagún there is an account of one special ceremony at which a young man of exceptional ability in warfare would actually volunteer himself to be a victim. After that he was treated with reverence, was given the choicest food, the most beautiful virgins for wives, and, after the sacrifice, was worshiped as a god.

When, as high priest of the Toltecs, Quetzalcoatl allowed only flowers, snakes, and small birds to be sacrificed on his altars, a cry of heresy went up from the gore-begrimed priests who were by his interdict put out of business; but Quetzalcoatl cast a spell over the people that rendered them deaf to the angry protests. He then went on to abolish war altogether and turned warriors into fabulously successful farmers capable of growing cotton in different colors! Toltec metalwork, jade carvings, pottery, and weaving were the finest produced in Mexico at that time.

The outraged priests summoned their ancient god, Texcatlipoca, to aid them in overthrowing Quetzalcoatl. Texcatlipoca, being evil, was Quetzalcoatl's opposite but was as necessary to him as black is to white, down is to up, and bad is to good. Knowledge of one meant inevitably knowledge of the other, and the two gods were considered inseparable.

When conjured up, Texcatlipoca with two evil colleagues

crept into the darkened sanctuary of Quetzalcoatl and there brought forth a new invention: the mirror. Quetzalcoatl, on seeing himself, was badly frightened and cried, "If my subjects see me they will run away." Whereupon the two minor gods obliged him by covering him with red paint, feathers, and a ridiculous mask. They then concocted a delicious stew of corn, beans, and tomatoes and produced a tempting beverage of intoxicating pulque mixed with honey. The holy man ate large helpings of the stew but declined the beverage, as he distrusted its effect. Texcatlipoca begged him to sample it with his little finger; he did so and promptly sampled it with four. Soon he was singing and drinking, and a beautiful dancing girl was brought in to join the hilarity. The next morning when he awoke, the room was empty except for the girl asleep beside him. To his horror he realized he had drunk himself into a stupor and had broken his priestly vow of chastity.

Wailing and tearing his hair, he wandered through the forest to Cholula (outside Puebla) where he lived in self-imposed exile for twenty years. He then went to Coatzacoalcos, taking with him four faithful disciples to whom he imparted all his knowledge. At the end of the tenth century he sailed off in a craft of his own design made of intertwined serpents and feathers. To his group of weeping disciples he promised to return from the land of the rising sun on Ce Acatl of some future time cycle. He disappeared below the eastern horizon.

The anticlimax to this dramatic parting is that he landed in Yucatán, only a few hundred miles away. There he was called Kulkulcan. The architecture of Chichén Itzá shows unmistakable traces of his influence; in fact, that great Mayan city is only a variation of the Toltec city of Tula. He finally died by climbing onto a self-made funeral pyre some thirty years later. According to legend, the flames consuming his body turned into doves that flew straight to the planet Venus.

It wasn't long before the butchering priests of Tula were back in business, but their sacrifices brought only disaster. A terrible drought drove hordes of people away and an invasion by the Huaxtecs scattered the rest. By 1200, Tula was completely deserted and was shrouded in dust and gloomy silence.

Out of the north came a wave of tribes called collectively the Chichimecs, who possessed a revolutionary weapon: the bow and arrow. Under the leadership of Xolotl (an unflattering name meaning monster) they conquered each town on or near the lake in the valley of Mexico and settled finally in the town of Tenayuca. Xolotl had many daughters for whom he found husbands by offering each, as a dowry, one of the towns he had conquered. In this way, towns in the valley became a kind of confederacy held together by bands of marriage to Xolotl's daughters.

Xolotl's son and grandson, Nopalzin and Tlolitzin, were not so assertive as he and allowed other towns to gain ascendancy over Tenayuca. The fourth ruler, Quinatzin, moved the Chichimec capital from Tenayuca to Texcoco and made Nahuatl the official language of the valley. His son, Ixtlilxochitl, when he came to power was murdered by Tezozomoc, ruler of the rival city of Atzcapotzalco. Thereafter the Chichimecs were never again a major power in the valley. Prince Nezahualcoyotl, son of the murdered Ixtlilxochitl, wandered disconsolately through the forests on the slopes of the two great volcanoes waiting for the tyrant Tezozomoc's downfall when he, the prince, would ascend the throne of Texcoco as its rightful king.

It was during the reign of Tezozomoc, who made Atzcapotzalco the most powerful town in the valley, that a nomad tribe of some one thousand strong, calling themselves Mexica-Aztecs, were given permission to settle on Chapultepec hill. They were thoroughgoing barbarians, eating uncooked meat, wearing skins, and living in caves; and their practice of skinning sacrificial victims and of performing dances while wearing the skin revolted the citizens of every town in the vicinity. When Coxcox, the king of Culhuacán, learned that his own daughter had been sacrificed and skinned at an Aztec ceremony, he sent his army to wipe out the entire tribe. Those Aztecs who escaped the king's wrath hid among the reeds in Lake Texcoco and later took refuge on a dank, snake-infested island a mile or so from shore. The island eventually became Tenochtitlán and, later still, Mexico City.

That is one version of the founding of Mexico City. Another version, and by far the more popular one, has it that the Aztecs were a wandering tribe searching for a sign spoken of by their prophets who had told them that where it appeared, there they should build their city. One morning in June 1325, while passing Lake Texcoco, they looked out over the shimmering waters and there on a small island was their sign: a giant eagle crouched on a prickly pear, his wings spread wide catching the rays of the morning sun and his beak holding a writhing snake. This sign has become the Mexican national emblem and can be seen on the Mexican national flag.

However that was, it is known that the Aztecs settled on the island where they later fought among themselves and split into two groups: Tenochtitlán on the south and Tlatelolco on the north. Old King Tezozomoc, fully aware of the barbarity of the Aztecs and of their potential danger as an enemy, appointed his own son and a nephew to rule over the island. These young rulers shaped the Aztecs into a formidable military power that fought and won many battles to keep towns in the valley subjugated to the will of Tezozomoc. At the same time the Aztecs displayed their talent for engineering by constructing across the lake of Texcoco magnificent broad causeways that connected their island to the mainland at three points.

When Tezozomoc died (he was reputed to have been 106 years old) his city of Atzcapotzalco was attacked by the Aztecs led by its ruler, Itzcoatl, who solicited the aid of Tlacopan (now Tacuba) and Texcoco ruled by Nezahualcoyotl. Their combined armies achieved victory in 1428, whereupon Itzcoatl formed a triple alliance between Tenochtitlán, Tlacopan, and Texcoco, making the Aztec city a hegemonic state whose powers would spread and would eventually dominate the major part of Mexico. In this alliance, the Aztecs were the army, Tlacopan was the quartermaster corps, and Texcoco was the lawmaker.

Between 1428 and 1502 the Aztecs were ruled by five different kings, each of whom drove his armies beyond the frontiers set by his predecessor until the Aztec empire (in reality not as much an empire as a confederation of towns, all paying heavy taxes to Tenochtitlán) stretched from the gulf coast to the Pacific and down into what is now Guatemala in the south. Its northern boundary was a diagonal line across the country from the Pánuco River to the Río Balsas.

By the beginning of the sixteenth century there were very few animals in pre-Columbian Mexico—no horses or mules, no sheep or goats, or even chickens. Men called *tamanes* did the work of horses, moving tremendous weights incredible distances without the aid of wheels or pulleys, the idea of which never entered their heads. Today we can hardly imagine how mere humans, however strong, could haul the large Aztec calendar stone from a quarry in Puebla to Tenochtitlán.

As there were no sheep, all clothes were made out of rough, crudely woven cotton, even the most gorgeous robes of the emperor. As there were no cows, goats or chickens, the Indian's diet was perniciously low in proteins. His meals consisted mainly of corn and beans, both carbohydrates, to which was added, on very rare occasions, fowl or fish. (Mexico's lower classes live on practically the same diet even today.) Moctezuma had fish from the ocean brought to him daily by runners. But God's very special gift to Mexico was the maguey plant, whose long, fleshy leaves, edged with tiny spikes, taper to a hard point as sharp as the tip of a bull's horns. The maguey provided the Indians with parchment, sewing needles, thread and twine; and the core of the plant, where its sap collected, provided honey, sugar, vinegar, and, most important of all, the milky-white beverage pulque. Pulque, the Mexican beer, is rich in proteins and is slightly intoxicating; hence the Indians drank it (and still drink it) greedily and often to excess. Perhaps their craving for proteins drove them to cannibalism—the Aztecs used to eat the arms and legs of their sacrificial victims—and to the practice of fattening up their hairless, elephant-hided dogs for eating at special repasts.

Aztec society was presided over by the emperor's retinue of lords and nobles, most of whom had risen to their high station through meritorious deeds in war; their titles, however, were not hereditary. They owned lands that were worked by serfs and the food produced thereon went to feed the emperor and his court of priests and artisans. The scraps remaining were given to the workers in the field. Priests stood below warriors on the social scale, and artisans—featherworkers, stone carvers, painters, and weavers—stood slightly below the priests. But warriors, priests, and artists were collectively the upper classes.

The island capital, Tenochtitlán, was like something out of *The Arabian Nights*. A tall *teocalli* at the center of the capital rose majestically over immense imperial palaces of stone and colored plaster. Before the pyramid was an enormous well-paved square used daily as a market place, but on feast days the scene of ceremonial dancing and singing. Three broad avenues cut through the city from the main square—to the south, to the north, and to the west—and led out onto massive causeways that ran like dikes across the lake. Many canals crisscrossed the city, through which flowed a lively traffic of canoes made from hewn-out tree trunks and rafts or barges laden with produce and flowers to be sold at the market place. Gardens were cultivated and many houses had aviaries filled with bright-colored *guacamayos* (macaws) or *clarins* (a tropical thrush). Poorer people lived on the rim of the island in bamboo huts raised on stilts because heavy rains often flooded the city.

In the fifteenth century the most amazing man in Mexico was Nezahualcoyotl: educator, architect, religious philosopher, writer of quite remarkable poetry, and the illustrious king of Texcoco. All his knowledge and skill he put into a temple or monument to "An Unknown God," the ruins of which are still to be seen in Texcoco. His poetry, preserved in *Codices*, astounds scholars by the profundity of thought and feeling it contains. And his disciples wrote poetry of equally high order.

In 1502 the tyrant king of the Aztecs, Ahuizotl, died. (Aztec armies, under his leadership, had more than doubled the size of the empire.) At the council of lords it was decided that a young man of twenty-two, a student of theology and a son of a former king (Axayacatl 1469–81), would be the next Aztec monarch. His name was Moctezuma Xocoyotzin II, better known as simply Moctezuma. Slender and well proportioned, he was lighter skinned than his golden brown countrymen, his shiny black hair hung to his shoulders (as was the custom with men), and he wore a sparse beard. Despite his life of ease as a youth, as an emperor he displayed courage and great physical endurance in leading Aztec armies to forty-three victories over towns in the south. He was preparing an assault on Tehuantepec when runners brought him news that strange vessels had been sighted off the east coast of Yucatán. He hastened back to his capital to confer with astronomers. That was in 1518. He was told that Ce Acatl, the date of Quetzalcoatl's promised return from the east, was completing its fifty-two-year time cycle and would fall due in March of the following year.

We may well marvel at the ingenious systems for recording time devised by cultures in ancient Mexico. As early as 1000 B.C. the Olmecs had discovered that it takes the earth 365 days to go around the sun. After that observation, no culture was without a calendar, and some (the Mayan, for instance) were as accurate as our own Gregorian calendar. Thus it was possible for Moctezuma to know almost to the day when to expect fulfillment of a prophecy made by Quetzalcoatl five centuries earlier. Much credit for their astronomical brilliance must be given to their system of mathematics which contained the concept of "zero." At first "zero" may not sound like much, but upon reflection it will be seen that it, in fact, precedes all quantity, all series. It represents an absolute "nothing" which is the beginning of everything and is therefore the source of all creative thinking. Europe was a thousand years behind Mexico in grasping this idea.

Perhaps Moctezuma's studies in theology caused him to take counsel with priests and his own intuitive feelings. He was a man of moods and often abandoned himself to melancholia. In the preceding years many strange phenomena had given him good cause to brood. In 1509, for instance, the lake of Texcoco was, for no apparent reason, rocked violently, causing temples and houses in the city to be swamped and flooded. In 1511 a temple atop a pyramid caught fire and burned for days despite frantic efforts to extinguish the flames. And in 1515 various comets were seen in the sky. One, extraordinarily bright and triangular in shape, hung in the eastern sky for days on end. Soothsayers saw these as portentous signs foretelling the downfall of the Aztec empire. Their remarks irritated Moctezuma, and once, in a fit of depression, he gave orders to have several of them sacrificed.

Moctezuma ruled an empire larger than any monarch before him. His army was invincible. His lords and nobles daily professed their loyalty. His subjects prostrated themselves in obeisance whenever he passed through the streets. His treasury was full, food was plentiful, and tribute poured in from all his provinces. Still he felt instinctively the fatal blow to come, but how it would come or from where, he had no way of knowing.

CHAPTER TWO

1519–1521

On April 21, Good Friday of 1519, a band of Spanish soldiers tugged their longboats up a wind-swept barren beach which their commander, in honor of the day, christened Veracruz. He was Hernando Cortés, swordsman, horseman, explorer, a Christian from Catholic Spain, statesman, orator, and historian—in short, a conquistador par excellence. Red-bearded, broad-shouldered, barrel-chested, a medium-sized, powerfully built man about thirty-three or thirty-four years old, he was sent by the governor of Cuba, a man named Velázquez, to explore the gulf coast and trade where possible with the natives.

His entire company of 555 men and 16 horses disembarked from his modest fleet of 10 galleons and encamped on the sand dunes behind the beach. Before long, however, the heat, the pestering insects, the dearth of water, and above all the racking sickness *"el vómito"* (probably malaria) which terribly weakened most men and caused the death of thirty, made them all clamorous to leave—either to march farther inland or to take to their boats.

Moctezuma, informed by runners of these odd creatures from the sea, plied his gods with offerings and prayers for some sign, some indication as to how he should treat them. Were they agents of Quetzalcoatl and was their leader Quetzalcoatl himself? Or were they mere mortals come to destroy his empire? Since his gods answered with stony silence, he decided to bribe the strangers into leaving. He sent down to the coast a train of gift-ladened *tamanes* (carriers)

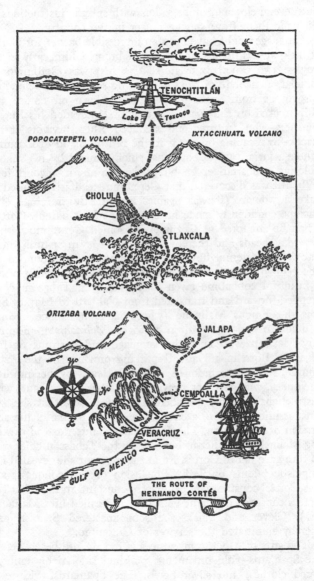

THE ROUTE OF
HERNANDO CORTÉS

and several eloquent ambassadors with specific instructions to dissuade them from staying longer in the country.

Language might have been an impossible barrier for Cortés if luck, always on his side, had not brought him early in his voyage two expert translators. The first was Geronimo de Aguilar, an acolyte of the Church who seven years before, on his voyage from Spain to Cuba, was blown off course and shipwrecked on the coast of Yucatán. He evaded his Mayan pursuers—who captured and sacrificed other survivors of the wreck—by escaping on a raft to the nearby island of Cozumel where a jovial cacique, or tribal chief, amused by his strange coloring and stranger babblings, kept him for a court fool. When it was discovered that Geronimo steadfastly refused to take a woman (it was against his priestly training), the cacique confidently made him overseer of his harem. Cortés, when he anchored at Cozumel, ransomed Geronimo with a few glass beads and thereby acquired a Mayan-Spanish translator. At Veracruz, however, Geronimo was confounded by the Nahuatl language spoken there. To the amazement of all, a beautiful concubine given to Cortés by a Tabascan chief stepped forward and translated from Nahuatl to Mayan. She was the famous Malinche (whose name has since become a derogatory slang word in Mexico: *Malinchista*, meaning any Mexican who apes the language and customs of foreigners). Born in a Nahuatl-speaking province of the Aztec empire, she was abandoned at ten or eleven by her mother, the queen, who gave her away to some Mayan merchants with instructions that she be killed. The queen felt that she was thus assuring her son, a child by a second husband, the succession of her throne. The Mayan merchants, instead of killing Malinche, sold her in bondage to the Tabascan chief who in turn gave her to Cortés. From the moment she revealed her linguistic talents until the conclusion of the conquest, she was Cortés' constant companion (so constant, in fact, that the Aztecs confused his name with hers and called him Malinche too). Clever and quick, she soon mastered Spanish and thereby eliminated the services of Geronimo.

The gifts of Moctezuma were laid out on the beach before the Spaniards—gold ornaments, polished jade, richly embroidered clothes, and silver bowls. The Spaniards, with eyes popping, saw that their wildest dreams were, in fact, realities. Here was tangible proof of Mexico's wealth. Cortés, after hearing the entire message of the Aztec ambassadors, calmly replied that he could not possibly leave Mexico without first visiting their great emperor in Tenochtitlán. The ambassadors, outraged by his refusal to take their advice, sternly lectured him, but when he showed no inclination to listen, they left, angrily hinting that an Aztec army would, at any moment, swoop down on them and take them captive.

Since there were dissensions in the Spanish camp—some officers longed for the peaceful, lazy life of their plantations in Cuba—Cortés ordered the ships to be stripped and sunk. Only one was spared which was used to carry a trusted envoy back to Spain to petition King Charles V for a royal decree granting Cortés the right to conquer and to colonize Mexico. By so doing, Cortés was defying the authority of Velázquez, governor of Cuba, and was therefore a mutineer.

Bernal Díaz, one of the soldiers with Cortés, and author of the classic account of the conquest, recalled the speech of Cortés after sinking the ships. "With the help of our Lord Jesus Christ," he wrote, "we must conquer in all battles and encounters . . . for if we were anywhere defeated, which pray God would not happen, we could not raise our heads again, as we were so few in numbers, and could not look to help or assistance, but that which came from God, for we no longer possessed ships in which to return to Cuba, but must rely on our own good swords and stout hearts."

Stout hearts indeed!

AUGUST 1519

They fought their first full-scale battle against Tlaxcala, a small kingdom lying east of the twin volcanoes: Ixtaccihuatl and Popocatepetl. The Tlaxcalans were a rugged, mountain people, one of the three tribes still unconquered by their powerful neighbor, the Aztecs, causing the Aztecs (who had besieged them time and time again) great embarrassment and annoyance. The chief Tlaxcalan cacique, concluding that Cortés was marching to Mexico to aid his archenemy the

Aztecs, ordered his army to fall on the Spaniards and destroy them. The hapless Tlaxcalan army was torn up by Spanish cannons, hacked by Spanish infantry, and trampled by Spanish cavalry. Still they pressed on and might have won by sheer numbers alone (they outnumbered the Spaniards 50 to 1) had not one of their top generals, to show his spite for a rival general (with whom he quarreled bitterly), withdrawn his troops—over half the army. The remaining Tlaxcalans were soon routed and Cortés marched triumphantly into the Tlaxcalan capital, not, however, as a chest-thumping hero but rather as a shrewd diplomat offering amnesty to all who would accept the Catholic faith and pledge allegiance to Spain. Such leniency among Indian tribes was unheard of. The Tlaxcalans dutifully paid homage to the victors and swore to support them if ever they fought the Aztecs. The alliance then forged was perhaps the biggest single factor in defeating the Aztecs.

OCTOBER 1519

Against the advice of their Tlaxcalan friends, they marched some twenty miles south to Cholula, the holy city visited centuries before by the great teacher and prophet Quetzalcoatl. Since it was a religious center for thousands of pilgrims from all over Mexico, Cholula was rife with spies and agitators. Three days after their arrival, Malinche, in conversations with the wives of Cholulan caciques, discovered a plot already afoot to slaughter the Spaniards as they left the city. Cortés arrested several people implicated and, after questioning them closely, satisfied himself that Malinche's fears were indeed well founded. He immediately announced to the Cholulans he would leave with his army the following morning but only on condition that two thousand *tamanes* be supplied to help with the ever-growing load of baggage. The Cholulans, unaware that Cortés knew of their planned treachery, feigned disappointment but complied with his request, supplying a thousand more *tamanes* than was asked for. Then in the gray, murky light of dawn when the main square was crowded with Cholulans, Cortés, instead of leaving, ordered his musketeers to open fire. His cavalry and infantry followed up the volley by charging into the howling, screaming mass. Those Cholulans who fled to the exits were blown back by exploding cannons which Cortés had posted there the night before. In two hours three thousand Cholulans were slain, and in two days the entire town was razed. This was the massacre of Cholula.

Moctezuma, who was said to have been the author of the Cholulan plot to murder the Spaniards, now felt compelled to invite Cortés to his capital. If he wasn't Quetzalcoatl, he was at least a man aided and abetted by some supernatural powers. He sent guides to conduct the Spanish general around the volcano Ixtaccihuatl, but Cortés, suspicious of an ambush, chose to travel on a rough, seldom-used trail leading between the volcanoes. At the top of the pass several of his more spirited soldiers scaled the snow-capped peak of Popocatepetl just for an extra thrill.

NOVEMBER 1519

Swarms of inquisitive Indians flocked around them, impeding their progress as they moved across the valley of Mexico. On November 12 they entered the great causeway stretching from Coyoacán to the heart of Tenochtitlán. The view of this magnificent city rising out of the water, with its gardens and gushing fountains, and its fine handsome buildings decorated with stone carvings and bright paints, seemed to them a dream. Moctezuma—borne on a canopied litter and attended by a retinue of lords and nobles all with eyes reverently downcast—came forward to greet them. Their home, he said, would be the palace of his father, Axayacatl, facing his own on the main square. In modern Mexico the building Monte de Piedad stands where Axayacatl's palace then stood, and the National Palace together with the old university now marks the site of Moctezuma's palace. That Axayacatl's palace could easily house the entire Spanish army plus several thousand Tlaxcalan warriors gives some idea of its gigantic size.

During the following week, Moctezuma proved a superb

host, taking the army on sight-seeing tours of the city and feasting them lavishly at state banquets where, with charm and courtesy, he asked many questions concerning Spain, the Catholic Church, and the royal families of Europe. The monarch's munificence, however, failed to impress Cortés, who was beginning to regret having ever brought his tiny army to the heart of Mexico.

Clearly Moctezuma's show of kindness and respect was based on the illusion that Cortés was Quetzalcoatl and not, as Cortés would have liked, on the military superiority of the Spaniards. One inadvertent wrong step could shatter the illusion and bring chaos upon their heads. Even cannons and cavalry would be no match against a city of three hundred thousand inhabitants. Musing thus over his predicament he concocted a plan as bold as any to be found in the annals of history.

Accompanied by six of his bravest and coolest officers, he called upon Moctezuma in his royal chamber and, when the room had been cleared of all except pages and attendants, announced that Moctezuma was under arrest. The Indian prince was thunderstruck. The charge, claimed Cortés, was that of ordering a coastal tribe to attack the Spanish colony at Veracruz, thus causing the death of several soldiers who died in the ensuing battle. The sentence was confinement to the Spanish quarters. When Moctezuma protested his innocence, an officer whipped out his sword and threatened to kill him on the spot. What thoughts must have raced through the poor man's mind. In that split second the future of Mexico hung in the balance, for if Moctezuma had bared his chest and allowed the officer to run him through, all conquistadors in Mexico would certainly have perished before sundown and the conquest of Mexico would certainly have been greatly delayed; indeed, it might never have been "conquered" at all. But Moctezuma chose life to honor and ignominiously allowed himself to be put in irons.

By holding Moctezuma prisoner, Cortés was the virtual ruler of all Mexico.

APRIL 1520

This extraordinary state of affairs lasted for eight months and might have gone on indefinitely if the governor of Cuba, Velázquez, had not then intervened. Hearing rumors of Cortés' daring exploits—all in violation of his orders—he outfitted a force of twelve hundred men to sail to Mexico, charging its leader, a man named Pánfilo de Narváez, to arrest and hang Cortés as a traitor. Narváez took possession of Cempoalla, an Indian village north of Veracruz where he dallied, uncertain as to how to proceed. The season of tropical rains had started, affording him an excuse to wait for more propitious weather.

Cortés, on the other hand, waited for nothing. Selecting seventy of his fittest men, he led a forced march to Cempoalla, leaving behind in Tenochtitlán all his cavalry, artillery, and most of his men, under the command of Pedro de Alvarado. In the middle of the night during a torrential downpour, he and his men slipped into Cempoalla, disarmed the guards, seized the cannons, and captured Narváez, who, in struggling frantically to defend himself, lost an eye. His blood-curdling screams of agony so horrified his men that they fought without spirit and soon surrendered.

1520

Meanwhile, back in the capital, Pedro de Alvarado, because of his quick temper and lack of discretion, committed the gravest blunder of the entire campaign. While attending an Aztec religious ceremony he mistook the frenzied dancing and chanting of the assembly as a general uprising against the Spaniards and ordered the cannons to open fire. Like the massacre of Cholula, he rushed upon the mob with cavalry and infantry and killed some 400 nobles and 3000 commoners. The next day the entire population rose up like one great howling ogre craving blood—Spanish blood. Heedless of the consequences to their monarch, they flung themselves against the doors of the Spanish quarters, shouting insults and daring the Spanish to come out. What had been almost miraculously avoided for so long had finally happened: open war raged between the Aztecs and the Spaniards.

Cortés was busily dismantling and sinking ships of Narváez when he heard of this calamity. Immediately he marched to Mexico at the head of his new army—taken from Narváez—numbering over a thousand. He arrived during a short respite in hostilities and was able, therefore, to join his harassed comrades in the besieged palace of Axayacatl without a casualty. But no sooner had the great door closed behind them than a shower of arrows and spears clattered against it, signaling the resumption of war.

For over a month the Spaniards withstood the unrestrained fury of mass hatred, fighting off daily suicidal attempts to scale the palace walls. At one point Moctezuma was brought on the roof to implore his people to make peace with the Spaniards, but jeers and whistles drowned his words and the raucous mob hurled stones at him. One struck him on the head and sent him reeling unconscious into the arms of his attendants, who quickly whisked him away. Although the wound was slight, he sank into a state of lethargy and depression and died within two weeks, probably of a broken heart.

With food and water almost exhausted, Cortés had no alternative but to evacuate. In the dead of night, a light rain falling to muffle the sounds of creaking cannons and the clattering hoofs of horses, the army filed out along the western causeway leading to Atzcapotzalco. They took with them a ponderously heavy portable bridge to throw over breaches in the causeway made by the Aztecs to prevent just such an escape. At the first breach the bridge became so tightly wedged down by the trampling army that it could not be extricated. The front file pushed to the brink of the second breach, called frantically for the bridge to be brought forward. The Aztecs, aroused by the commotion, sounded the general alarm. At that pandemonium broke loose. The Aztecs, incensed by their enemy's temerity in attempting to escape, assailed them with unprecedented fury. The Spaniards plunged or were shoved into the water, some of them, weighted down with gold and silver loot, sinking straight to the bottom. Others fell into Aztec canoes and were borne away to the sacrificial altars. But more made good their escape by swimming to shore or by scrambling up the sides of the causeway. It is reckoned the Spaniards lost 400 men, killed or missing, and their Tlaxcalan allies lost 2000. When dawn broke on the debacle of dead and dying strewn along the causeway and cannons and valuable equipment abandoned there, Cortés is said to have fallen down beneath an *ahuehuete* tree (which can be seen to this day in Tacuba) and wept unconsolably. This episode is known as La Noche Triste (The Sad Night).

The little Spanish army limped away toward Tlaxcala, traveling by a northern route around the lakes. They thought their Aztec pursuers would be awaiting them on the southern route which they had traveled nine months before on entering the valley. Despite their painful wounds and low morale, they had to fight running skirmishes with rural tribes and to garner food by foraging the countryside. After five days they collapsed from exhaustion and needed two days to recuperate. Resuming their trek, they met, east of the pyramids of Teotihuacán, in the valley of Otumba, a sprawling Aztec army so large and closely assembled that their white plumed helmets and white tunics gave the impression that the valley was covered with snow. Cortés' force could neither retreat nor make a stand. Their only hope was to stun the enemy with a charge. Abandoning all thoughts of personal safety, they found a new, almost superhuman strength from the sheer hopelessness of the situation, a strength that sent them yelling, lunging, running into that vast throng, fighting with the ferocity and courage of wild tigers. For several hours they battled, slaying hundreds but moving not one inch toward victory till Cortés, rising in his stirrups, spied a richly garbed Indian chief who seemed to be directing enemy operations. Rearing up his horse, he galloped straight for him and pinned him to the ground with a lance. The bewildered Aztecs, seeing Cortés prancing above their slain commander, holding aloft their highly prized banner, fell back in disorder. Confusion spread and retreat became a stampede. When the field was clear, the Spaniards staggered, limped, and hobbled into friendly Tlaxcalan territory.

NOVEMBER 1520

For five months they nursed their wounds, sharpened their weapons, taught the Tlaxcalans military tactics, and, most amazing of all (at least to the Tlaxcalans), started construction on a fleet of brigantines with which to assault Mexico City.

Back in the Aztec capital, a terrible plague of smallpox ravaged the populace. Introduced into Mexico by a Negro soldier in the Narváez expedition, the disease swept the country like a raging prairie fire since the natives had neither immunity nor means to combat it. One of its first victims was Cuitlahuac, the successor to Moctezuma. The next emperor to follow is considered the first great military hero of Mexico: Cuauhtémoc.

JANUARY 1521

The conquistadors marching at the head of a multitudinous army of Indian allies re-entered the valley of Mexico and occupied the town of Texcoco, an important stronghold in the Aztec defenses. From there they went marauding the countryside, going as far afield as Cuernavaca, which fell to a handful of Spaniards and Tlaxcalan warriors who entered the barricaded town by swinging like acrobats from tree to tree over a deep ravine and dropping down behind the startled defenders who were intently watching for a frontal attack.

Returning to Mexico, Cortés divided his army into three divisions; one for each of the three causeways. By this time the 20 brigantines made in Tlaxcala had been brought overland and launched in Lake Texcoco. They had been carried by 2000 *tamanes* roughly 180 miles, through forests and across mountains in a procession that took six hours to pass any one spot.

MAY 1521

In one concerted assault involving all three divisions and the flotilla, the Spaniards bore down on the city. They gained the main square, but a ferocious counterattack forced them to withdraw hastily to their camps along the causeways. Cortés then changed tactics. Instead of gambling everything on a series of knockout blows, he advanced slowly, steadily into the city, wrecking everything as he went. When he reached the main square, Cuauhtémoc and his famished army had withdrawn into the slums of Tlatelolco, refusing to surrender on any terms. The once glorious Tenochtitlán was by then in ruins; its streets and canals were littered with putrefying dead that polluted the air with an almost unbearably foul stench. Cortés sent envoys to Cuauhtémoc beseeching him to surrender. Total amnesty was promised. Cuauhtémoc killed the envoys and said to the remnants of his court, "Let no man who values his life speak to me of surrender." Cortés could not help but admire his fortitude and courage, but his admiration did not deter him from mercilessly attacking the last redoubt of the Aztecs. Cuauhtémoc was captured in his attempt to flee the island in a canoe. His hands were bound and he was brought to the main square where Cortés had established his headquarters. Haggard and emaciated, the Indian prince prostrated himself before the victorious Spanish general, and then rose slowly to his feet. "Malinche," he said in a faint voice, "I have done all I could to defend myself and my people, till I am reduced to this wretched state. You can do with me now what you will." He lurched forward and grasped the dagger in Cortés' belt. "Better for me that you use this," he said, "and kill me at once."

Thus ended the three-month siege of Tenochtitlán.

For sheer suffering and misery on the part of the besieged, the fall of the great Aztec capital can be matched by but very few accounts in history.

CHAPTER THREE

1522–1535

The night of Cuauhtémoc's capture winds and driving rain tore at the vanquished city and flashes of lightning, with its eerie white light, heightened the horrors of desolation and destruction. Those awakened by the crashing thunder thought the abandoned gods of the Aztecs were wreaking their vengeance on all mortals—Spaniards and Indians alike.

The next day disease-ridden survivors of the siege filed slowly out of the city. Alderete, the king's treasurer, picking over the ruins, collected only a pathetic pile of trinkets which the army looked upon as sorry compensation for their hard-won victory. They complained noisily to Cortés that Cuauhtémoc knew more than he would admit, and that he should be tortured until he revealed the whereabouts of Moctezuma's treasure—that great pile of gold, silver, and precious stones which they had seen with their own eyes a year before filling sealed rooms in the palace of Axayacatl. Cortés reluctantly turned Cuauhtémoc over to his torturers. The chief cacique of Tacuba who was tortured with him screamed in agony when white-hot irons were pressed to the soles of his feet, but Cuauhtémoc bore the same treatment without a whimper. His only utterance was a reproof of his wailing companion. "Do you think, because I don't scream, that I am enjoying this foot bath of fire?" When nothing could be wrung from them but an admission that much gold had been flung in the lake, Cortés stopped the proceedings and released Cuauhtémoc. Alderete sent divers down to probe the murky depths of the lake, but they brought up only bits of broken pottery. Though extensive searches have been made both before and since the draining of Lake Texcoco, the whereabouts of Moctezuma's treasure remains to this day one of the greatest mysteries of Mexico.

News of the Aztec defeat traveled with the wind from valley to valley and down the great *barrancas* (ravines) to the palm-fringed shores of both coasts, and tribal chiefs came from near and far to gaze on the smoldering ruins of the once invulnerable Aztec capital. Willingly they made peace with the Spaniards, whom they looked upon as some kinds of gods in human form. No less wonderful were their horses, an animal they had never seen before. And they eagerly received baptism from Father Olmedo, the army's chaplain. It was the custom in ancient Mexico to adopt the religion of the conquering tribe, since it was thought that the strongest tribe obviously had the best gods aiding them. But Father Olmedo, in baptizing each Indian singly, soon exhausted his supply of Christian names and resorted to mass baptisms, using the name of the saint being honored that day according to the church calendar. Thus, on St. John's day, he would sprinkle thousands of Indians with holy water and loudly announce, "You're all called John!" (Women became Jean—Juanna.) To this day babies in Mexico are named after the saint of that day on which they are born, making saint's days the same as birthdays.

Cortés was displeased to learn that many tribes in the south had not appeared to pay homage, and so dispatched expeditions to various parts of the country to exact from tribal caciques a pledge of loyalty to the Spanish flag. Pedro de Alvarado was sent south to Guatemala and Cristóval de Olid sailed from Veracruz with instructions to found a Spanish colony in Honduras and to explore the coast for a rumored river linking the Atlantic with the Pacific.

In the meantime the strenuous work of clearing debris and rubble from the war-ravaged city and of laying foundations for Spanish mansions and government buildings went on, with the Spaniards treating the once proud Aztecs like slaves. It was Aztecs, in fact, directed by Spanish engineers, who did the manual work.

1522

Almost a year to a day after the fall of Tenochtitlán, a boat was rowed slowly shoreward from a great ship lying at anchor before Veracruz, and sitting aft in rigid attention was a rather beautiful woman in black, her pallor and darting eyes revealing a state of great inner excitement. She was Doña Catalina Xuarez, wife of Don Hernando Cortés. She had been the daughter of a merchant in Havana when Cortés, then a captain in the army of the island, had, in the heat of passion, proposed marriage to her. But later his passion cooled and he tried to break his promise. It was Doña Catalina's three husky brothers who put Cortés under duress until he was on his knees beside their sister and before a priest, swearing eternal fidelity. Soon after that, Cortés sailed away with his fleet to Mexico. Doña Catalina, by following him, was showing her determination to live with her husband wherever he went.

The port captain, Gonzalo Sandoval—the most trusted captain of Cortés—gave her a royal welcome and personally escorted her up to Mexico City, as Tenochtitlán was thereafter named. Cortés, however, received her with formal courtesies that but thinly disguised his great disappointment at seeing her. Perhaps he felt his marriage to a merchant's daughter would keep him from being accepted into the highest levels of court society in Spain. If so, he successfully hid his feelings behind a front of good manners and presented her to each of his officers at a party he gave some weeks after her arrival in his recently completed house in Coyoacán (which is not only still standing but serves as the town's police station). Several times that evening guests heard Cortés exchange sharp words with his wife, and she, at an early hour, retired from the party complaining of a severe headache. This was not regarded as unusual since she was known to be easily fatigued and was continually falling into dizzy spells and fainting. At midnight, after the guests had gone, Cortés found her in a small chapel fervently telling her beads. "Leave me alone," she was heard to say, "I feel like letting myself die." Before dawn the servants, answering their master's frantic calls for help, burst into his bedchamber and found Cortés holding the limp body of Doña Catalina. "My wife, I think, is dead," he said solemnly. She was buried that very morning.

Scandalmongers, of course, circulated stories that Cortés had murdered his wife. Years later a servant testified that he saw blue bruises on the poor woman's throat—probably strangulation marks. If these stories ever reached the ears of Cortés, he affected not to notice them and he maintained to the end an aloof silence on the subject. Perhaps he considered the accusations too ludicrous to warrant any comment whatsoever. In those days it was quite common for newcomers to Mexico to die of a fever soon after arriving. Nevertheless, the death of Doña Catalina has been a subject to excite many imaginative minds, and pulp magazines in Mexico to this day retell the story in lurid detail with strong implications that Cortés was actually guilty of slaying his wife.

For the conquest to bear fruit, Cortés well knew that soldiers would have to be transformed into responsible landowners who, to protect their own interests, would help preserve law and order. So he offered his veterans large tracts of land if they promised to: 1) live eight consecutive years on their allotted land; 2) bring out their wives from Spain immediately or marry locally within two years; 3) train the Indians on their land in the ceremonies and customs of the Catholic religion; and 4) plant all vines, trees, and plants that were sent from Spain. Failure to keep any of these promises would forfeit land titles.

OCTOBER 1522

All during the conquest the young king of Spain, Charles the Fifth, had been in Germany attempting to suppress religious heresies that had broken out there. Adrian, the scholarly friar and former teacher of Charles, ruling Spain in the king's absence, had acted on the advice of Governor Velázquez and had issued a warrant for the arrest of Cortés. When the king, after his return to the throne, heard the whole story of the conquest of Mexico, his admiration for Cortés was boundless. He immediately rescinded Adrian's arrest warrant and called together a group to study the matter more fully. Don Martín Cortés, the proud father of Hernando, and a certain Duke of Bejar (an influential nobleman who had chosen to champion the cause of Cortés) appeared before this group to declaim the merits of the *gran conquistador*. Their words must have had some effect, for the group decided that Cortés was to be made governor, captain general, and the chief justice of New Spain. The order was signed by Emperor Charles V (Charles I of Spain) on October 15, 1522. Hardly had the ink dried on the parchment than the Bishop of Burgos, a burly man who, for no apparent reason (perhaps he was jealous), passionately despised Cortés, assailed the king's ear with arguments calculated to sow doubt in the young monarch's mind. Cortés was undoubtedly a man with great personal ambition, said the bishop, who had repudiated the authority of his superior Velázquez to achieve his ends. Would he not, then, become equally disaffected toward the king and tear Mexico away from Spain to form an independent kingdom? These thoughts caused Charles to regret having entrusted so much power to Cortés, and so, to allay his fears, he sent two notaries to Mexico, ostensibly to verify that the king's royal fifth was being exacted from the booty of conquest but in fact to spy on Cortés and to report any irregularities in his character.

Twelve Franciscan friars, chosen after much consideration by Pope Adrian VI (he who, as a friar, had ruled Spain in Charles's absence), arrived in Veracruz and traveled the whole arduous way to Mexico City on foot. When they entered the main square, haggard, bearded, and in tattered robes, Cortés, in full view of the public, fell on his knees and kissed the hem of their robes. The Indians were astounded! Here was the great general, the conqueror of all Mexico, voluntarily humbling himself before impoverished priests. This incident and, later, the merciful and selfless acts of those early monks changed radically the Indian's notion of religion.

One of the first acts of these twelve friars—called the "Twelve Apostles"—was to found a language school in Texcoco for the study of Indian dialects and for teaching Spanish to the Indians. From the beginning the friars had no doubt whatever that the Indians were sons and daughters of Adam and Eve, but considered them a branch of the great family of mankind that the devil had led astray. It was Catholic Spain's duty, therefore, to Christianize them and to instruct them in morals. That duty, and that alone, justified the conquest, they said, and the Spaniard's exploitation of the Indians they categorically condemned as a wicked crime.

1524

Toward the end of this year Cortés collected an army of 100 horses, 50 foot soldiers, and 2000 *tamanes* and marched off to Honduras. He took with him Cuauhtémoc as a hostage, knowing that the popular Indian prince, despite his scars and broken health, was capable of inciting a revolt if left unwatched. The government he placed in the hands of two soldiers—Estrada, the treasurer, and Albornoz, the auditor— and gave Roderigo de Paz power of proxy to handle his own affairs. Precisely why Cortés left Mexico at this time is not clearly understood. Several reasons have been suggested, none of which singly seems strong enough to have warranted such an ambitious undertaking. Undoubtedly it was a combination of causes. News reached him that Captain Olid, sent to colonize Honduras, had there mutinied and in defiance of Cortés had established an independent kingdom. Cortés had dispatched a kinsman, a captain named Las Casas, to arrest Olid, but Las Casas was shipwrecked on the rocky Caribbean coast and was presumed to have drowned. According to some historians, it was the news of Las Casas that determined Cortés to march. There were, however, other pressing reasons urging him to leave. The spying notaries sent out by Charles V were becoming insufferable with their tactless questioning and shameless prying. Also, life as a desk-bound official was, for him, unbearably dull and he longed to plunge once again into the unexplored regions of Mexico in search of gold and exotic cultures. In any case, by deciding to go he was making the biggest mistake of his life.

First of all, Las Casas had, in fact, escaped drowning. Being a strong swimmer, he reached shore safely and then traveled

overland to Olid's camp where he was promptly jailed as
a spy of Cortés. But he managed to persuade his jailers and
several soldiers to remain loyal to their old commander of the
conquest, and from his cell he initiated a revolt against the
camp's commander, Olid. In the fighting that ensued Las
Casas—released from jail by sympathizers—engaged Olid in a
knife fight. After a horrific struggle Las Casas emerged the
blood-stained victor and Honduras was thereafter a colony
loyal to Cortés. But by the time this news reached Mexico
City, Cortés and his army were crashing through tropical
jungles in Chiapas.

The march itself was like one long dreadful nightmare from
which no one could awake. Few marches in recorded history
can match it for sheer horror. They trudged through dank,
misty, snake-infested jungles and through a steady downpour of rain—though in the mountains drinking water was
perniciously scarce. Mountain trails were so rain-soaked that
sixty-three horses floundering in the mud slipped off preci-
pices and fell to their deaths. Rivers were all flood-swollen
and almost impossible to ford. The terrible strain of this venture apparently unhinged the mind of Cortés temporarily, for
he became obsessed with the idea that Cuauhtémoc was planning a revolt. He set up court, ranted and raved over flimsy
evidence, and declared Cuauhtémoc guilty of treason. Spanish soldiers were shocked to see the Indian prince hanged.
Bernal Díaz, a witness to the event, writes ashamedly of his
general's behavior and concludes: "The execution of Cuauhtémoc was most unjust and was thought wrong by all of us."
When finally, more dead than alive, they reached Honduras, Cortés seemed indifferent to the fate of Olid. He
planned another expedition to Nicaragua, but news of deplorable developments in Mexico during his absence determined him to sail immediately for Veracruz. Two attempts
to leave ended in shipwreck and filled him with a heavy dis-
may. He took to dressing in the black robes of a Dominican
monk and spoke morosely of dying in Honduras. Only after a
lapse of several months did he again venture another voyage
by sea, this time successfully reaching Mexico by way of
Cuba.

During the twenty months Cortés was away on his Honduran adventure, the government, which under his watchful eye had seemed stable enough, fell to ruin. Estrada and Albornoz were swindled out of their offices by two disreputable merchants who later noised it abroad that Cortés had died in the swamps of Chiapas. They even held a mock funeral service for him and then claimed possession of his property. Roderigo de Paz, Cortés' proxy, in attempting to defend the land was overpowered, beaten up, and hanged from a tree like a common thief.

1526

Soldiers in Veracruz gaped incredulously at the thin, haggard, and wasted figure that announced itself as Hernando Cortés. When his identity was confirmed, bells rang joyously and cannons roared their salute. Indians in each town he visited on his journey up to the capital strewed his path with flowers, and his old comrades-in-arms embraced him and wept with joy at seeing him alive. In Mexico City the dishonorable merchants were seized by a crowd and clamped into wooden cages which were put on exhibition in the main square. A holiday was declared by the jubilant populace to celebrate the homecoming of their illustrious conquistador. This happy occasion was like balm to the shattered nerves of Cortés; soon after, he regained his customary courage and confidence. His recovery came none too soon, however, for within a month a legal body called the *Juez de Residencia* arrived from Spain empowered to relieve him of command. Its leader, Ponce de León, a man of high principles but poor health, handed Cortés a letter from Charles V explaining in high-flown phrases that the *Juez* in no way reflected the court's distrust of Cortés but rather showed its desire to clear him of ugly charges being made against him in Spain. The king suggested that, for his own good, Cortés should return to Spain to defend himself. Ponce de León, after ruling only twenty days, died of a fever. (Gossips said Cortés killed him.) His successor, Marcus de Aguilar, already very old and extremely ill, died two months later. (Another murder, said the gossips.) That left the court notary, Estrada, in charge. Like all little men entrusted with power, he took pleasure in mistreating and insulting those towering over him in ability and character. For no apparent reason he ordered Cortés to leave the city. When a soldier refused to carry out the order, he had the soldier's hands cut off. Cortés suffered these humiliations in silence. He retired to his house in Coyoacán where he bided his time until April of 1528 when he returned to Spain, taking with him (as gifts for the king) Indians, parrots, gold bracelets, sculpture, and jade carvings.

1528

In December of this year four *oidores* of the royal *Audiencia* of New Spain and the rotund Bishop Zumarraga—all passengers on the same ship—arrived in Veracruz. The *Audiencia*, a kind of judicial and administrative body authorized to rule Mexico, was formed in Spain when Charles heard of Estrada's incompetence to rule. On reaching the central plateau, however, this group, like the *Juez de Residencia* before it, lost in quick succession its two senior members who were, unfortunately, the most mature-minded members of the group. The third member, into whose hands the government fell, Nuño de Guzmán, was perhaps the blackest scoundrel that ever ruled Mexico. His cruelty to Indians and his use of royal funds to finance unscrupulous schemes to make a fortune quickly were opposed by only one man: the church dignitary, Bishop Zumarraga. Commissioned in Rome to be the protector of the Indian, Zumarraga had listened patiently to the whole long list of grievances made by the Indians against Guzmán. Then from the pulpit on Sunday he would rail directly at Guzmán, sitting pompously in the front pew, for his atrocities which, when exposed, shocked the congregation. Guzmán, after mass, advised the bishop to stick to scripture when sermonizing, but each Sunday the bishop would deliver another searing diatribe against him. Finally Guzmán could stand no more and signaled his henchmen to silence him by pulling him bodily from the pulpit. The faithful, horrified to witness this sacrilege, surged forward to protect the priest; and they angrily warned Guzmán that arms would be used to defend the bishop if another attack were made upon him. Frightened that news of this incident would leak back to Spain, Guzmán confiscated the mails and personally read each letter before allowing it to be sent. But the crafty Zumarraga bribed a sailor of a cargo vessel to carry back a tub of tallow in which a letter had been hidden. This letter was so clear and so compelling that the Spanish court, on the strength of it, outfitted a new *Audiencia* and sent it off to Mexico posthaste.

1529

Hearing that a second *Audiencia* was on the high seas, coming to replace him, Nuño de Guzmán gathered up a small army of mercenaries and set off to "conquer the west." It was entirely unnecessary at that time to conquer anything in Mexico, since most tribes had already sworn their loyalty to the conquistadors of Cortés. Nevertheless Guzmán stomped through what is today the states of Michoacán, Nayarít, Jalisco, and Sinaloa, inflicting on the natives his abominable cruelties and leaving behind him a trail of charred ruins and broken idols. His only noteworthy accomplishment was founding Guadalajara, but his cruelty instilled such a hatred in the Indians that it took nearly a century of patient missionary work before those regions could again be entered. The second *Audiencia* when it arrived, immediately issued a warrant for his arrest, and he, to escape capture, made a heroic coast-to-coast trek over Mexico's rugged plateau but was apprehended near the mouth of the Pánuco River on the gulf coast (now Tampico). He was sent back to Spain in irons.

While a new Mexico rose on the ruins of an old—classical mansions and government palaces, cobblestone streets and wide plazas—the Franciscan friars were quietly establishing standards in morals, education, and religion that would thereafter provide the mold for the Mexican character. One friar, Bernardino de Sahagún, arriving in Mexico in 1529, spent his first few years mastering Nahuatl and other Indian dialects at the language school in Texcoco; he then wandered freely from village to village probing into every aspect of Indian life—from religious beliefs to the way they cooked corn. To his questions about history, the Indians often answered with hieroglyphical writings which were interpreted for him by Indians learning Spanish at the Texcoco school. The results he compiled into a monumental, four-volume work which he entitled *The History of Things in New Spain.* (See Chapter One.) It remains to this day the richest mine of information on life in pre-Columbian Mexico. Another friar, Pedro de Gante, had the infinite wisdom to incorporate the Indians' religious dancing and chanting into the Catholic services. In translating the sacred books of Mexico he found that their version of creation ran more or less parallel to that of Genesis, the Christian version, and that the two religions had, after all, many points in common.

The Indian was by nature attracted to the Catholic religion with its pomp and pageant, its gorgeously garbed priests, its highly decorated altars ablaze with candles and swathed with clouds of incense, and its plain-song chants. All this satisfied his sense of piety. But the great work of planting Christianity in Mexico took more than impressive religious ceremonies and the selfless service of scholarly monks. It took a miracle.

1531

On December 9 of this year a newly baptized Indian named Juan Diego, passing the hill of Tepeyac on his way to morning mass at the convent in Tlatelolco, stopped at the sound of his name being called from afar. Turning, he saw a beautiful lady standing in the sun, surrounded by shimmering rays of light. Trembling with fear, he fell to his knees. "Go to the Bishop Zumarraga," said the vision, "and tell him to build me a chapel on this hill." Juan, finding his voice and courage, asked timidly, "How will he believe me, a poor, ignorant Indian?" "Gather up roses," she said, "and take them to him as a gift from me." With that she vanished. Although it was a frosty December day, Juan saw a nearby bush laden with roses in full bloom. Quickly he gathered them up in his *tilma* (a toga-like garment worn by the natives) and hurried off to the bishop's house in Mexico City. When after a long wait he was admitted into the presence of that august dignitary, Juan threw open his *tilma,* tumbling the roses on to the floor, and there, to the gasping surprise of all present, was the picture of Our Lady of Guadalupe, the same beautiful lady Juan had seen in the sky.

She is shown as a dark-skinned Madonna draped in a long mantle of blue patterned with stars, and wearing a white robe embroidered with gold designs. She stands demurely on a crescent moon which is supported by a solemn-faced cherub. The Spaniards could boast of their national saints; the Indians now had one of their own. After much proof of her miraculous powers, she was declared the patroness and protectoress of New Spain by a papal bull of 1754.

Juan Diego's *tilma* is on view above the central altar of the cathedral of Our Lady of Guadalupe. Many people pronounced incurably ill by medical science have made miraculous recoveries after having visited her shrine. Art historians conclude that no painter living in Mexico in the sixteenth century could possibly have painted it. Chemists who have studied its paint under microscopes and have tested its reaction to special acid cannot determine from what it is made. In fact, attempts to explain the painting away logically call for greater gullibility than to accept it simply as a miracle.

The second *Audiencia,* although competent and conscientious, was swamped with problems of government crying for prompt action. Since their most urgent letters would take three to six months to get an answer, they implored King Charles V to send out a viceroy authorized to make on-the-spot decisions. A viceroy was a king by proxy. Only men of the very highest caliber could possibly be made viceroys, and it is to Spain's everlasting credit that she chose men wisely for the post. The first of a long line of sixty-one was one of the best: Don Antonio de Mendoza, who arrived in November 1535 in a stately carriage drawn by teams of white horses and announced by the trumpeted fanfares of liveried heralds. This was the official beginning of Mexico's colonial period.

There was perhaps only one man in Mexico not elated by the viceroy's arrival and that was Hernando Cortés, who had himself coveted the job of ruling the land of his conquest. He had been made, instead, the marquis of Oaxaca, ruler of all the territory south of Cuernavaca, including Guatemala—an area as large as all Spain. He built his palace in Cuernavaca which today serves as the assembly hall for the congress of Morelos and which is pointed out, by all Mexican guides, to tourists. There he lived with his second wife, the young and beautiful Doña Juana de Zuñiga, daughter of the Count of Aguilar. Cortés died on his last trip to Spain at the age of sixty-three on December 2, 1547. His mortal remains were brought back to Mexico and were immured in a wall of the Chapel Niño Jesús behind the Hospital de Jesús (founded by Cortés) on 20 de Noviembre—the broad avenue leading into the capital's main square, the Zócalo.

After Mexico achieved her independence in 1821, a campaign was started to discredit the name of Cortés. Neophyte politicians professed their patriotism by urging vandals to deface or destroy anything that honored the great Spanish general. During the riots of 1828 his tomb was ransacked, but found empty. Descendants of Cortés had rescued his funeral urn the night before and kept it in a family vault until the rioting had ended. In 1840, William Prescott, writing his celebrated *History of the Conquest of Mexico*, deplored the fact that not one single statue or monument to one of the most amazing men in history could be found anywhere in the Mexican republic. To this day, little to commemorate him exists; indeed, during the twenties and thirties of this century, he was most strongly vilified when Mexico's outstanding painters (Rivera, Orozco, and Siqueiros) covered the walls of public buildings with murals depicting Cortés as a kind of moronic monster branding and flogging docile Indians. As paintings, they are undeniably decorative; as history, they are malicious distortions of fact. They give no credit to his indomitable courage, his genius in organizing and carrying out a campaign, his great generalship (which Prescott compared to that of Caesar and Alexander the Great), his humanitarian acts of founding hospitals (some of which still exist), and of forming a government based on coexistence with the Indians, not in extinguishing them (as Pizarro did in Peru) or in driving them like animals from Christian colonies (as the

Puritans did in New England). The words of Antony might well have been applied to Cortés instead of Caesar when he said:

> *The evil that men do lives after them;*
> *The good is oft interred with their bones . . .*
>   Julius Caesar, Act III, scene 2

CHAPTER FOUR

1536–1650

1536

One year after the arrival of Viceroy Mendoza, residents in the capital were greatly excited over a rumored civilization in the unexplored north, supposedly richer and more fabulous than that of Tenochtitlán. The center of all this flurry of talk was a soldier of fortune named Cabeza de Vaca, who had escaped from a famished and disease-ridden colony, planted and abandoned, near what is now Tampa, Florida. He had wandered along the gulf coast (now Mississippi, Louisiana, and Texas) and across northern Mexico, picking up, as he went, stories about some kind of Indian promised land called the "Seven Cities of Cibola." Viceroy Mendoza himself was interested. He dispatched an itinerant monk named Marcos de Niza (who had acted as chaplain in Pizarro's conquest of Peru) to retrace the steps of Cabeza de Vaca and verify the story. With him, as a guide, went a giant Negro from Morocco called Esteban, who had accompanied Cabeza on his overland odyssey. After wandering all over what is now the state of Sonora, Fray Niza returned, minus Esteban (he had deserted to join an Indian tribe), but filled with glowing reports of a golden city he had seen from afar. Hostile Indians, surrounding the place, kept him from going nearer, he said. What he saw were obviously hallucinations caused by the heat, or else he was a terrible liar. In any case, he started one of the biggest wild-goose chases in history.

Mendoza organized a huge expedition and chose Vásquez de Coronado to lead it. Riffraff and vagabonds, eager to rush off on any wild adventure that promised loot, flocked to his banner; they walked through Mexico, into Arizona and New

Mexico, going as far north as Kansas before turning back. The endurance of these men, their capacity to suffer hardships of thirst and hunger, is almost beyond belief. On April 1, 1542, with only a handful of his original army, Coronado staggered into a northern outpost of New Spain, having discovered only scrubby wastelands and arid deserts, but having completed what historians have considered one of the most amazing land explorations of all time.

1540

On Christmas Day, 1540, began the Mistón rebellion. Caciques of the Chichimec Indians, a tribe living in the hills around Guadalajara, noting the disappearance of Spanish soldiers (most had joined Coronado's expedition) seized the opportunity to rally their warriors and avenge the cruelties inflicted on them by Nuño de Guzmán. "Throw off the shackles of Christianity," they cried, "and return to human sacrifices, orgies, and devil worship." Luckily for the Spaniards, neighboring tribes in the area found the Chichimecs repugnant and declined to join them. Even so, the Chichimecs, by themselves, were enough to terrify the citizens of Guadalajara, who sent back desperate calls for help to Mendoza, in Mexico City. Mendoza considered this a job for a seasoned conquistador and called Pedro de Alvarado from Tehuantepec to put down the revolt. That valiant veteran of a thousand battles charged headlong into the Indian ranks but, through a miscalculation of the enemy's reserves, was thrown back and forced to retreat. His horse, in the confusion of the rout, slipped and fell on him. Alvarado died eleven days later from injuries received from the accident. Mendoza himself then gathered an army and marched on the Indians. He was victorious everywhere and finished the war with a signal victory in the region called Mistón. Hence the name: the Mistón rebellion. This was the only serious Indian uprising against the Spaniards after the fall of Tenochtitlán, although the Indians did revolt against the Mexican government, even as late as 1870.

1542

When Cortés, acting as governor, captain general, and chief justice of New Spain, granted land to his veterans of the conquest, he was instituting a system of landownership which, in its fedudalistic tenure, outraged many conscientious friars. They argued that the Spaniards had no right either to the land or the labor of the Indians, and that the conquest could only be justified on religious grounds: "Spain was bringing Christianity to the heathens." Up until 1542 landowners depended entirely on food supplied them by the Indians living on their properties. In some cases Indians were branded like cattle, worked to exhaustion and, slowly but surely, to extinction. The most outspoken protagonist in the Indian's defense was Fray Bartolomé de las Casas, who had renounced a promising career in law to become a Dominican priest. Sent first to Cuba and thence to Guatemala, he tirelessly wrote books and articles damning his fellow countrymen's mistreatment of the natives. His works were read with avid interest by the Council of the Indies, a scholarly group (most of them Dominicans, like Las Casas) held responsible for writing government policies applicable to all Spanish possessions. Under the influence of Las Casas, they wrote a remarkable edict called the *New Laws of the Indies for the Good Treatment and Preservation of the Indians.* "The Indian," it said, "is henceforth free." (This was written three hundred years before Abraham Lincoln's Emancipation Proclamation.) "To enslave them or to mistreat them in any way, is a misdemeanor punishable by law." Furthermore, they said, landownership was not hereditary. Upon the death of the owner, land titles reverted to the crown.

The howl of protest that rose from colonists all over New Spain carried grave warnings of revolt. Mendoza, recovering from his battles with the Chichimecs in Guadalajara, was besieged by enraged landowners, arguing that unless the laws were modified the colony would collapse for want of laborers. As it was, only the sternest discipline kept the Indians at their jobs. If they were freed, no work would be done at all.

And why, they asked, should they attempt to improve the land if, when they died, their children received no benefit whatsoever? Their wailing and ranting moved Mendoza to take some of the teeth out of the laws, and by so doing he probably averted a revolution. In Peru and Panama, where the laws were enforced to the letter, pitched battles were fought between colonists and government troops.

Spain's policy (into which neatly fit *The New Laws of the Indies*) was always to "centralize." Everything revolved around the king, who was omnipotent. Beneath him were his carefully chosen viceroys whose kingdoms, or colonies, were dotted with villages, towns, and cities. Towns of New Spain were patterned after the towns in Old Spain. Each had its own legislative and judicial body, called the *cabildo* (council), made up of *regidores* (elders) who appointed *alcaldes* (mayors), and the whole functioned as a self-sustaining unit. Most of the land surrounding the town was owned by rich townsmen, except for the *ejidos*, which were communal lands for grazing and threshing, owned by the town itself. The mayor was overseer of the *alhóndiga*, the communal warehouse for grain. By keeping it full, grain supply was constant, and the price was thereby stabilized.

Colonists soon found a legal loophole in the hated *New Laws* by broadly interpreting the rights of the town to force citizens to do work necessary for the support of the commonwealth. Though the Indians were forced to work the fields, to build public buildings and churches, and to mend the roads, they were not called slaves, but citizens, working under the grand title of *repartimiento*—assessment. Indians were put in a sort of work pool from which landowners could draw however many they needed for a week's work, provided they gave the Indian food and shelter for that week. Such was the fate of Indians living in Spanish towns.

But there were Indians, possibly better off, living in purely Indian communities. Many of these communities, deep in the uncharted back country of Mexico, were hardly disturbed by the conquest, except that human sacrifices had been abolished and a Catholic church or a shrine of some kind had been installed. Caciques, acting as judges and councilmen, saw to it that taxes were paid.

And so, three distinct social levels emerged early in the colonial period, so sharply drawn and so inviolable that the social structure of colonial Mexico was not unlike the caste system in India. On top were the Spaniards from Spain called *peninsulares*. They occupied all the important government posts, and either held titles themselves or came from titled families. Second came the Creoles, Spaniards born in Mexico of Spanish parents. They could never rise above secondary posts in the government, although as landowners and merchants they could—and did—amass fortunes. Third and far behind the first two, were the Indians: silent, joyless, and inscrutable. They could never be anything but common laborers. Authors of legislature did their best to protect all three classes, but they completely overlooked the possibility of yet a fourth class, a few of whom then existed and were treated as outcasts to be shunned and avoided. They were Mestizos, offspring of Spanish and Indian parents. The full consequences of this oversight would not be felt until two centuries later, at which time, during the wars of independence, Mestizos were found on all social levels and as a race made up one fifth of the population.

One need only look at a Mexican landscape to appreciate the tremendous impact the Catholic Church has had on Mexico. Twin spires of cathedrals mark the center of every town and village, and in the country they rise like lookout towers, protecting the moorish-styled monastery surrounding them. This prevalence of churches was the result of Spain's government, which, at the time of the conquest and during her colonial period, was quasi-theocratic. The viceroys assisted, unstintingly, the ambitious undertakings of those early monks and friars, many of whom were truly remarkable men. Fray Francisco Tembleque is a good example. He arrived in Mexico in 1540 and, after learning the Nahuatl dialect at the language school in Texcoco, preached the gospels to the Indians of Otumba. But he was horrified to discover that the Indians were dying at an appalling rate because of the polluted drinking water of the area. So he scouted the countryside and found in Zempoala (now in the state of Hidalgo), some 30 miles away as the crow flies, a bubbling spring of clean, clear water. Though no engineer, he organized a team of stonecutters and masons and worked with them 17 years constructing an aqueduct 48 miles long that spanned three deep ravines—one with 46 arches, the second with 13 arches, and the third with 67 arches. So well was it constructed that it supplied fresh water to Otumba for over three centuries, till in 1914 a renegade band of Carranza's rebels destroyed a part of it.

Even more extraordinary is the story of Father Urdaneta. Born in the Basque country of Spain, he sailed, as a lowly crewman, with Jofre Loaisa, a Spanish explorer, on his ill-fated expedition to the Orient in 1525. Loaisa actually reached the islands of the East Indies, but all his many strenuous efforts to return to Mexico, then Spain's far western outpost, ended in disaster. He was beaten back by high winds, storms, and even hurricanes. Consequently those Spanish adventurers were stranded in the east for eleven years, sailing from island to island in defiance of the Portuguese, who, by the famous papal bull of 1493, were given legal possession of that half of the world. Urdaneta, by sailing eastward around Africa, finally reached Lisbon in 1538 and proceeded to Spain. He entered an Augustinian monastery and, after being ordained a priest, was sent in 1553 to a monastery near Mexico City called Desierto de los Leones. About this time King Phillip II of Spain was eying with envy the lucrative trade Portugal was carrying on with China, and exhorted his viceroy in Mexico, then Luis de Velasco, to find some west-to-east passage across the Pacific.

Velasco, knowing of the seafaring past of Father Urdaneta, went to his monastery to ask him to take command of an expeditionary fleet to explore the Pacific. Father Urdaneta, then somewhere in his fifties, declined the command but agreed to accompany the expedition as an adviser. So in November 1564, four ships sailed from Acapulco with Miguel de Legazpi in command, and Father Urdaneta at his elbow telling him what to do. As expected, the westward journey was clear sailing, and they arrived safely in the Philippines, February 13, 1565. Legazpi, a better soldier than a sailor, decided to stay and colonize the islands. He told his nephew to take a boat (the worst one) and return to Mexico as quickly as possible. Father Urdaneta was assigned to go with him. They left Manila on June 1, 1565. Four days out the pilot and the sailing master suddenly and inexplicably died. Scurvy broke out and soon there were hardly enough able-bodied men to handle the ship. At this point Father Urdaneta took the wheel. Reasoning, rightly, that the trade winds of the Pacific must follow the same clockwise motion as those of the Atlantic, he steered due north about two thousand miles, through reefs, shoals, and squalls, and against the frantic opposition of his crew who thought, because they were going north instead of west, that the good father had gone mad. Finally (probably near Japan) he caught the prevailing westerlies, ran before the wind to the coast of California, and sailed down to Acapulco. Sixteen men had died; those alive were prostrate with scurvy, and only two could walk. One, standing grimly at the wheel, his tattered robes whipped by the wind and his hoary head held high, was Father Urdaneta.

The passage had been found. The course was now set for heavily laden cargo ships bearing silks, spices, and ivories from the Orient which were exchanged in Acapulco for Mexican silver. Thenceforth, the Pacific was spanned with lively trade routes. Father Urdaneta, stoutly refusing plaudits of any kind, returned to his monastery and there quietly died on June 3, 1568.

CHAPTER FIVE

1650–1810

Mexico's colonial period lasted from 1521 to 1821, exactly three hundred years, and ended with a series of wars against Spain. Because of these wars it is generally believed that Spanish rule throughout this period was tyrannical. Spain, in fact, was no more tyrannous than England, France, Italy, or Austria, ruled during those years by monarchs whose methods of governing would, today, be considered heartless and cruel. It was an age when feudal lords and serfs were gradually being replaced by constitutional governments.

In the sixteenth century Spain was without a precedent in colonizing and could look to no one for advice as to how to proceed. Considering the gigantic size of her operation—to plant the seeds of Spanish culture over an area nearly eight times larger than all Europe—and the ponderously slow methods of communications—by galleons on the sea, and by horse-drawn carriages overland—it is remarkable that she made as few mistakes as she did. What most critics of Spain and her colonial empire fail to recognize (the most obvious fact of all) is that it lasted three hundred years, or nearly ten generations. No government as despotic as Spain's is reputed to have been could have so long endured. Furthermore, peace during this period was practically undisturbed except on two occasions in the seventeenth and eighteenth centuries, when street riots were reported.

As early as 1550, Spain realized the efficacy of using mendicant monks instead of swashbuckling conquistadors to explore regions where hostile tribes were reported to be. Nuño de Guzmán proved what disastrous and long-lasting effects brute force and violence could have. The monks were able to teach—not only with sermons spoken in the native's own dialect but also by leading lives of poverty, chastity, and obedience—that peace in this world was its own reward and that union with God was all that mattered.

Franciscan, Dominican, and Augustinian orders, and later the Jesuits, founded missions in all major Indian villages from Guatemala in the south to wigwam camps in the north in what is now the state of California. Missions were primarily schools where Indian and Mestizo children were taught reading, writing, arithmetic, and Catholic catechism. Brighter students were taught Latin. Antonio Valeriano, for example —a pure Aztec Indian who graduated from, and later taught at, the Santa Cruz College in Mexico City—wrote excellent Latin and was called by Father Sahagún (who knew him as a teacher) one of "the foremost and best-educated men in Mexico."

Early in the sixteenth century a lay member of the second *Audiencia,* Vasco de Quiroga, established his Hospital de Santa Fé near Mexico City. It began as an orphanage for abandoned Mestizo children but gradually grew into a hospital for the poor, and served also as a guesthouse for itinerant monks. Later, Vasco de Quiroga was ordained a priest and in time was made bishop of Michoacán. There he founded the most famous of all his *hospitales,* to which was added a trade school for teaching the Indians shoemaking, carpentry, masonry, hide tanning, wall painting, weaving, and other crafts. The aims and principles of his *hospitales* he set forth in a small book called *Las Ordenanzas,* a work that greatly influenced missionaries who founded similar institutions in Oaxaca and Guatemala.

But it wasn't until the eighteenth century that the greatest missionary of Mexico appeared. He was Father Kino. With a parish 1000 miles long and nearly half that wide—an area that covered the whole great northwest of Mexico, including the long peninsula of Lower California—he traveled 30 miles a day on horseback over mountains and deserts and through dense jungles, stopping at Indian villages to baptize and, when possible, to celebrate mass. He founded numerous missions which so flourished that they in turn became the parent houses of other missions. In this way Father Kino, almost singlehandedly, brought the words of Christ to a semi-barbaric people in a region twice the size of modern Italy.

The Hapsburg kings, who had ruled Spain during the conquest and up until the beginning of the eighteenth century, tended to regard Mexico (and all their New World possessions) as merely a pump to keep the coffers of Spain filled with silver and gold. The only industry they wished to see develop was mining. Consequently those areas rich in mineral ore were settled first, and towns such as Taxco, Guanajuato, Querétaro, and Zacatecas (to mention but a few) grew quickly. Money accumulated there was lavished on massive cathedrals and on classical manors in which lived church dignitaries and town magistrates. So well-planned and constructed were these villages that they remain to this day excellent examples of Spanish architecture in Mexico. It was forbidden by law to grow mulberry bushes and trees (food for the silkworm) or olive trees or to cultivate vineyards, and violators were heavily fined or imprisoned or both. This law protected the silk, wine, and olive industries of Spain. What few industries Spain allowed in Mexico—hide tanning and weaving—were so tightly bound by government restrictions that they were seldom profitable.

And so for two and a half centuries Mexico's only industry, to the exclusion of almost everything else, was mining gold and silver, but mainly silver. Between 1560 and 1821, she, with other countries in New Spain (principally Peru) minted *two billion dollars* in silver (in an age when a penny bought what half a dollar buys today) and sent another two billion to Spain in ingots to be minted there. It is said that before the nineteenth century two thirds of all the silver in the world passed through the port of Veracruz, and that the mines of Zacatecas alone produced one fifth of the total amount of silver then in circulation.

But the curse of dealing solely in gold and silver was, of course, irrepressible and flagrant robbery. Mule trains carrying bags of silver ingots to Veracruz and Acapulco or to the Casa de Moneda (the government minting house in Mexico City) were constantly being waylaid by masked bandits whose more sensational exploits became the subjects of ballads sung

by tavern bards. In the spirit of Robin Hood, the more benevolent brigands shared their loot with the impoverished peasants and became in time legendary heroes of folk tales. But
the most famous bandit of them all, strangely enough, was a
woman named Catalina de Erazu.

Doña Catalina was born in Spain early in the seventeenth
century. Her parents, after deciding that no man was likely
to be attracted by her powerful physique, consigned her to a
convent where it was hoped she would take the veil. But she
soon escaped, disguised as a man, to Peru and Chile, where
she posed as a soldier of fortune. She won fame as the best
swordsman in America before being arrested for gambling,
dueling, and robbery. The discovery that she was a woman
confounded the local judges who, not knowing what to do
with her, returned her to Spain for trial. So unique was her
case that the pope himself was consulted and he, intrigued
by her story, granted her special permission to wear men's
clothes. King Phillip IV of Spain, for some reason, ordered
the charges against her to be dropped and even promised her
a pension of five hundred pesos a year.

She sailed to Mexico and was soon back at her old trade of
holding up *diligencias* (stagecoaches). One of her many wild
escapades in the ten years that followed was an affair with a
Spanish nobleman who accused her of molesting his wife.
Doña Catalina, indeed passionately in love with the woman,
challenged the nobleman to a duel which he declined, claiming that his honor as a gentleman forbade him to use arms
against a woman. (More than likely he was terrified of Doña
Catalina's prowess as a swordsman.) She died peacefully in
1650 with no one to weep for her except historical writers of
later periods who told her amazing story in chronicles and
novels, the most popular of which is *La Monja Alférez*.

But if the loss of silver to road bandits was a problem, it
was a mere trifle compared to what sea bandits, the pirates,
were taking. The English sea dogs and the pirate ships of
Frenchmen and Dutchmen lurked in palm-screened coves of
the Caribbean islands waiting to pounce on the great lumber-
ing galleons of Spain plowing through choppy seas and ocean
swells, their holds filled to overflowing with silver and gold.
On the Spanish Main—from Veracruz to Florida (St. Augus-

tine was founded as a fortressed shelter for Spanish ships)
to the Bermudas to the Azores to Cadiz—pirates lived like
parasites, and many grew fat and respectable. England
knighted her more prosperous pirates and made the most
notorious sea dog of them all, Henry Morgan, governor general of Jamaica. Sir Francis Drake left such an indelible impression on the west coast of Mexico that even to this day
Indian mothers, when scolding their children, say, "The
Draque will get you if you don't behave!"—his name being
synonymous with the bogeyman.

The Church at this time was suffering (if it could be called
that) from its own success. After the first wave of mendicant
monks had swept over Mexico leaving behind them scores of
missions and the foundations of cathedrals and monasteries,
the friars that followed were not so zealous to Christianize
and help the Indians, but rather attended the spiritual needs
of rich Spanish merchants and landlords who, upon dying,
bequeathed them property, cattle, and great endowments in
gold and silver. As a consequence the clergy, while preaching
to the natives to despise all earthly goods, were themselves
accumulating such riches that eventually they had to give
money away on loan (at very reasonable rates) or else see
Mexico's economy collapse. By the end of the eighteenth century the Church owned almost two thirds of all the money
in circulation and over half Mexico's land.

In 1700 the Hapsburg dynasty ended with the death of
Charles II of Spain, the lunatic (who was never trusted to be
alone for fear he would kill himself), and the first of the
Bourbon kings came to power. The third Bourbon king,
Charles III (who reigned from 1759 to 1788) initiated radical
reforms in the Spanish government and thoroughly revamped
Spain's antiquated policy toward her colonies. He sent José
de Galvez (founder of Galveston, Texas) to Mexico to verify
rumors that public trust was being abused by town officials.
Galvez, in his reports, recommended so many sweeping and
sensible changes that Charles made him minister of the Indies to insure that his suggestions were enforced. After that,
Mexico's trade restrictions were greatly reduced and for the
first time in its history trading ships traveled from Veracruz
to other ports in South America and could sell to other ports

besides Cadiz. Town mayors (*alcaldes*) were replaced with *intendentes* who were duty-bound to serve the will of the people. Charles also sent out better viceroys to Mexico. Bucareli (after whom a main street in Mexico City is named) was viceroy from 1771 to 1779, during one of the most prosperous times in Mexico's history. Revilla Gigedo, who succeeded him (besides a street, there are also islands off Mexico's Pacific coast named in his honor), has been called by Mexican historians the finest viceroy of all the sixty-one that ruled Mexico. After his dismissal in 1794 (by the weak and irresolute King Charles IV), the viceroyship fell into the hands of inferior men incapable of dealing effectively with the complicated political situation which began with the rise of Napoleon and which culminated with Mexico's independence.

CHAPTER SIX

1794–1820

1808

Political upheavals in Europe had their repercussions in Mexico. Spain's king, Charles IV, had been duped by his wife into making Manuel de Godoy, an ambitious youth of twenty-five, prime minister. But Godoy's good looks and fine figure were hardly the qualities needed for handling the complicated affairs of state, and the government soon deteriorated. Godoy sold favors to lobbying merchants and gave men more inexperienced than himself posts of importance. One such man was José de Iturrigaray who was made viceroy of Mexico, though he had little to recommend him for the job. It was not long before the Spanish people were complaining against the outrageous graft and corruption undermining their government, and they beseeched Ferdinand VII, the king's eldest son (who had consistently opposed Godoy), to ascend the throne. On March 19, 1808, Charles IV, under a barrage of criticism, abdicated in favor of his son and retired to his country estate near France.

Napoleon, then at his zenith, watched these developments with interest and thought he saw an opportunity to steal another crown for his brother Joseph. He invited former King Charles to France and, using his best persuasive powers, got him to sign a statement renouncing his abdication. At the same time, General Murat—Napoleon's most trusted officer—was sent to Madrid with instructions to bring Ferdinand to France by fair means or foul. Ferdinand was tricked into traveling to Bayonne, France, where Napoleon politely informed him he was a prisoner. After extorting an abdication from Ferdinand, Napoleon proclaimed his brother Joseph king of Spain.

Spain, by then, was seething with discontent. On May 2, 1808, the famous Segundo de Mayo, Spain's day of independence, the people of Madrid organized a partisan army and attacked the French battalion sent to protect Joseph Bonaparte. Towns and villages in the south followed their example and formed guerrilla armies. Independent juntas sprang up everywhere, pledging their loyalty to Ferdinand. Thus began the Peninsular War of Spain.

As early as 1794, Mexico had viewed with alarm the storm clouds gathering over Europe. Against the remote possibility of invasion, the viceroy stored up arms and ammunition and called for volunteers to join a Mexican army loyal to the crown. Response to his call was so enthusiastic, particularly from San Miguel, Celaya, and Dolores, that he soon had fourteen thousand men under arms, all of whom he sent into field maneuvers near the town of Jalapa. In the cavalry regiment was a dashing twenty-seven-year-old second lieutenant, a Creole named Don Ignacio de Allende (after whom the town San Miguel Allende was later named), whose excellence as an officer soon won him a promotion to captain.

When news of Ferdinand's imprisonment reached Mexico, a wave of patriotic loyalty to Spain swept the country. Viceroy Iturrigaray was deluged with letters from mayors from all over the country stating that though Napoleon's brother sat on the throne of Spain, the mayor and his Mexican village were still staunch supporters of Ferdinand. The Creoles of the capital were even more vehement. They insisted that Iturrigaray swear allegiance to Ferdinand and that he ignore any document from a Spanish junta that did not have Ferdinand's signature. Mexico would then function as an independent nation with Iturrigaray as nominal head, until Ferdinand returned to the throne.

The Spaniards of Mexico, the *Peninsulares*, were strongly against the idea. First of all, they disliked Iturrigaray because of his close connections with the notorious Godoy, whose disreputable habits of dealing in graft Iturrigaray was emulating in Mexico. It was well known that the viceroy's lucrative trade in contraband was the chief cause of the country's economic distress. But more important, they detected in the Creole demand a subtle hint of Mexican independence. After the

Second of May uprising in Spain, the *Peninsulares* proposed that Mexico accept the authority of some independent junta operating in the south of Spain. Iturrigaray saw this as a move to curtail his power and therefore peremptorily rejected the plan of the Spaniards.

On the night of September 15, 1808, a small group of armed Spaniards burst into Iturrigaray's house, dragged him out, and locked him in a carriage which rumbled off to Veracruz. There a boat was waiting to carry him back to Spain. The Spaniards then elected a new viceroy, an old man practically in his dotage, named Pedro Garibay, whose only act of importance was to end the army's maneuvers in Jalapa. Garibay's ponderous deliberation over matters of petty importance exasperated the Spaniards, and he was soon replaced by Francisco Javier de Lizana y Beaumont, the archbishop of Mexico who proved to be not much better than Garibay.

But the wind of independence was blowing. Captain Allende, when informed the army was being disbanded, picked up a piece of chalk and wrote on the barracks walls, "Independence! you cowardly Creoles!"

In 1810 the population of Mexico was roughly estimated to be 6,000,000 people—40,000 Spaniards, 1,000,000 Creoles, 3,500,000 pure-blooded Indians, and 1,500,000 Mestizos. From this it can be seen that the Spaniards were a small ruling minority—an oligarchy—whom the Creoles bitterly resented and the Indians and Mestizos hated. War, when it finally broke out, became a class war and one can only assume that the savagery with which the lower classes fought was the inevitable outcome of an oppression too long endured. Independence, it seemed, was but the by-product of a battle to rebalance a disintegrating class society.

Late in the eighteenth century it had become fashionable among cultured Creoles to form literary societies, which would meet for tea and cakes and a lively discussion of the classics. But before long, books banned by the Church, those of Rousseau, Voltaire, and Descartes—all smuggled into the country—were avidly read and discussed, and the societies, although outwardly literary, became secret political societies. In 1810 the most active group in Mexico was operating in Querétaro under the inspired leadership of Captain Allende.

After many discussions of liberty, equality, and fraternity, the only point on which all members could agree was: get rid of the Spaniards! By this time, the Spaniards had acquired the derogatory nickname *gachupines,* which then meant "spurs," which is how the Mexican felt the goadings of the Spaniards. Allende was in a quandary over the ideals of his society, and he, at length, confided his plans to a much-beloved priest from the village of Dolores who occasionally attended his meetings, one Father Miguel Hidalgo y Costilla.

Hidalgo, although a priest, had a voracious appetite for banned books. Born in Pénjamo on May 8, 1753, he studied for the priesthood in Valladolid (now Morelia), at the same time acquiring a wide reputation as an authority on Otomí, an Indian language. He was a man of strong passions and opinions, and his penchant for gambling was well known. Once the clergy of Valladolid raised a fund to finance his studies at the University of Mexico, where he was to receive a degree in theology, but somewhere along the way he fell into a card game, lost the money and his opportunity to earn the much-coveted degree. Assigned to an impoverished parish in the tiny town of Dolores, he worked tirelessly at ameliorating conditions for his Indian charges. How, he asked, could he attend their spiritual needs, when their physical needs had been so long neglected? In defiance of Spanish law, he planted mulberry trees and vineyards and the profits he obtained therefrom went to improve the community. He taught the Indians how to tan hides and started a small industry for making porcelain and tile. Being himself a self-taught musician and a master of many instruments, he organized an Indian orchestra that "oom-pahed" and blared at all the fiestas, and there was nothing he enjoyed more than a Mexican fiesta. When Hidalgo was drawn into Allende's society, he was already a man fifty-seven years old; his bald patch was rimmed with long, hoary hair; his complexion was swarthy; he stooped; he habitually wore a flat, broad-brimmed black hat, a long black frock coat, knee breeches with long black stockings, and a pleasant smile, though his brow was creased with two deep lines of worry. The two men decided to start an insurrection on December 8, the day of the fair at San Juan de Los Lagos.

But there were leaks among the conspirators, and the magistrate of Querétaro was soon aware that trouble was brewing. Knowing his wife to be an ardent supporter of Allende, he locked her in an upstairs room and took the key with him on his errand to alert the militia. His wife, Josefa Ortiz, signaled a fellow conspirator, Ignacio Pérez, living in the house next door, who came quickly to her locked door and received through the keyhole news of her husband's intention to arrest Allende. Pérez raced to San Miguel to warn Allende but found he had already gone to Dolores to consult with Hidalgo. That was September 15, 1810.

At two o'clock in the morning of September 16, Pérez, Allende, and others burst into Hidalgo's house and urged the old priest to escape before the Spaniards arrived. Hidalgo calmly and slowly dressed, thinking over this untimely turn of events, and, while pulling on his long black stockings, said, "Gentlemen, we are lost. Now there is no alternative but to go and catch *gachupines.*" (*"Caballeros, somos perdidos, no hay más recurso que ir a coger gachupines."*)

At gun point the tiny band forced the town jailer to release his prisoners; then rich Spaniards were rounded up and shoved into the empty cells. By daylight, country people were filing along the roads on their way to early Sunday mass. But vigorous, insistent ringing of church bells aroused the townspeople and they came in droves to discover the reason for the commotion. When the church was filled to overflowing, Hidalgo climbed into the pulpit and delivered what has since been regarded as Mexico's proclamation of independence. *"Mexicanos, viva Méjico,"* he cried, a cry that millions of Mexicans take up every September 15—Mexico's day of independence. In Mexico City today, the president, at eleven o'clock at night, appears on a balcony of the National Palace and leads patriotic crowds, jamming the plaza in roars of "Viva!" But what seems to be forgotten, in all these annual demonstrations, is the rest of Hidalgo's speech. Nowhere in it is the word "independence" mentioned. What he said was that Spain had fallen into the hands of the infidel Napoleon and that Ferdinand VII, Spain's rightful king, was being held a prisoner by the French. All *gachupines* were agents of Napoleon and should, therefore, be run out of Mexico. He ended with: "Long live Ferdinand VII! Long live Mexico!" If that meant independence, it was well dissembled. It did, however, fire the congregation with a self-righteousness, especially that part about running *gachupines* out of Mexico.

With a following of three hundred men Hidalgo marched on San Miguel. From the church at Atotonilco he carried off the banner of Our Lady of Guadalupe and the cry then ran, "Long live Our Lady of Guadalupe! Death to the *gachupines!*" When they reached San Miguel, the Spaniards had barricaded themselves inside the city hall. Allende and Hidalgo shouted for them to surrender at once or suffer the consequences of an angry, unruly mob. When Allende swore on his word of honor that no harm would be done to them, their families, or their property, they surrendered peacefully. That night, however, after Allende retired, the mob ran riot through the town, sacking and defacing houses of the Spaniards. Allende, awakened by tumultuous shouting, flew from bed, pulled on clothes and ran to the street, where he leapt on his charger and drove headlong into the rabble, beating them down with the flat of his sword. When a semblance of order had been restored, Hidalgo came forward and severely reprimanded Allende for mistreating the people. This was the first of many bitter quarrels that the two insurgent leaders were to have. Allende argued that the mob was an utter nuisance and that a small, compact body of well-trained men would far better serve their purpose. But Hidalgo wanted his mob. He loved the masses and would not hear a word against them. This important argument, upon which turned the question of how the war would be fought, was won, in the end, by Hidalgo, who won also the command of the army and was given the title Captain General of America.

Hidalgo led his crowd to Celaya. He had now 6000 followers, nearly all of them barefoot, ragged Indians and Mestizos armed with knives, clubs, machetes, and slings. Women, herding flocks of children and carrying baskets of beans and *tortillas*, cluttered the ranks, and the whole procession looked something like a macabre circus. Celaya fell without a shot being fired and was sacked despite the tearful pleadings of its citizens to spare it. His ragtag mob now swelled to 20,000, Hidalgo rolled on to Guanajuato.

Guanajuato is still one of Mexico's most picturesque towns. In 1810 its mines were pouring out the bulk of Mexico's silver. The town itself was a charming pattern of handsome houses and quaint shops, and through its narrow, cobbled streets rumbled many fashionable carriages. The whole effused an air of stable prosperity and decorum. Near the edge of the town still stands an enormous fort-like structure called the *alhóndiga* (communal grain warehouse) completed in 1803. Hearing of Hidalgo's approach, the intendant of the town, Don Juan Antonio Riano turned the *alhóndiga* into a huge vault and a refuge for rich Spanish families. In its grain bins were stored an estimated three million pesos in cash, bullion, and valuables, and on its ramparts were posted Spanish soldiers.

On September 28, 1810, Hidalgo deployed his army around the city and sent in a messenger asking Riano to surrender. When Riano refused, Hidalgo unleashed his horde, who quickly overran the town except for the area around the *alhóndiga*. Musket fire from its high walls pinned down the mob and beat back every attempt to storm the doors. Early in the battle, Riano was killed and the arguments that raged as to who should succeed him diverted the soldiers' attention momentarily from the mob. In that moment, three Indian miners pulled stone slabs on their backs to shield them from the rain of bullets and ran, in a crouch, to the doors, where they started a fire. Flames licked up the heavy wooden beams and soon devoured the doors.

Pushing, shoving, and howling, the mob surged forward and simply overwhelmed the defenders with their numbers. With their primitive weapons they mutilated and massacred soldiers and wealthy Spaniards alike, then, frenzied with greed and hate, they fell upon the money and bullion, fighting each other for its possession.

"The building presented the most horrible spectacle," wrote Lucas Alamán, an eyewitness to the scene. "The food that had been stored there was strewn about everywhere; naked bodies lay half buried in maize, or in money, and everything was spotted with blood." Hidalgo's shouts to stop were lost in the din, and the looting and wrecking went on for two and a half days, ending only with Hidalgo's command to march again. They were off to Valladolid (Morelia).

The citizens of Valladolid were paralyzed with fear, locking themselves in houses or running off to hide in the hills. The town was left practically defenseless. Canon Betancourt of the cathedral, in contempt of this despicable show of cowardice, walked at the head of an unarmed group to meet Hidalgo on the road. There, before the town, he exacted from the rebel leader a promise that the shameful plunderings of San Miguel, Celaya, and Guanajuato would not be repeated at Valladolid. Hidalgo, however, when he entered the town and found the cathedral locked (he had wanted to say a prayer of thanksgiving, he claimed), angrily jailed all Spaniards, replaced the city officials with his own men, and confiscated four hundred thousand pesos from the church treasury. Heady with this success, he felt certain that his army, which was still growing, was now invincible.

With 2000 regular soldiers and a meandering, disorganized mob of 80,000 Indians and Mestizos, he swung through Toluca and started up the mountain pass toward Mexico City. In the National Palace the near-hysterical Viceroy Venegas, lacking his best officer, General Calleja (who was on the march from San Luis Potosí), commissioned a military novice named Trujillo to intercept Hidalgo in the mountains. Trujillo went off with 7000 men and two cannons. The two armies met on October 30 in a mountain pass called Monte de las Cruces (Mountain of the Crosses), a place where road bandits, when caught, were crucified. The battle raged all day with neither side giving ground, although by nightfall Trujillo was nearly surrounded and, under cover of darkness, withdrew. He returned to Mexico City claiming a great victory, but the viceroy wailed in despair. He had the Virgen de los Remedios brought from her shrine in the hills and placed in the grand cathedral, where he formally commissioned her captain general of all Spanish forces in America and then fell on his knees and prayed for divine intervention. His prayers, it seems, were answered.

Every now and then the unfolding of history takes an unexpected turn. The chain-like pattern of cause and effect is suddenly upset by some altogether different and unexpected cause, with its subsequent startling effect. With victory lying in the palm of his hand, Hidalgo did not seize it. By turning his army around and marching back to Toluca, he confounded both military strategists and historians, who have looked in vain for the reason for this move. Many have been suggested: that Trujillo, in fact, defeated him; that another argument arose between himself and Allende; that his army was falling apart with desertions. But the real reason can probably be found only by carefully studying the character of Hidalgo. He may have felt mercy for the people in Mexico City. Or he may have felt the lack of principles guiding his movement. In any case, his insurrection, from this point onward, went into a steady decline from which it never recovered. General Calleja, with 7000 men, caught up with him at Aculco and soundly defeated his dwindling army of 40,000. Hidalgo escaped to Valladolid and Allende managed an orderly retreat to Guanajuato.

Undaunted by this defeat, Hidalgo dispatched several of his more capable officers to various parts of the country to sound his "Cry of Dolores"—to Guadalajara and to rural regions in the south. A priest and former pupil of his, Father José María Morelos, was sent south to capture Acapulco. Don José Antonio Torres was sent to Guadalajara, which received him with such a resounding welcome that he induced Hidalgo to take up residence there. All Guadalajara, including its clergy and officials, hailed him as a great liberator, gave him fiestas, and celebrated high mass in his honor, during which he sat in the canopied chair regularly reserved for viceroys. They bestowed upon him the title Alteza Serenísima (Supreme Highness), while he, in quiet moments, worked at writing precepts for his government. Meanwhile Calleja advanced on Guadalajara.

Despite Allende's heated objections, Hidalgo chose to fight Calleja outside the city. Defenses were prepared on the banks of the Lerma River, near a bridge called Puente de Calderón, some miles northeast of the city. He had 100,000 men, and Calleja, when he arrived after a forced march, had but 7000, although his superior discipline and strategy more than offset this numerical difference. After several hours of hard fighting, a well-aimed Calleja cannon sent a heated iron ball into Hidalgo's munitions dump, starting a holocaust behind the rebel lines. A wind fanned the flames till the whole countryside was a burning inferno. Hidalgo was again defeated, and Calleja entered Guadalajara in triumph.

The *insurgentes* regrouped in Zacatecas where Allende, furious with Hidalgo for his bungling at Guadalajara, demoted him to a civilian in charge of political affairs and put himself at the head of the army. But it was too late. The redoubtable Calleja was again on the march. In 40 coaches with an armed escort of 1000 men, the rebel army of Allende struck off for San Antonio de Béjar (now San Antonio, Texas) where, it was rumored, a new uprising had started. While they were wending their way through the mountainous district of northern Coahuila, an ex-rebel leader named Ignacio Elizonda ambushed them and captured their entire train. Under a heavy guard they were marched across a scorching desert to Chihuahua where all except Hidalgo were given a quick court-martial and were subsequently shot. Hidalgo, because he was a priest, was handed over to the bishop of Durango, who defrocked him and returned him to the army for execution.

Don Miguel Hidalgo is revered as Mexico's greatest patriot. Against his shortcomings which were, admittedly, many, stands one attribute which he possessed in abundance and which in Mexico is more admired than military genius or intellectual brilliance. He had sympathy for the underdog. He, more than any leader in his movement, sought to alleviate the misery of the Indians and Mestizos. His highly emotional nature undoubtedly made him rash and headstrong, but it also made him burn with compassion for all suffering, sentient beings, including animals. A paper he wrote in prison expresses those same depths of emotion found in passages of the Old Testament. "Who will give water for my brow and fountains of tears for my eyes? Would that I might shed from the pores of my body, the blood that flows through my veins, to mourn night and day for those of my people who have perished, and to bless the eternal mercies of the Lord! Would that my laments might exceed those of Jeremiah!"

He was shot in Chihuahua on July 30, 1811. His day as a lion had lasted but a brief six months, long enough, however, to shake the whole social structure of Mexico. Hidalgo was, in fact, a portent of his times. Mexico was in transition, and much turmoil and trouble were yet to be endured.

The corpses of Hidalgo, Allende, and two other rebel leaders were decapitated and their grisly heads were sent to Guanajuato where they were stuck on poles fixed to the top of the *alhóndiga*. There they remained, a gruesome reminder of Spanish retribution, until 1821, when Mexico finally won its independence. Remnants of Hidalgo's army still continued, after his death, to harass the government. Father José Morelos, commanding a band of hand-picked, well-trained guerrilla fighters, captured Chilpancingo on May 24, 1811, then marched to Cuautla, near Cuernavaca, in the heart of the sugar-cane country and within striking distance of Mexico City. From February to May he fought nettling battles with government forces but could never gain a decisive victory. The unbeatable Calleja was sent to Cuautla to capture him, but in his attempt to storm Cuautla's defenses he was repulsed and suffered heavy casualties. So he encircled the town and waited for a surrender by starvation.

With Morelos and his men reduced to eating soap and the bark from trees, victory was almost within Calleja's grasp. Morelos, however, through a series of brilliant maneuvers, broke Calleja's encircling ring and made good the escape of all but a few of his emaciated followers. For the next six months he roamed the rugged terrain around Tehuacán and Puebla, and finally, on November 24, 1812, after a short three-hour siege, occupied Oaxaca, the largest and richest city in the south. Former followers of Hidalgo took heart at this triumph and rallied around Morelos, acclaiming him the new leader of the insurrection. Towns from the gulf coast to the Pacific pledged their support to his movement, whose principles and objectives he was at pains to clarify.

On September 8, 1813, he convoked a congress of partisans in Chilpancingo at which was approved and ratified his declaration of independence. Briefly it stated: 1) that Mexico was no longer property of Spain; 2) that the Catholic religion was the official religion of Mexico; 3) that slavery was abolished; 4) that all men were equal before God and the law; 5) that government monopolies were to be broken up; 6) that his government would be supported by a 5 per cent income tax and by a 10 per cent import tax on all foreign goods; 7) that Spaniards were to be deported. He was unanimously elected commander in chief of the new government, whose first task was the same vexing one that faced Hidalgo: to get rid of the Spaniards.

At the head of an army 5600 strong, he marched on Valladolid. As his men took up positions in the hills surrounding the town, the commander of government troops within the city called for the support of a nearby cavalry regiment commanded by a young lieutenant named Agustín Iturbide. While probing for weaknesses in the enemy's line, Iturbide, on a sudden impulse, dashed straight up the hill to the heart of the rebel camp and so stunned its defenders that Morelos himself was in danger of being caught or killed. In the confusion that ensued, rebels fired on rebels and then ran in disorder from their positions. The following day Iturbide looked in vain for his enemy but found only abandoned stores of food and munitions scattered among the trees.

The star of Morelos was going into its descent, and there were many Creoles who would have liked to hasten its fall. These were the Creoles with vested interests—landowners and government officials—who certainly despised *gachupines* as much as anybody but who found Morelos' terms for independence too harsh to accept, especially the part about paying an income tax and breaking up government monopolies. Morelos lost military and political followers and wandered with his waning congress through mountains and jungles, sometimes holding sessions in forest clearings. Government troops were doggedly hunting him down, and he fought now only to escape being captured. While leading his congress to Tehuacán, the proposed capital of his new government, he was surprised by a Spanish patrol and sent his congress one way while he, drawing the patrol's attention to himself, struck off in another. His congress reached Tehuacán without a loss, but he was pursued by the patrol and caught by an ex-officer of his rebel army named Carranco. Carranco stumbled onto Morelos while the latter was resting peacefully beneath a tree. Without making a move to resist, Morelos said calmly, "Señor Carranco, it seems we have met before."

Morelos was resigned to his fate. In the last years of his nomad existence, he had realized the futility of fighting against hopeless odds. By order of the bishop of Oaxaca he was defrocked, and had the holy oils of his consecrated hands removed by scraping. This painful ordeal he suffered without a whimper, though the onlooking bishop and priests wept openly. The authorities of Mexico City, alarmed at his tremendous popularity (which could easily have erupted into a serious demonstration) took him to San Cristóbal Ecatepec —twenty miles north of the capital—where on December 22, 1815, he was shot. A large monument has been erected over the very spot where he stood when executed.

With him fell his congress, the bulwark of his government. Most deserted and made peace with the royalists, but Vicente Guerrero proclaimed himself the successor of Morelos and held out with a band of guerrilla fighters in the hills of the Mixteca country near Oaxaca.

Meanwhile, the Spaniards in Mexico tried to follow the political cavortings of Spain, whose judicial pendulum was swinging crazily from right to left. The junta of Cadiz (to which the viceroy of Mexico was legally bound) concocted a constitution so extremely liberal that the Spaniards in Mexico and the rich Creoles hesitated to accept it and toyed with the idea of themselves declaring Mexico's independence. That was in 1812, when Morelos had just published his own proclamation of independence. But he, with his plan to exact import and income taxes, was, in the eyes of Mexico's upper classes, as repellent as the constitution of Cadiz, and so it was decided to do nothing till Ferdinand returned to the Spanish throne. When Ferdinand VII resumed his royal duties in May, 1814, he at once rejected the constitution of Cadiz, showing by this that he was no liberal nor had any liberal tendencies. Rich Mexicans were thoroughly delighted with his act. But the Spanish people in Spain were not willing to regress to the centralized government of the Bourbon kings. They had tasted freedom when, without any help from the crown, they had fought and defeated Napoleon's armies. In 1820, Colonel Rafael Riego, a stalwart among the liberals, upon receiving orders to sail with his regiment to Argentina, revolted and marched on Madrid instead. As most of the army supported him, the revolution was practically bloodless, and, by March of that year, King Ferdinand was forced to recognize and uphold the constitution of Cadiz. This change set the Mexican rich thinking once again about the benefits of an independent Mexico.

CHAPTER SEVEN

1820–1824

1820

In times of trouble Mexican cafés become public forums, where political differences can be thrashed out for merely the price of a coffee. When Viceroy Apodaca was ordered by the king to uphold the republican constitution of Spain, cafés overflowed with old-guard monarchists, railing against liberalism and liberal governments. Dr. Matías Monteagudo, a devout Catholic and a debater of renown, met with groups in cafés and in private houses to work out some method of saving Mexico from what he considered to be the evils of liberalism. The king, he argued, had been forced against his will to swear allegiance to the Cadiz constitution, therefore all orders emanating from that document were, *ipso facto*, invalid. Viceroy Apodaca should not be imposing the liberal constitution of Spain on Mexico, but should be taking orders from the Council of the Indies—that scholarly group of priests and lawyers that had been ruling Mexico so well since the beginning of the sixteenth century. His reasoning made sense to many, but how, they asked, could they force the viceroy to accept their plan—called the *Profesa* plan—when they lacked military backing? Dr. Monteagudo was ready with the answer: Don Agustín de Iturbide would lead them.

Iturbide, a Mestizo (with a Spanish father and a Mexican mother) though he claimed he was a Creole, was then thirty-seven, tall, handsome, affable, and a military leader whose skill and bravery had been amply tested on the field of battle. Since retiring from active service in 1816, he had been closely associated with a quasi-political group of Catholic laymen—

headed by Dr. Monteagudo but directed by priests of the convent of San Felipe Nervi—called *La Profesa* (from which the plan took its name) on the corner of Avenida Madero and Isabel la Catolica. Iturbide listened with interest to the unfolding of Dr. Monteagudo's logic, but he made no binding agreement with him. During these many political discussions Iturbide probably formulated his own plan, one which he thought about deeply but which, at that time, he mentioned to no one.

In November of 1820, Viceroy Apodaca, who was extremely fond of Iturbide, promoted him to brigadier general and sent him south with funds and 2476 men to put down, once and for all, the annoying rebel forces of Guerrero. Iturbide's troops, attempting to drive the leonine Guerrero from his lair, were decisively defeated, doubtless because Iturbide was not attentive enough to the problems of battle but was, rather, preoccupied with working out details of his plan. He had reached a critical stage in his life; conditions demanded that either he act immediately or forever hold his peace. After some deliberation he took the plunge and entered into communications with Guerrero. He proposed that the two armies join forces in a fight for Mexico's independence but only on condition that they both accept a plan which he, Iturbide, would soon make known. Guerrero, mildly suspicious of a trick, at first refused, but Iturbide agents in his camp persuaded him to think otherwise. When the alliance was concluded, Iturbide confiscated 525,000 pesos from a mule train transporting silver to Acapulco, where ships were waiting to carry it to the Orient. Merchants, whose money had been so expropriated, received vouchers signed by Iturbide redeemable only when Mexican independence had been won.

On February 24, 1821, he published in the town of Iguala his famous plan—*Plan de Iguala*—which was admittedly a far cry from the high ideals of Morelos. But it was workable and it appealed to a war-weary country. First, it proclaimed Mexico an independent constitutional monarchy, to be ruled by Ferdinand VII, if he so desired, or by some other prince from one of Europe's royal, reigning families. Second, it made citizens of all people—Spaniards, Creoles, Indians, and Mestizos—and they were thenceforth to be known simply as Mexicans, with equal rights and equal opportunities. Third, it tolerated no religion but the Catholic religion, the official religion of Mexico.

As if by magic, the Plan of Iguala appeared on billboards in plazas of towns all over Mexico, and citizens, in defiance of the law, gathered in groups to argue its merits. All warring factions found appeasement—Spaniards saw an end to their persecution, Creoles saw an end to Spanish domination, monarchists and conservatives saw an end to the encroachment of liberal ideas, and the Church (to which everyone belonged) saw its unrivaled supremacy assured. And behind all this stood the army of Iturbide to guarantee the enforcement of each point—the army of the three guarantees, called in Spanish the *Trigarante*.

Military leaders—Guerrero, Negrete, Nicolás Bravo, Guadalupe Victoria, Santa Anna, and many others—flocked to his banner, which has since become the Mexican national flag: red for union, white for religion, and green for independence. Rural towns immediately and enthusiastically supported the plan. Viceroy Apodaca had been outmaneuvered. Powerless to check the landslide desertions of towns, and constantly menaced by pro-Iturbide officials within his own government, he resigned with only four towns still flying the Spanish flag —Mexico City, Durango, Veracruz, and Acapulco. To resign was a wise move, since he was, in any case, soon to be replaced by a new viceroy from the liberal government of Spain.

The new viceroy, Don Juan O'Donoju (pronounced O'Donohue), arrived on July 30, 1821, and took his oath of office before Mayor Davila of Veracruz because the road to Mexico was blocked by the army of the *Trigarante*. By arrangement, he conferred with Iturbide in the town of Córdoba, where they worked out and signed a treaty by which Spain accepted, in its entirety, the *Plan de Iguala*. Four minor amendments were conceded to O'Donoju, one of which granted Spaniards residing in Mexico the right to return to the mother country with all their accumulated capital in cash; another pledged the Mexican government to pay for the evacuation of Spanish troops from Mexican soil. What Hidalgo and Morelos failed to achieve with all their heroic and heart-breaking battles, Iturbide accomplished with the stroke of a pen. Mexico, at last, was independent.

On September 27, 1821, Iturbide, at the head of his handsomely uniformed army of the *Trigarante*, paraded through the decorated streets of Mexico City. A profusion of flags—red, white, and green—hung from balconies and fluttered above the wildly cheering crowds. Bands blared, bells rang, and cannons roared. People lining the streets cried and laughed. It was Mexico's most jubilant hour.

A clause in the Treaty of Córdoba empowered Iturbide to form a council of governors of thirty-eight members to rule the country, until a constitutional government could be established. Their first task was to handle elections of representatives to a constituent congress, but in their zeal to be fair they entangled themselves in a long series of elections—electing electors to elect further electors who, in the end, produced a body of men representing only the wealthy upper classes. At their first session on February 24, 1822, Iturbide, acting as the nominal head of the government (in the absence of a monarch) in his address to the assembly, stated emphatically that writing a constitution was the greatest and most urgent task before them.

Three weeks before this historic session, Ferdinand VII gained the upper hand in Spain and began having liberals arrested and shot; he denounced the Treaty of Córdoba and claimed that O'Donoju was a traitor to the crown for having signed Mexico's document of independence. Spanish troops in Veracruz waiting to embark for Spain promptly seized the island fort of San Juan de Ulúa, which remained, for the next four years, the last Spanish stronghold in Mexico.

The hundred and twenty members of the constituent congress were mostly political amateurs who wasted precious hours haggling over inconsequential matters such as statues and monuments for war heroes, or indulging in long pointless debates about the subtle meanings of Voltaire. Iturbide, in his speeches, begged them to give more attention to the pressing problems of state, principally to that of writing a constitution, but his exhortations only won him enemies, especially among rabid Jacobin liberals. The national economy was in a state of disaster because of the large withdrawals of capital made by Spaniards returning home with their fortunes. Congress, in a move to economize, put the army on half pay, and when Iturbide remonstrated they, to show their disdain of him, promptly discharged half the soldiers. The government by then was teetering on the brink of ruin. Its critical condition provoked accusations and counter-accusations which were hurled back and forth between liberals and conservatives, freemasons and the Church, Iturbide and his congress. In the midst of it all was discovered a plot (implicating the mayor of Veracruz) to give Mexico back to Spain.

On the night of May 8, 1822, there occurred a "spontaneous" demonstration outside the palace of Iturbide, touched off, it is said, by a sergeant named Pío March, of Iturbide's own Celaya regiment, who, with a band of soldiers, ran through the streets shouting, "*Viva Agustín Primero, Emperador de Méjico*" ("Long live Agustine First, Emperor of Mexico). A gathering crowd swelled these shouts to a roar. Iturbide appeared briefly on his balcony and signaled for them to go away, but their shouting increased. Finally in an impromptu speech he promised to accept the crown, on condition that congress offer it to him. The crowd went wild with delight; cathedral bells were rung and cannons were fired. By seven o'clock the next morning congress was in session and, after listening to many long-winded speeches in praise of Iturbide, voted at four o'clock in the afternoon to make him emperor. There were 71 yeas, 15 nays, and 23 abstentions.

So, on July 21, 1822, in the great cathedral of Mexico, with *Te Deums* being sung and the bishop of Guadalajara conducting the solemn ceremonies, the president of congress placed the crown of emperor upon the head of Agustine I, ruler of an empire stretching from Oregon in the north, down to the Isthmus of Panama in the south.

His first act as emperor was to dissolve his ineffectual congress and to form a small council of his own choosing to rule until congress would again convene. He was now a virtual dictator. His gravest problem was to feed the monster he himself had created: the army of the *Trigarante*. Salaries of generals and colonels had been shamefully neglected for months, and the brutish monster, for want of food, was threatening to devour its maker. Pamphlets of mysterious origin, calling the emperor a tyrannical despot ". . . who wants to hitch you to his triumphant chariot with chains a thousand times heavier than ever were clamped upon us by our former oppressors," were being circulated in Veracruz. Iturbide was undoubtedly aware that his Napoleonic-style empire was in danger of being stillborn and made frantic efforts to keep it alive. He offered generous concessions to the liberals and printed paper money with which to pay off long overdue debts—particularly to the army—but this only brought on a terrible spiraling inflation that further aggravated the situation. In his deep concern to avoid ruin, he completely overlooked Don Antonio López de Santa Anna, an upstart general in Jalapa who had been brooding over a supposed slight to his honor. In November of 1822, Iturbide, passing through Jalapa on his way to Veracruz, discovered Santa Anna prefixing his name with *Jefe Político* (Political Boss). This utterly empty title sorely rankled the authorities of Jalapa and they begged the emperor to forbid its use. Iturbide mildly reprimanded Santa Anna and passed on, probably forgetting in the next few minutes whatever it was he said. But Santa Anna swore to avenge this inconsiderate blow to his pride.

The time was ripe for the appearance of such an unscrupulous egotist as Santa Anna. He was short and paunchy; he had a large bulbous nose, and heavy-lidded eyes that gave him a look of unrelieved boredom. In the heat of hating Iturbide, he concocted a plan, called the Plan of Casa Mata, which demanded the immediate reinstatement of congress. Several generals, at odds with Iturbide, used this plan to instigate a revolt, the most formidable of them being Vincente Guerrero.

Plans are studded all along the course of Mexican history. Between 1821 and 1921, one hundred "plans" were written, some of them good, most of them preposterous, serving only as a pretext for some general (usually self-made) to grab power and the spoils that went with it. The "plan," then, is an attempt to justify the overthrow of the government and win, it is hoped, the support of the people. It must be conceded that historian Leslie Byrd Simpson is right when he states: "The plan . . . may be considered the fundamental constitution of Mexico." Concerning the *Plan de Casa Mata*, Santa Anna laughingly admitted years later that when he wrote it, he did not know the meaning of the word "republic."

Though Guerrero and his motley army were defeated, Iturbide dreaded the prospect of dragging the country into more war, and so he abdicated on March 19, 1823. Congress, which he had hastily reinstated in a futile attempt to quell the uprising, granted him a pension of twenty-five thousand pesos a year so long as he remained in exile.

He sailed on the British frigate *Rowillins*, May 8, 1823, accompanied by his wife and eight children. More than a year later, congress, then under the sway of radical liberals, branded him a traitor, subject to be shot if ever found on Mexican soil. But this edict never reached him. He had left Italy, where his presence was found objectionable to authorities of the Holy Alliance, and had taken up residence in London, where he uncovered a Spanish plot to retake Mexico. An ex-secretary of his, Torrente, then living in Paris, greatly exaggerated the size of a pro-Iturbide party in Mexico and begged him to return to the homeland to lead the Mexican armies against the impending Spanish invasion.

He did so, landing at Soto la Marina, a gulf-coast town north of Tampico. Almost immediately he was captured and jailed by a small patrol commanded by Felipe Garza, formerly an officer in Iturbide's army of the *Trigarante*. Local authorities voted for his immediate execution, and he was shot by Garza's squad on July 19, 1824. Fourteen years later his remains were taken from Padilla to the Chapel of San Felipe and later to the great cathedral of Mexico where they were immured behind a large bronze plaque which reads:

AGUSTÍN DE ITURBIDE, AUTHOR OF THE MEXICAN
INDEPENDENCE.
COMPATRIOT, WEEP FOR HIM.
STRANGER, ADMIRE HIM.
THIS MONUMENT HOLDS THE ASHES OF A HERO.
HIS SOUL RESTS IN THE BOSOM OF GOD.

CHAPTER EIGHT

1823–1855

1823

Mexico's high central plateau, extending over its entire length, and nearly its breadth, is an awesome series of mountain ranges that surround and separate one valley from another. Now highways snake through mountain passes, permitting traffic to reach the most provincial village and forming, as it were, a network of veins and arteries that binds the country into one functioning, national-conscious whole. National-consciousness is relatively new in Mexico and developed, it could be argued, with the growth of such internal communications as roads, railroads, and the telegraph. In 1823 roads were deplorable and national-consciousness was practically nonexistent.

For three centuries under Spanish colonial rule provincial towns such as Oaxaca, Guadalajara, Querétaro, Zacatecas, Mérida—in fact, nearly all major towns in Mexico, cut off as they were from the rest of the country—nurtured a regional pride in their costumes, customs, cuisine, songs, and dances. Each town was governed by a rich and often titled Spaniard whose loyalty to the viceroy in Mexico City was unswerving. With loyalty, then, the entire Spanish empire was held together. When the viceroy was removed, the main support of an extremely complicated system of loyalties was withdrawn and the entire system collapsed. The withdrawal of Spanish noblemen from provincial towns worsened the situation. The country fell into a loose confederation of states, each resenting and distrusting the rule of professional politicians, particularly those in Mexico City who wished to dominate the entire country.

Distrust not only divided the country horizontally into autonomous towns and provinces, but vertically, setting class against class in an unholy struggle for political power. The upper classes were dominated by rich Creole landowners who were almost at one with the high priests of the Church. Politically they favored a strong central government presided over by a monarch. The middle class in 1823 was so diversified that classification, as such, is almost impossible. In general it could be said that it was made up of Mestizos, the pure Mexican with a Spanish and Indian ancestry. To follow the rise of this uniquely Mexican interracial blood group from zero, at the time of the conquest, to over forty million today, is to follow, in effect, the main trend of Mexico's history. When Hidalgo sounded his "Cry of Dolores" in 1810, the Mestizos numbered a million and a half—a fifth of the population—and made up the bulk of Hidalgo's army. By soldiering in the wars of independence, Mestizos were, for the first time, asserting their right to a voice in deciding Mexico's destiny. Compared to the Indian, the Mestizo was ambitious, adaptable, mentally quick and inquisitive, and too proud to accept the poverty to which the Spaniards had relegated him. Compared to the Spaniard, he was more humble, more tolerant, softer in speech and manner, and with a keener sense of humor. He was emotional rather than intellectual, brave rather than prudent. Mestizos were found all along the political scale but were in a preponderance on the left. The bottom class, still as ever, then as now, were the pure-blooded Indians—quiet, patient, inscrutable, highly superstitious, and politically indifferent though easily persuaded to follow any group that promised them better conditions, so long as the group respected the Virgin of Guadalupe. In 1823 all three groups were suspicious of each other and a stifling atmosphere of fear enveloped the country.

The Church, which usually tried to stand apart from all questions of class strife and politics, now found itself very much a part of them. The Church in Mexico, like the Church in Spain since Isabel la Catolica (in the fifteenth century) had been, during the reign of the viceroys, an integral part of the government. The powers of the Church and those of the government were mutually overlapping, and people tacitly understood that to be a good Catholic was, in effect, to be a good subject of the crown. But in Mexico, when the crown's representative, the viceroy, disappeared, the Church was left without any government support. She floundered, temporarily, having never been in such a situation, but gradually gained strength and confidence by consolidating her holdings and becoming a kind of private business. During the colonial period she had been given choice land for her monasteries and convents, lands which were converted into pastures for cattle and fields for farming. Her income, then, from agriculture was considerable, and neither her income nor her property—by a decree of the Hapsburg kings—was taxable. In 1820 over half the country's wealth was in the hands of the Church, making her far richer and stronger than the young Mexican government struggling to get to its feet.

The first congress of that new government convened in November 1823. The problems facing this congress were intrinsically different from those facing the first American Constitutional Congress of 1786. Mexico grappled with deep-rooted beliefs and prejudices that had grown like weeds in a culture three hundred years old, whereas the original thirteen states were comparatively young and were, in almost every way, better suited for a democratic form of government. It is, therefore, truly without point to compare the growth of democracy in the two countries since their backgrounds, up to the time democracy took root, were utterly different. If comparisons must be made, France in her trials after the revolution of 1789 has more in common with Mexico than has the United States. Both France and Mexico were dominated by the Church, and both governments swung violently from the extreme right to the extreme left, from conservative to liberal, from monarchy to anarchy. Mexico's road toward democracy was fraught with dangers, but a handful of spirited men were determined to travel it, whatever the price.

The constitution which congress passed and ratified in 1824 was mainly the work of two liberals: Miguel Ramós Arispe and Dr. Valentín Gómez Farias. Quite obviously they used the Constitution of the United States as their model, omitting, of course, freedom of religion, since the Catholic religion was still the only religion tolerated in Mexico. The country was cut up into thirteen states, and by making each state autonomous the demands of congressmen from the provinces were satisfied. The government was to be financed (principally) by a 20 per cent import duty on all foreign goods, to be collected by government customs houses at all ports of entry. Many congressmen were unhappy with the constitution, particularly the conservatives and the centralists, but as they had produced no alternative plan, they were obliged to accept it, although they did so grudgingly.

1824

Guadalupe Victoria was honored with being elected the first president of the Mexican republic. Unfortunately his military background was not a good one for the high office of president. Hardly had he settled at his desk than his government was threatened with bankruptcy. He was spending over 18,000,000 pesos annually (12,000,000 went to the army alone) but collecting only 9,000,000 from revenues. Money, therefore, was desperately needed. At that time Britain was building its empire, sending troops to India and China and ambassadors to Latin America with instructions to make favorable trade pacts backed by loans. The able diplomat H. G. Hart, then Britain's chargé d'affaires in Mexico, charmed Guadalupe Victoria into accepting two loans from England for over three million pounds each, negotiated by the English banking houses of Goldschmidt, Barclay, and others. The interest rates were exorbitant, but Guadalupe Victoria was backed to the wall and could hardly quibble. The loans temporarily staved off bankruptcy and kept down rebellion, but they put control of the nation's economy in the hands of the British. By 1828, when Guadalupe Victoria retired from office (he held the distinction of being the only president in over fifty years to serve a full term), two political parties had emerged from heated debates over the nation's finances.

On the left were the liberals, divided into *moderatos* who favored mild liberal reforms—their leaders were Gómez Farias and Luis Moya—and the *puros* (extremists) who preached a rabid Jacobin philosophy, their most outspoken leader being Lorenzo de Zavala. On the right were the conservatives—the landed aristocracy and the clergy—whose most brilliant spokesman was then Mexico's greatest scholar, Lucas Alamán. He favored a monarchy, but, failing this, he preferred a military dictatorship to even the mildest form of liberalism.

Both political camps were teeming with freemasons, although they were more numerous and stronger among the liberals. Various masonic lodges were founded in Mexico City, and rivalries between different rites (emanating from New York) became important factors in deciding political disputes. The grand master of freemasonry in Mexico was the energetic and affable American Ambassador to Mexico, Mr. Joel Poinsett—from whom the Mexican winter-blooming Christmas flower, the *noche buena,* gets its English name: the Poinsettia. So successful was he at turning Mexican politicians into masonic neophytes that by 1828 both presidential candidates were freemasons, although the conservative candidate, General Gómez Pedraza, was less under Poinsett's control than the liberal, General Vicente Guerrero.

1828

The conservative, Pedraza, won the election by the narrow margin of *one* electoral vote. Vicente Guerrero grumbled (he was by far the more popular candidate) but might have accepted defeat peacefully if Santa Anna hadn't jumped up and shouted "Fraud!" Government troops drove Santa Anna into hiding and later ferreted out liberal leaders who were allegedly aiding him. This had the effect of unifying the liberals and of making a hero of Guerrero, around whom gathered veterans of past wars urging him to lead a revolt. But the revolt, when it came, actually started in the Acordada jail in Mexico City where the radical Lorenzo de Zavala was imprisoned. He, with fiery speeches, won the sympathy of his jailers, who released him and then assisted him in gaining command of the militia stationed there. At the head of these troops, he led an assault on the National Palace. Rabble from the city slums took advantage of the confused street fighting to rob and wreck stores, particularly those of foreigners, and they burned the Parian market, then the largest in Mexico City. President Pedraza's rapid departure should have ended the mclee, but riotous lootings and burnings went on for another two weeks. Damage done was estimated at over two million pesos, and Mexico incurred claims against her by foreigners which later would have disastrous effects.

1829

By January order had been established over the smoldering city and congress proclaimed Vicente Guerrero the new president. Anastasio Bustamante, the conservative, who had been the running partner of Pedraza, was allowed to stay in office as vice-president.

It will be remembered that Guerrero, after the death of Morelos, had been the last resolute fighter for independence who alone held out for six years in the hills surrounding Oaxaca. But it seems that the rigors of waging nerve-straining, guerrilla warfare sapped his energies, for as a president he was listless and indifferent. Only once was his old leonine spirit aroused: that was in July of 1829, when General Barradas, the Spaniard, acting on the instructions of King Ferdinand VII landed on the coast of Tamaulipas near Tampico with 2700 men in an idiotic attempt to reconquer Mexico. He, like the great conquistador Cortés, whose success he meant to emulate, voluntarily cut off means of escape by sending his fleet back to Cuba. After capturing Tampico his army collapsed from malaria, thirst, and hunger. Guerrero stomped about his presidential office and finally commissioned Santa Anna to lead 3000 Mexican soldiers against the Spaniards. In the meantime, over 900 men of the Barradas army had died of tropical diseases and the rest lay prostrate with fevers and sickness. By the time Santa Anna arrived, the Spaniards could do nothing but beg humbly for honorable terms of surrender. Santa Anna, in his reports, called this a great military victory for Mexico and Guerrero hailed him as the "Hero of Tampico." After this, Guerrero sank back into his chronic state of lethargy.

1830

But his congress could not tolerate the deplorable state of affairs. Crimes were going unpunished, the treasury was practically empty, and the country's economy was in chaos. Impeachment proceedings were started, but General Bustamante, the vice-president, ended them by overthrowing Guerrero by force and by proclaiming himself president.

1831

Though Bustamante was a tool of the conservatives and the puppet of Lucas Alamán, he was a vigorous administrator and for two years Mexico enjoyed an efficient government. Crime was cut down, roads were cleared of bandits, and the takings at the customs houses increased because he had practically stamped out smuggling. But Bustamante ruled with the hand of a tyrant, and before long his enemies far outnumbered his friends.

The outcries of liberals against Bustamante's dictatorship (especially loud in the northern provinces) sounded like revolt to the politically sensitive ear of Santa Anna, and he set the country on fire by seizing the customs house at Veracruz and pocketing the money collected there. Government troops sent down to capture him were stricken with malaria and were, therefore, easily repulsed and routed. Northern states, emboldened by Santa Anna's audacity, formally announced that they would no longer accept the dictates of a centralized government. At this Bustamante threw up his hands. In a fit of temper he resigned and sailed to England where he meant to remain the rest of his life in exile. His departure was hailed by the liberals as a great victory for the democratic cause, and congress, infected by their jubilation, proclaimed Santa Anna president of the republic and Gómez Farias, co-author of the constitution, his vice-president.

1833

At the root of Santa Anna's many faults was his overweening *amour-propre*. He hungered after titles, honors, and prestige but never once took seriously the obligations that went with them. He rather used (or abused) these privileges to get whatever he wanted. His spineless character was held up solely by pride, and when that was pricked (as it was on several occasions) he deflated like a balloon. Whenever his responsibilities became too heavy, he retired to his large hacienda, Magna de Clavo, near Veracruz, where he was entertained with cockfights and bullfights, banquets and speechmaking. On the day set by congress for his inauguration, he pleaded sick and remained on his hacienda. Gómez Farias was therefore made provisional president in his absence.

Gómez Farias, by this time, had become a drum-beating, anticlerical fanatic. Congress, lashed by his whip of hate, enacted several reform bills which dealt sledge-hammer blows to the Church. Appointments to ecclesiastical offices were to be made by the government; monks and nuns could retract their vows; and a government branch of secular education was instituted. These were but a few of his reforms. The clergy was in an uproar and the army was no less enraged when he passed a bill cutting their pay, size, and privileges. The chorus of complaints against him was now deafening, but somehow he managed to stay in power. In fact, it took nothing less than an act of God to dislodge him. In 1833, Mexico was swept by a plague of cholera. An eerie silence fell over the capital, broken only by the tolling of church bells and the rumblings of death carts heaped high with corpses. The superstitious said this was an anathema of God, punishing them for allowing Gómez Farias to attack the Church. Santa Anna, bored with life on his hacienda, agreed and returned to Mexico City to throw Farias out of office. The clergy nearly wept with gratitude and urged him to accept the role of dictator. With the air of one sacrificing himself for the good of the country, he accepted. He dismissed congress, repealed all anticlerical laws, returned to the army its special privileges, sent liberals into hiding or into exile, and settled down to a life of self-glorification as the "Liberator of Mexico." But his insufferable pretensions were soon to be humbled by a tall, broad-shouldered Texan who, despite his rough manners and simple dress, was a self-taught Greek scholar. His name: Sam Houston. At the time, Houston was an unemployed soldier of fortune living with an Indian tribe in the wilds of Texas. Several years before he had left Louisiana pursued by creditors and a garrulous wife and had established a reputation in Texan towns for his great strength and courage and his uninhibited recitations of Homeric poems, many of which he knew by heart.

1835

Texas then was the upper part of Mexico's northern state of Coahuila. It is estimated that at the time 50,000 of its 68,000 inhabitants were Americans. Many were bona fide colonists, others were drifters escaping creditors in the States, and some were adventure-hunting frontiersmen, but all were united by their disaffection for the Mexican government. Trouble flared during the dictatorial reign of Bustamante in 1830 when government troops patrolled the Louisiana border to nab smugglers. Riots resulted. In 1832, Texas supported with troops the revolt of Santa Anna against Bustamante and simultaneously convoked a congress which petitioned Santa Anna's government to abolish customs houses and border patrols along their American frontier which, they claimed, only disrupting vital trade routes between Texas and the United States. Santa Anna, the dictator, not only refused their petition but sent an army under General Cos to ensure that import duties were collected there. In December 1835 a Texan partisan army intercepted Cos at San Antonio and drove him back behind the Rio Grande.

Santa Anna himself collected a motley army of some 3000 Indian conscripts and marched them across the frozen and parched plains of Coahuila where scores of his poorly clothed peons perished from cold and hunger. In February 1836 he arrived at San Antonio, which was defended by Bill Travis and 150 men holding an old abandoned mission house called the Alamo. For two weeks the Texans successfully beat off every Mexican attempt to storm the walls, but an all-out, concerted attack led by Santa Anna overwhelmed the exhausted defenders and the Texans were slaughtered to a man. Santa Anna felt that the core of Texan resistance had been crushed and pushed northward in search of rebel leaders.

The congress of Texas, five days before, had made its declaration of independence and had elected David Burnet provisional president of the new republic. Sam Houston had been asked to lead the army—a volunteer outfit of farmers, backwoodsmen, mercenaries, and adventurers, which at full strength numbered only seven or eight hundred men. People fled in terror before Santa Anna's advancing army, which sacked and burned towns as it swept northward and eastward toward Galveston, where Burnet was reported to be. Houston fought a retreating battle until he was backed up against a dense wood near Lynchburg Ferry where Santa Anna had intended to ford the San Jacinto River. On April 21, 1836, the two armies faced one another over an open field. Santa Anna, confident that Houston was cornered and beaten, succumbed to the warm, balmy air of spring and, not bothering to post guards, took a siesta. His soldiers settled down to a meal of beans and tortillas. That was when Houston struck. With his sword raised in classical Greek style, he led a charge of hacking, swinging, shooting Texans who rent the air with their famous battle cry, "Remember the Alamo!" In exactly eighteen minutes 600 Mexicans were slain, 220 were wounded, and 730 were subsequently captured. Houston's losses were three men killed and eighteen wounded, including himself. Santa Anna was caught trying to escape in a disguise so ineffective that his own men gave him away by respectfully saluting him wherever he appeared. The Texans were all for shooting "Santy Any" then and there, but Houston wisely spared him. He offered Santa Anna his freedom in exchange for the recognition of Texan independence. Could there be any question about what the fat little man would do? Life at any price. On May 14 he signed the Agreement of Velasco which called for the immediate withdrawal of Mexican troops to south of the Rio Grande and a promise to ratify in congress the independence of Texas. Santa Anna was chained to an iron ball and shipped to Washington where he conferred with President Jackson, and then was released to make his way back to Veracruz.

Though the dictator fell, his party, the conservatives, kept control of the government. They refused to acknowledge any document signed by Santa Anna and ordered General Urrea to occupy the strip of territory between the Rio Grande and the Rio Nueces. They then revoked the liberal constitution of Gómez Farias and wrote their own, calling Anastasio Bustamante back from England to be their president (dictator) once again.

1838

The fiery French minister to Mexico, Baron Deffaudis, presented Bustamante with a claim of 600,000 pesos for damages suffered by French citizens in Mexico during the riots of 1828 (when the Parian market was burned). He also demanded a preferential trade agreement between his country and Mexico. Bustamante, reading over the list of damages, found one claim made by a French baker whose shop in Tacubaya had been allegedly plundered of 60,000 pesos worth of pastry. This he considered to be preposterous and he returned the claim unpaid. The French baron was outraged and exasperated—what he actually wanted was for Bustamante to sign the trade agreement—and he summoned the French fleet from Martinique to blockade Veracruz till a settlement was reached. The blockade had lasted seven months when Baron Deffaudis was replaced by Admiral Baudin, commander of the fleet, who slapped another 200,000 pesos on the claim to cover blockade expenses. Bustamante finally agreed to the 600,000 but refused to honor the blockade bill or to sign the trade agreement. It was then that Admiral Baudin ordered a bombardment of Veracruz.

Santa Anna was relaxing on his nearby hacienda, Magna de Clavo, nursing back to health his pride that Sam Houston had so mercilessly battered, when the sound of explosions came rumbling through the trees. He buckled on his long saber (he was so short it nearly trailed on the ground), climbed on his white charger, and galloped off to Veracruz— to his country's defense! When he arrived, the town was quiet —French frigates were lying at anchor offshore—and he decided to take a short siesta before the shooting started. At that moment, however, a French raiding party entered town and advanced on the very house in which he was resting. Capture seemed imminent, but he escaped by flouting convention and running through the streets in his underwear, holding aloft his saber which in the panic of flight he managed to seize. By the time he found clothes, the French were already in their boats rowing away. Nevertheless, he mounted his trusty steed and charged! A French cannon ball came whistling through the air and hit him in the right leg below the knee, and he fainted away. Friends and followers carried him into a nearby house and laid him out on a bed where it was thought he would die. Doctors and surgeons were rushed down from Mexico City.

In a room packed with weeping women and men fighting back tears, he dictated in gasping breaths a fifteen-page report to the nation. San Jacinto was forgotten. The "Hero of Tampico" became the "Hero of Veracruz." The doctors successfully amputated, and (unfortunately for Mexico) it was only his shattered leg that was then buried at Magna de Clavo. Bustamante agreed to pay the French in full, the French fleet sailed away, and the wits have ever since referred to this tragicomic incident as the "Pastry War."

1841

The conscientious conservative Bustamante remained doggedly at his presidential post for four stormy years. The country was by then seething with discontent and the army, with its never-ending clamor for more revolutions, further aggravated the situation. Yucatán set up its own liberal government and was on the verge of seceding. Gómez Farias, the messiah of the liberals, came out of exile to lead a revolt in Mexico City. Santa Anna came up from Magna de Clavo to join the fight, although he claimed to be a mediator. The country was rapidly disintegrating into anarchy. General Paredez in Guadalajara "pronounced" against the government; General Valencia in Mexico City "pronounced" against Bustamante (that made two revolutions within the city); and Bustamante left the city and "pronounced" against himself!

It was a *danse macabre* and Santa Anna piped the tune. On October 6, 1841, he rode into the National Palace in a luxurious carriage drawn by four white horses to become, once again, dictator of Mexico. No cheering clergymen greeted him this time. Mme. Calderón de la Barca, the Scottish wife of Spain's ambassador to Mexico, an eyewitness to those events, wrote in her diary (later published under the name *Life in Mexico*), "This revolution is 'the apotheosis of egotism transformed into virtue,' and it must be confessed that with most of the actors, it has been a mere calculation of personal interest."

1842

Santa Anna's unmitigated cheek served him well for raising money. He made forced loans on the Church, he sold phony mine shares to British investors, and he upped taxes on imports, thus doubling the government's revenue. But the money, unfortunately, he frittered away on a three-year spree. He formed his own personal army and outfitted them with gorgeous uniforms. Each week some national fiesta was gaudily celebrated and any excuse at all served for a national fiesta—his birthday, the archbishop's birthday, his friend's birthday, and so on. The most mawkish ceremony of all was the entombment of his leg, of which he was almost psychopathically proud. At the Santa Paula cemetery of Mexico City, military cadets from the Chapultepec academy stood stiffly at attention, cannons were fired, while the grisly thing was slowly lowered into a grave before an ugly but expensive cenotaph. This mad, comic opera ended on a dying discord when the treasury was drained and money sources dried up. The army clamored for its back pay. General Paredez, again in Guadalajara, "pronounced" against him. When Santa Anna marched across country to crush Paredez, another rebellion broke out in the capital. His cronies and stooges were driven out of office and liberals filled up congress, which immediately elected the liberal José Joaquin Herrera president. Beaten by Paredez, his army disorganized and undermined with desertions, Santa Anna limped back to Veracruz, taking a circuitous route around Mexico City. With a cook, a batman, and a cage of fighting cocks, he went into hiding in the hills above Veracruz.

1845

President Herrera was faced with the highly explosive problem of Texas, whose independence Mexico still refused to recognize. The self-proclaimed republic, since 1838, had waited with apprehension for a Mexican army to reconquer them and had, in that time, made many appeals to the United States for help. But senators from northern states had ignored them, claiming that Texas, if admitted into the Union, as was proposed, would enter as a slave state. As they saw it, the whole issue was political claptrap created by the South to gain more seats in the Senate. Texas, then, despairing of aid from the United States, turned to England, who had been persistently offering to make them a British protectorate. When President James K. Polk heard of this possibility, he exhorted Congress to annex Texas immediately or else be faced with defending the Monroe Doctrine against England.

At the same time Herrera was ready to compromise with the Texans. He would recognize their independence if they would promise to maintain their sovereignty and not be swallowed up by the United States. But his offer came too late and was turned down. He thereupon authorized General Arista stationed in the north to fire on any American troops found south of the Rio Nueces. Such troops were to be considered invaders of Mexican territory.

1846

Under these conditions, war was inevitable. The fire-eater General Paredez felt Herrera wasn't being tough enough and led a successful revolt to overthrow him. But while Paredez was certainly tougher, he was also a heavy drinker, and he proved a hopeless failure at organizing his country for war. In April, General Arista, following out Herrera's orders, clashed with and captured a cavalry patrol of Zachary Taylor's army encamped beside the Rio Grande. Blood had been spilt! For some strange reason, legal minds always consider this a just provocation to spill more blood. Polk asked Congress for a declaration of war on Mexico, April 25, 1846. Zachary Taylor, "Old Rough-and-Ready," decamped and moved south, defeating General Arista's army at Matamoros and again farther south at Monterrey. In August, Colonel Kearney took Santa Fe, New Mexico, and marched westward to take San Diego and Los Angeles.

Paredez, finding consolation only in drink, was pushed out of office by Juan Alvarez, who turned the government over to the liberal Gómez Farias. He reinstated the constitution of 1824 and then announced that the new president and commander in chief of Mexico's armies would be none other than Santa Anna!

A year before, Santa Anna had been found by government troops among cannibalistic natives near Veracruz who, it is said, were fattening him up for eating. Congress voted to have him banished, and the troops were instructed to pack him off to Havana, Cuba, where he was to remain in exile for at least ten years. But in Cuba he corresponded with President Polk, boasting that if *he* were back in Mexico the boundary dispute over Texas would be settled quickly and peacefully. Polk took the bait and ordered American warships patrolling Mexican waters to allow his ship safe passage to Veracruz. No sooner did Santa Anna set foot on Mexican soil than the promises made to Polk vanished from his mind, and he threw himself into preparations for war.

1847

Considering that the treasury was practically empty, Santa Anna worked miracles to raise an army of 18,000. Nearly starving and shivering with cold during the frosty winter nights, he force-marched them 300 miles. Before reaching Saltillo (held by Taylor) he had lost 4000 men, most of them through desertions although many had perished from exposure or starvation. Taylor, reveling in the glory of his recent victories, was nearly taken by surprise and had to withdraw hastily to Angostura where he set up defenses in a mountain pass around a hacienda called Buena Vista. On February 22 the Mexican army drew up in battle array before the American forces. Santa Anna's seasoned eye was quick to perceive a weakness in the American defenses—a stretch of ground between the American-held hacienda and the eastern side of the mountain pass, deemed untenable by Taylor. He made first a feint to the front and then poured troops through the gap. At bayonet point the Mexicans carried one American defense ditch after another, while Taylor's deadly artillery tore holes in the Mexican ranks. Still the Mexicans ran on, stumbling, falling, and carrying the battle up to the very walls of the hacienda. By day's end, Taylor had abandoned all his defense ditches but the last. The ground gained by the Mexicans was strewn with carnage, mostly their own. Neither side won. Both sides lost. Taylor, dreading the onslaught of the next day, made plans to retreat. Santa Anna, inconsolably depressed by his long list of casualties and realizing that his exhausted troops could never again make such a heroic charge, withdrew under the cover of darkness, leaving night fires burning to deceive the enemy. When the first streaks of dawn penetrated the valley, the Americans, peering over their parapets and finding the enemy camp deserted, whooped and shouted for joy. Taylor danced a jig and then reported to Washington that a great victory had been won.

On March 7 some ten thousand American troops were landed on the beaches south of Veracruz. Their commander was General Winfield Scott, a meticulous man who abhorred risks of any kind and had no faith in luck. He called for a devastating bombardment of Veracruz before occupying the city. After that he led his troops quickly inland to minimize their exposure to tropical diseases. At Cerro Gordo, Santa Anna, in a strongly fortified position, intended to smash the advancing American army. Scott probed his enemy's defenses and found that a frontal attack was tactically impossible, so he sent a company of engineers off on a flank to cut through a jungle. With Yankee ingenuity they hacked out a path for the artillery which, once in position, poured shells into the Mexican army and sent them scattering in all directions. Retreating Mexicans streamed past Puebla, governed by the clergy, who stoutly refused Santa Anna's offer to defend it. Scott moved forward and took Puebla on May 14 without firing a shot. The clergy and town officials planned to poison the entire American army at a large banquet, but Scott somehow guessed their intentions and foiled the plot by having a member of the clergy taste the food before it was served to his troops.

Gómez Farías, acting president in Santa Anna's absence, in a frenzied attempt to raise money, demanded that the Church give him 5,000,000 pesos. Church officials indignantly refused, whereupon he empowered the army to seize the church treasury which amounted to 1,500,000 pesos. The citizens of the capital, egged on by the enraged clergy, rose up in defense of the Church and drove Gómez Farías out of office. Remnants of the liberal government, however, fought the Church, and a full-scale civil war raged in the capital. The confusion then was indescribable.

Scott waited with exasperation in Puebla for some kind of order to be restored, for while bedlam reigned, negotiations for surrender were impossible. It was, finally, the blustering Santa Anna who gained ascendancy and managed to impose his authority on the city. He notified Scott that the war could be concluded if ten thousand dollars were forwarded to him immediately, which money he would use to finance a government amenable to signing a peace treaty. The gullible Scott believed him and forwarded the money by special courier. Needless to say, every cent went toward strengthening the

Mexican army, which worked frantically at bolstering the city's defenses.

Scott, outraged by this swindle, marched on the capital following the route taken by Cortés—through the snow-capped peaks of Popocatepetl and Ixtaccihuatl.

The first and most important battle of Mexico City was fought at Contreras, a small village behind San Angel. There Santa Anna and General Valencia successfully withstood the first assault waves of Scott's army; but Santa Anna prematurely sensed a Mexican victory and ordered Valencia to fall back. The glory of defeating the Americans he wanted to be exclusively his own. General Valencia ignored his order, whereupon Santa Anna, like a rebellious schoolboy, withdrew his army and marched off to sulk at Guadalupe, leaving Valencia and the entire city to its fate. Scott carried Contreras and marched on Churubusco, which was held by a battalion of Irish immigrants who had changed sides during the war. They thought the Mexicans were fighting a religious war against that "dirty Protestant Scott." Called *"Los Patricios"* by the Mexicans, they fought ferociously and were only subdued by a do-or-die charge of Scott's army. Fifty of them were captured and hanged from a gallows erected beneath Chapultepec hill. Chapultepec Castle was defended by a handful of young cadets who, without the aid or assistance of the Mexican army, fought Scott's war machine to a standstill. When after three days they could hold out no longer, some wrapped themselves in Mexican flags and leapt from the precipitous cliffs shouting *"Viva Méjico!"* Each year on September 15 these valiant cadets are commemorated with patriotic speeches and wreath-laying ceremonies and one wonders if Mexico, in honoring her boy heroes, is not at the same time expressing her contempt for the Mexican army of Santa Anna who had abandoned them.

On September 15, a column of ragged, battle-weary American marines straggled into the main square of Mexico City led by a general wearing only one boot! Scott came galloping up to receive from his men exuberant cheers for his victory; but it was a victory that had depended on the very element which Scott so abhorred: luck. Had any general but Santa

Anna been fighting beside Valencia at Contreras, it is more than likely that the American army would have been put to rout.

1848

Santa Anna from his redoubt in Guadalupe swore to continue the war indefinitely with guerrilla warfare, but the congress was sick of war and longed for peace at any price. The price was ruinous. Mexico was to hand over Texas, and what is now New Mexico, Arizona, and California in exchange for fifteen million dollars. From this distance in time, that looks like a swindle (which it was), but it was justified by a simple catch phrase: "manifest destiny." This phrase, which has since fallen out of fashion, was at that time used glibly by American journalists and politicians to explain away the Mexican War. The Mexican congress, upon receiving these humiliating terms, at first balked, but when Scott threatened to resume hostilities, they quickly accepted. On March 10 the newly elected president, Peña y Peña, signed for Mexico the Treaty of Guadalupe Hidalgo, and Scott and Nicholas Twist, President Polk's personal emissary, signed for the United States.

There is not a Mexican today who does not feel somewhat bitter about the war of 1847.

It is said that the word "gringo" came out of this war. American troops while marching along often broke out with a lusty rendition of the ancient ballad "Green Grow the Rushes, Oh!" and the Mexicans, mispronouncing and misinterpreting the words, shortened it to "Grin Go," which thereafter became a name for Americans or American-looking English-speaking people living in Mexico.

By the end of July the last regiment of American marines had been evacuated from Mexico. The Mexican people were depressed and disillusioned. Their mines and farms had been neglected for so long that commerce had practically come to a standstill, and their roads were overrun by gangs of armed bandits whose brutal crimes were going unpunished. Anarchy would most certainly have followed if two highly conscien-

OREGON
TERRITORY
1846

THE TERRITORIAL LIMITS OF NEW SPAIN (MEXICO) 1810

GUADALUPE-HIDALGO
TREATY 1848

GADSDEN
PURCHASE
1853

TEXAS
INDEPENDENCE
1836

GULF OF MEXICO

REPUBLIC
OF
MEXICO

PACIFIC
OCEAN

GUATEMALA
1821

MEXICO'S LOSS OF TERRITORY
DURING THE NINETEENTH CENTURY

tious and energetic men had not been made president—Joaquin Herrera, succeeded by Mariano Arista. Both worked economic miracles to stave off bankruptcy, but Arista, in cutting down government expenses, made the fatal mistake of cutting down the army. Immediately generals in various provincial towns "pronounced" against him, and he, either unable or unwilling to cope with the growing dissension, resigned in disgust.

1853

That was in January. In quick succession two bombastic generals, distinguished only by their long sabers, played at being president. People in the capital, discussing politics over coffee, talked frequently and nostalgically of the good old days when viceroys ruled the land. Lucas Alamán, cultured and aristocratic, heading the conservative party, was, therefore, enthusiastically supported when he took control of the government in February. "The liberals," said he, in addressing the first session of congress, "have brought us nothing but one appalling disaster after another. They should be thrown out of high places and never be allowed to contaminate the government again." This was greeted with wild applause. He proposed that a military dictator should rule the country until some European prince could be found to accept the crown of Mexico. More wild applause. And the man to be dictator, he continued, should be none other than Santa Anna. There followed a pregnant silence.

Lucas Alamán obviously thought that Santa Anna, despite his many faults, was still the only man experienced enough to hold the country together till a monarch could be found. So the old war horse was dragged away from his peaceful pasture in Venezuela where he was living in exile and harnessed once again to the Mexican government. Though fifty-eight, he was still true to form—spending money frivolously on uniforms, beautiful horses, expensive carriages, and extravagant parties. Unfortunately the only man capable of controlling him, Lucas Alamán, died on June 2, shortly after completing his invaluable five-volume *Historia de Méjico*. His death was a great loss to Mexico but particularly to the conservative party, which realized unhappily that there was no one with sufficient talent or integrity to replace him. Santa Anna, without the restraint of Alamán, threw money away like a drunken sailor. Not even Iturbide at his height ever had so much power as Santa Anna then had. Without compunction he told the conservatives, who had put him in power, that any attempt to replace him with a European prince would be met with armed resistance. In one year he depleted the treasury and his "patriotic" army threatened to revolt if he defaulted on a single payroll.

1854

Relief came in the nick of time and from the most unexpected source: the United States. They offered to buy the lower portion of New Mexico and Arizona for ten million dollars, which offer, we can imagine, was no sooner uttered than Santa Anna banged the desk and shouted "Sold!" The Gadsden Treaty was signed April 25, and Santa Anna again had money with which to inject "patriotism" into his disgruntled army. His biggest problem, however, was not to keep the army paid, but rather to suppress a new brand of Mexican patriot that was making itself felt. This was the new generation which had grown to maturity while wars and revolutions ravaged their country, and while puffed-up and insincere generals (notably Santa Anna) grew fat at the nation's expense. They were idealists who met secretly in cafés or in private houses. A few ringleaders, such as Benito Juárez and Porfirio Díaz, had been caught and run out of the country. But in March, Juan Alvarez held a conspiratorial meeting at his large hacienda, La Providencia, in the state of Guerrero, with Ignacio Comonfort (a customs official from Acapulco), Eligio Romero, and Florencio Villareal. Comonfort presented the group with a plan calling for a new president (preferably some general of the rebel army) who would rule till a new constitution was written. All enthusiastically approved of the plan, and Villareal published it in the town of Ayutla, from which the plan gets its name.

1855

News of the Plan of Ayutla spread quickly throughout the country, and in Mexico City it was discussed in whispers at all the cafés. It soon reached the ears of Benito Juárez, who was in New Orleans supporting himself and his family by rolling cigarettes. Rebel bands of guerrilla fighters quickly seized control of the states of Guerrero and Jalisco; the towns of Guanajuato and Nueva León "pronounced" against the government; and most of the northern provinces professed their support of the plan.

The old dictator was confused and baffled by what faced him. This was no ordinary uprising. This was a war of ideals, a war he could not comprehend. His army of ninety-thousand commanded by contented and "loyal" generals was worse than useless in a battle of ideals. He was, by then, too old and too full of sins to start learning new tricks, and his opponents, the rabid idealists, terrified him because they were impervious to bribes. While the road to Veracruz was still held open by his army, he dashed down it, stopping only at Perrote where he gave an impassioned speech, stating that he ". . . turned back to the nation the powers it had entrusted to him, so as not to serve as a pretext for a civil war." He then scrambled aboard the first boat sailing for Venezuela, a boat called—irony of ironies—the *Iturbide*, after the man whom he, thirty-two years before, had driven into exile.

On November 14, the swarthy Juan Alvarez, a Mestizo with Negro blood, rode into Mexico City at the head of an Indian army gaily garbed in the colorful costumes of their native provinces. By a vote of a liberal congress which had convened at Cuernavaca, Alvarez was elected president, and Benito Juárez was made his minister of justice.

The age of *santanismo* was over. No one would ever again play Santa Anna's game of political duplicity, for by then the two political parties, the liberals and the conservatives, were irreconcilably separated and between them yawned an unleapable gap. The country was divided, but the split was by no means in two equal halves. An overwhelming majority were conservative because on that side stood the sanctity of the Catholic Church to which all Mexicans belonged. The church guns were manned by the army whose "loyalty" had been bought by the rich landowners, also conservatives. The liberals, on the other hand, were poor in number and funds, but they possessed something far greater: intelligence. The best minds in the country were with them: Melchor Ocampo, the famous scholar and scientist; Santos Degollado, professor of law at Morelia; Benito Juárez, the irreproachably honest lawyer and administrator of Oaxaca; and Guillermo Prieto, the brilliant young poet. The liberals also had the advantage of being the aggressors, for they were to wrest from the Church her lands. They began by enforcing anticlerical laws which were gradually incorporated into their constitution. That constitution, if enforced, would forever pauperize the Church and the Church, therefore, was forced to fight for her very existence. What followed was civil war, called the three-year War of the Reform. It was atrocious and destructive because it was the most vicious kind of war: a war of opposing ideologies.

CHAPTER NINE

1856–1867

General Juan Alvarez became a national hero for the part he played in overthrowing Santa Anna, and a wave of popularity carried him into the president's chair. But as president he was not happy. His meager education and his vulgar speech made him painfully aware of his great shortcomings as a statesman. So when a military junta backed a political rally to make Ignacio Comonfort president, Alvarez offered no resistance; indeed, he graciously stepped aside and offered his chair to the more cultured Comonfort.

Comonfort, the author of the Plan of Ayutla, was a bachelor of just over middle age when he became president. Under Santa Anna he had been supervisor of the customs house at Acapulco. Like most of his liberal contemporaries, he was well versed in the writings of the late eighteenth-century French philosophers, and he had reached the conclusion (not at all original) that the Catholic Church was to be blamed for all Mexico's problems. But while he wrote many articles in support of this theory, his heart, it seems, was not entirely convinced. He was a born Catholic, and, although he no longer attended any services, he retained a certain respect, even a fear, of the Church's power. As president he held up for ridicule the mawkish sentiments encouraged by the Church—all that groveling before priests and statues and relics—and he published a newspaper which he filled with scurrilous stories about members of the clergy—some of them true, some of them sheer calumny. The Church suffered these indignations in silence, but when the laws of Tejada were enforced, church officials exploded with heated diatribes against the government.

1856

Enacted in June, the *Ley Tejada* (Tejada's law) was written by Comonfort's secretary of treasury Miguel Lerdo de Tejada; they were laws authorizing the government to confiscate all church property except that land actually covered by the Church itself. It was a drastic measure, obviously written in the heat of a blinding rage. Admittedly the Church had vast land holdings, but she could never be accused of mistreating or neglecting the land. Indeed, the Church, with her efficient administration, operated the finest and most productive farms in all Mexico. Furthermore, within the shadow of each church was a school of some kind, and within the walls of almost every monastery was a public hospital attended by nuns. Tejada was, in effect, stripping the country of its schools, disrupting its hospitals, and interfering with a steady supply of farm produce. Why, then, it may be asked, was his law ever passed?

It was hoped that the impoverished Indian and Mestizo would buy up small pieces of land when church property was put on the block at government auctions. Mexico would thereby be transformed quickly into a nation of small landowners. At the same time, the government, on each sale, would impose a small tax which would accrue to the treasury. In theory, everyone would benefit. In practice, however, it was an utter fiasco. Whereas few Mexicans (especially the Indian or the Mestizo) had any money with which to buy land, the foreigner (especially the French) did; consequently land holdings were still large, but foreigners instead of the Church were the landlords. There were, however, some alert Mestizos who by juggling their finances bought up many acres of choice land at bargain prices and who, by so doing, assured their progeny of being the landed gentry of Mexico. The revenue collected by the government from this colossal rape was a disappointing three million pesos—a sum far below expectations.

1857

By February the new constitution had been drawn up and was ready for ratification. It was filled with radical reforms all aimed at humbling the Church. Article 3 established secular education, 5 gave priests and nuns the right to renounce their religious vows, 6 granted freedom of speech, 7 granted freedom of the press, 9 granted freedom of assembly, 13 abolished church courts, 27 forbade corporations (the Church) from holding land, 123 gave the government (not the Church) authority to decide in matters of religious worship.

No less a person than the Holy Father himself, Pope Pius IX, lashed out at this document, saying it was ". . . corrupting manners and propagating the detestable pest of indifferentism by tearing souls away from our Most Holy Religion, and it allows the free exercise of all cults and admits the right of pronouncing in public every kind of thought and opinion. . . . We raise our Pontifical voice in apostolic liberty . . . to condemn, to reprove, and declare null and void the said decrees and everything else that the civil authority has done in scorn of ecclesiastical authority and of this Holy See . . ." The Church would excommunicate any Catholic who signed these reforms.

So in February a dramatic signing ceremony took place. Gómez Farias, the elderly and now semi-paralyzed dean of the liberals, was given the honor of being first to put his name to the constitution. Leaning heavily on the shoulders of two disciples, he shuffled forward onto the stage, wrote his name with a shaky hand, and then solemnly swore to uphold the new constitution of the Mexican republic. Congressmen and deputies followed, each signing, each swearing. Many absented themselves because, being Catholics, they feared the anathema of the Church.

1857

On December 1, Ignacio Comonfort, under the new constitution, was reinstated as president, and Benito Juárez was made his vice-president, and, as vice-president, president of the supreme court. Almost immediately Comonfort was torn by his divided loyalties. Congress urged him to deport the cantankerous archbishop of Mexico who had been tirelessly inveighing against the government and its new constitution, but Comonfort, in deference to the old priest's venerable years and failing health, desisted and thereby lost the popular support of his party. Moreover, the liberals were bothered by Comonfort's constant demand for more power as president, as well as disapproving of his conciliatory methods in dealing with the Church. The truth was that Comonfort detested being an excommunicate and shrank from any ultimatum that could pitch the country into civil war. His dilemma was somewhat resolved by a revolution led by a self-styled general named Felix Zuloaga, who had formerly been a cardsharp in a gambling house and who had written a *plan*—the Plan of Tacubaya—calling for Comonfort to be dictator and, as dictator, to repeal the constitution. Before government troops could be mustered, Zuloaga stormed the National Palace, drove congress from its chamber, and shoved Juárez into a windowless room where he was kept a prisoner. Comonfort, bewildered and confused, accepted halfheartedly the dictatorship offered to him and dutifully repealed the constitution. Liberals regrouping in Querétaro branded him a traitor and proclaimed Juárez the new president.

Events now occur at a dizzying speed. Comonfort, finding no balm for his troubled conscience with the clergy, repudiated their conservative government and, to make restitution to his old liberal comrades, released Juárez from his stuffy confinement in the palace and then himself slipped out of the capital. After a long hectic journey he arrived finally in New York where he remained in exile.

Juárez fled to Querétaro and tried to set up a government, but Zuloaga, marching on the town with a large army, nearly recaptured him. Juárez journeyed to Guadalajara where his army mutinied (they had not been paid for months) and would have shot him if the poet Guillermo Prieto had not pleaded for mercy on his behalf. He then ran off to the tropical Pacific port of Manzanillo and boarded a ship bound for Panama. There he crossed the isthmus on muleback (the canal had not yet been dug) and caught a ship on the east coast sailing for Veracruz—then the last stronghold of the constitutional government. He remained there behind barricades throughout the War of the Reform, successfully guiding his battered government through some of the most appalling disasters ever to assail Mexico.

When the Plan of Ayutla was announced in 1854, Benito Juárez was well past middle age and was rather obscured by the dazzling personalities of Melchor Ocampo, Santos Degollado, Ignacio Comonfort, and Juan Alvarez. Only after a close study of character would one have picked Juárez out of all that brilliance as the man destined to become Mexico's greatest patriot, for his iron will and unflagging determination—the stuff of greatness—had, at that time, not yet been tested.

He was born near Oaxaca, on March 21, 1806. Before he was three, both his parents—pure Zapotec Indians—died and his grandparents took custody of him and his three sisters. As a boy he tended sheep and milked cows, but a burning ambition "to make something of himself" sent him to the town of Oaxaca where his sister worked as a servant for a certain Maza family. Sr. Maza, a bighearted man, took in young Benito as if he were one of his family. Don Antonio Salanueva, a friend of Sr. Maza and a devout Catholic—a lay member of the Franciscan order—taught Juárez reading, writing, arithmetic, Spanish grammar, and bookbinding and was so greatly impressed by his pupil's zeal to learn that he sent him to the Franciscan seminary in Oaxaca where, he thought, the friars would mold him into a priest. While Benito, then, was immersed in the philosophy of St. Thomas Aquinas, Iturbide fell, Gómez Farías and his constitution had put Guadalupe Victoria in the president's office, and the threat of revolution hung in the air. The friars praised Juárez for his "exceptional diligence and particular application," but after eight years he knew for certain that the priesthood was not his vocation. Since a career in the army held no glamour for him, he entered law and read avidly and with great excitement the philosophers of the "Age of Enlightenment." He mixed with local revolutionary parties, opened a law office in Oaxaca, and soon married Margarita Maza, daughter of the man who had befriended him. During the Mexican War, in which he took no part, he gained national notice by backing a controversial law, introduced into the Oaxaca legislature, calling for the confiscation of church lands. His importance grew and won him a seat in the constituent congress of 1847. The next step was governorship of Oaxaca which he held from 1847 to 1852. There he collaborated with a burly, black-eyed general named Porfirio Díaz, a Mixteca Indian who, like himself, was consumed with ambition. They both despised Santa Anna, and for daring to say "no" when asked if they favored Santa Anna's tyrannical dictatorship, they were both thrown out of the country. During Juárez's exile in New Orleans (then a haven for Mexican refugees in exile) he conversed often with Melchor Ocampo, who at that time was Mexico's greatest political philosopher. From their talks Juárez probably formed a resolution to give Mexico a steady, stable, and lasting government. When news of the Plan of Ayutla broke on his circle of liberal friends, Juárez left and traveled with all possible haste to Acapulco where he offered his services to General Juan Alvarez.

1858

General Zuloaga, the gambler and the deposer of Comonfort, was made president of the church-backed conservative government of Mexico, and a young general in his twenties named Miguel Miramón was made his vice-president. England and Europe quickly recognized him as the official president of Mexico by instructing their consuls and ambassadors to negotiate with him for unsettled claims pending since 1821. John Forsyth, the United States minister to Mexico, who allegedly gave political asylum to members of the Juárez government in his house in Mexico City, sounded out the

Zuloaga government but, finding it unsympathetic to the interests of the United States, withheld American recognition. Soon, and without the fanfare of protocol, he left the country.

In August, three months later, the American warship *Quaker City* docked at Veracruz and down its gangplank walked a Mr. McLane. At the improvised presidential office of Juárez, he withdrew from his brief case the papers of the McLane-Ocampo Treaty, stating that if Juárez signed the treaty, the United States would grant recognition to his constitutional government. The first of the terms called for the ceding of Lower California to the United States; the second "stipulated that the United States shall enjoy a perpetual right-of-way across the Isthmus of Tehuantepec."

The United States, since the discovery of gold in California, felt the urgent need of a short route from the Atlantic to boom towns springing up on California's coast. It was deemed an exasperating and needless waste to travel 20,000 miles by sea—down to the tip of South America—to reach towns only some 3000 miles away by land. If a canal could be dredged through a narrow isthmus in Central America, shipping costs would be cut to a fraction. The isthmus of Tehuantepec had been probed by American engineers who followed its rivers and sounded its lakes and concluded that the Atlantic and Pacific could indeed be joined at that point. Juárez was agreeable and signed the treaty, but the United States Senate, then the scene of fiery debates over the slave issue, failed to ratify it. Northern senators saw in it a move to make Lower California another slave state, and quashed the treaty on the grounds that it was a violation of Mexican sovereignty (which it was). Fortune had favored Juárez. The United States Government by referring to him as the representative of Mexico's sovereignty was, by the same token, granting his constitutional government recognition. And he had not given up one foot of Mexican soil to get it. The canal project then became a dead issue, but periodically Mexican presidents have taken it up for consideration—the last being President Ruíz Cortines in 1957. With the present flare-up in Panama over control of the canal, a new canal through the isthmus of Tehuantepec may, quite likely, become a topic of serious discussion once again.

1860

President Zuloaga, who had never been popular with the clergy (mainly because of his disreputable past), was replaced by the youthful General Miramón. Miramón began his term as president with vim and vigor by laying siege to Veracruz. Through agents he had purchased in Havana two small warships, both commanded by a Mexican captain named D. Tomás Marin, who was instructed to blockade and then bombard the docks of Veracruz. Three American warships—the *Saratoga*, the *Wave*, and the *Indianola*—lying at anchor nearby, having escorted American diplomats to Veracruz, decided to intercede for Juárez and steamed out to ram the oncoming Mexican vessels. A boarding party captured Marin and locked him up on a charge of piracy. Legal authorities in New Orleans, on reviewing the case, found Marin guiltless and sent a sharp note reprimanding Captain Turner, commander of the American fleet, for his uncalled-for action. However that was, the unlucky Miramón had lost his sea force, and his land force, wracked by fevers and malaria, were without energy or inclination to fight. He therefore returned hastily and ingloriously to the capital.

Except for Veracruz, Miramón's conservative government controlled all the major towns of the country, though guerrilla armies of the liberals were still prowling the countryside and were growing steadily in size. Also the untrained generals of the liberals—all lawyers, professors, and scientists by profession—were gaining finesse in waging war. Santos Degollado, a liberal leader of Morelia, led a daring raid on Mexico City, capturing Chapultepec Castle where he ill advisedly waited for an uprising within the capital to support him. General Márquez, defending the capital, rushed out and in four hours completely routed his army. Although the raid was not a success, it threw a terrible fright into the clergy, who thought the liberals had been safely bottled up in Veracruz.

The clerics were also beginning to feel the pinch of shortages, particularly of money. The Church had already sold as much as she could to finance the army; any more might irreparably cripple her. With the liberals holding Veracruz, supplies from Europe became a mere trickle, and revenues from customs—usually the government's greatest source of income—was nil. Juárez, on the other hand, by controlling the customs at Veracruz, was gradually gaining an economic superiority. As a consequence, the armies of Miramón and those of his generals, Márquez and Mejía, were losing mercenaries in droves; they drifted over to the liberal side where salaries were being paid occasionally at least.

The death knell for the conservatives was first sounded at Silao, where Miramón and his army of 3000 men were decisively defeated by a liberal army of 7000. For the conservatives this marked the first defeat in a pitched battle with the liberals. Within three months only Puebla and Mexico City were held by the conservatives, and both were under bombardment by the sieging armies of the liberals. On December 21, Miramón marched out from Mexico City to meet the liberal army of General Ortega camped at Calpulalpan nearby. The battle ended in a complete rout of Miramón's army and a collapse of his conservative government.

1861

On January 1 the victorious General Ortega and his liberal army paraded through the streets of Mexico City led by a marching band while people jammed sidewalks and balconies, joyfully cheering and waving Mexican flags.

Ten days later a simple black carriage entered the city almost unnoticed. It bore a small, somberly dressed, grim-faced figure whose coal-black eyes looked fixedly ahead. This was the entrance of Benito Juárez, the unemotional, legal-minded first citizen president of Mexico—and the first, perhaps, to feel deep in his heart a grave responsibility for his country.

There was little glory and certainly small remuneration for being president of Mexico then. The treasury was empty, and neither soldiers nor bureaucrats could hope to see a cent of salary for months. The army therefore disintegrated and soldiers resorted to looting. At first they ransacked the well-stocked houses of the rich, but when these were gutted, they sank to the degraded depths of robbing the poor. The city took on a ghastly appearance. Wrote Manuel Payno, a partisan of Juárez: "Some [people] abandon their houses to seek safety in hiding places; the streets are filled with furniture, and if you enter the homes you see women and children weeping." Generals would trade an entire hacienda (one they had confiscated) for a horse that struck their fancy. Soldiers collected books from libraries for making bonfires, and they destroyed, unforgivably, Aztec codices which they took to be dirty, heavy wrapping paper. Without money, Juárez was powerless to stop them.

To add to the confusion, General Márquez had rallied remnants of his conservative army and ranged it over the mountain pass between Toluca and Mexico City. Juárez issued a decree granting full amnesty to Márquez and all his soldiers if they would lay down arms and join the liberal fold. Melchor Ocampo could not abide this decree, claiming it made a mockery of their hard-won victory. In a fit of anger he broke with Juárez and went off to live in retirement on his hacienda in Michoacán. Soon after, General Márquez raided his home and had the captured Ocampo bound hand and foot, stood up against a wall, and shot. Degollado and Valle, two prominent liberals, incensed almost to madness by this brutal act, rushed off in search of Márquez, vowing to shoot him on sight. But the wily Márquez ambushed them and had them shot also. Within one month, then, the liberals had lost three of their most capable leaders, and General Márquez, intoxicated with his success, led a foolhardy raid on Mexico City; but it was Porfirio Díaz, commanding a liberal army, who drove him back into the hills.

The most critical problem within the government was the treasury. Juárez was unable to keep a secretary in that office. As soon as one learned the hopeless state of the nation's finances, he would resign in despair. The government was losing 400,000 pesos a month and a sum total of 80,000,000 pesos in bona fide claims were owed to foreign powers. Juárez pledged his government to liquidate all its foreign debts, eventually, but at that time he announced that all payment to foreigners would be suspended for two years.

Naturally, under such conditions, the president's critics

were legion. Fifty-one members of congress signed a petition demanding his resignation, but fifty-two signed a counter-petition demanding he remain. If his critics thought they could intimidate him into giving up in disgust—as presidents before him had done—they were underestimating the iron will of Juárez. He was like an Old Testament prophet, unshakably determined to prove that an honest government could and would be built on the will of God working through the people. His most crucial test, however, was still before him: Maximilian and the French army.

As early as October 25, 1842, Madame Calderón de la Barca had written about a pamphlet prepared by a Señor Gutiérrez Estrada, a Mexican diplomat in Europe, proposing that some European prince establish a constitutional monarchy in Mexico. This pamphlet caused a sensation in Europe and became the most exciting topic of conversation in various court circles. After all, Europeans had before them the example of Bernadotte, the excellent French general in Napoleon's army who was asked by the Swedish government to become their king. Why then should not an emperor be found for Mexico?

By December 1, 1852, the principal characters in the drama of Maximilian were beginning to assemble when Louis Napoleon Bonaparte, son of Louis Bonaparte (for a short time king of Holland) and nephew of Napoleon I, was made Napoleon III, emperor of France.

On January 29, 1853, the second key character entered the scene when Napoleon III took for his wife Eugénie de Montijo, daughter of Count de Montijo of Spain and a Scottish noblewoman named Kirkpatrick. Eugénie was then one of Europe's most celebrated beauties, and she would soon become the pacesetter in fashion; whatever she wore was immediately imitated by English and continental women of *haute couture*.

The principal actor, Archduke Maximilian (brother of Franz Josef, emperor of Austria), made his first appearance of importance when he paid an official call on the court of France on May 17, 1856. His imposing height, his elegance, his handsome (though weak) face, and his great charm delighted Eugénie and left a lasting impression on Napoleon III. Later in that same year, Maximilian married Carlotta, daughter of King Leopold I of Belgium, and took up his duties as governor general of Venice and Lombardy, then under Hapsburg rule. The cast was then complete.

1861

When Juárez announced a suspension on payment of all foreign debts, Napoleon III called for a conference to be held in London at which England, Spain, and France would jointly decide on some means of collecting from Mexico their long-pending claims. To understand the outcome of that conference, it is necessary to sketch briefly the character of Napoleon III.

He, like Santa Anna, suffered from delusions of his own self-importance. In his speech he frequently dropped hints that he could be as great—and maybe even greater—than his illustrious uncle, Napoleon I. But he felt handicapped by the complicated network of treaties and alliances binding Europe together, and he looked about for a less organized continent. Latin America? Why not? After all, England was successfully snatching up land in India and Africa; and Holland, Denmark, and Belgium were planting colonies all over the globe —from the archipelagos in the South Pacific to the icebound islands of the North Atlantic. In this race for colonies France could easily outstrip them all by sweeping aside the young republics of Latin America and setting up a Catholic monarchy that would rule an empire stretching from the Rio Grande on the American border down to the Tierra del Fuego at the tip of South America. Mexico, with her pile of unpaid bills, would serve as an excellent excuse to begin building his empire there. His troops would overthrow the constitutional government of Juárez and would prepare the ground for the entrance of some prince of his choosing who would rule as emperor. And there was a plethora of princes to choose from.

The only country that could possibly interfere with this plan was the United States, but she was then too preoccupied with her great civil war to be concerned with defending the

Monroe Doctrine. The battle of Bull Run had been a resounding success for the South, and Napoleon III, like England (who needed southern cotton for her textile mills), fervently hoped the South would roll on to a quick victory. His plan, in fact, was a reckless gamble that she would.

Not a word of this was mentioned at the London conference. A pact was drawn up and signed by each country. Spain, England, and France were to land at Veracruz a contingent of troops that would be instructed to respect—at all times—the sovereignty of Mexico. They were being sent, said their pact, "to offer a friendly hand," and "to preside at the grand spectacle of Mexican regeneration."

1862

So by January of this year Veracruz was teeming with brightly uniformed soldiers of three nations. The Spanish and English commanders got their first clue that France was seeking more than a settlement of claims when they heard that the French minister had demanded 12,000,000 pesos from the Mexican government. This was a fantastic sum, far beyond what Mexico could pay to all three nations combined; and even if, by some miracle, she did pay France there would be nothing left over for England or Spain. The truth was that France didn't expect to be paid, but hoped rather that by making such an impossible demand Juárez would be driven into declaring war on all three powers. Juárez, however, was not so easily trapped. He sent down to Veracruz his secretary of foreign affairs, Manuel Doblado, to interview the Spanish commander, General Prim, and the English commander, both of whom swore that under no circumstances would they meddle in Mexico's internal affairs. The French minister, however, persisted in his demand for 12,000,000 pesos. In the meantime a large French army, commanded by General Laurencez, arrived; and General Almonte, Napoleon's emissary, set up a provisional government with himself as head. In view of these developments, England and Spain withdrew. They wanted no part in the game France was playing, a game which could easily explode into an expensive and profitless war. They also expressed their resentment at having been drawn into Napoleon's private scheme to occupy Mexico. By April, then, France alone had troops in Veracruz.

General Laurencez, commanding 6000 well-trained and handsomely uniformed dragoons and foot soldiers, was given orders to occupy Mexico City. On the path of his march to the capital was Puebla, defended by 4000 Mexicans armed with antiquated guns—many of which had seen service at the battle of Waterloo fifty years before, and had been bought at a bargain by Mexico's ambassador to London back in 1825. Commander of Puebla's forces was Ignacio Zaragoza, an amateur in tactical warfare, as were most of his officers, but a seasoned warrior in guerrilla fighting. Laurencez, to show his contempt for that ragtag army, called for a charge up the middle of the Mexican defenses at Zaragoza's most strongly fortified position. The charge carried his cavalry through soggy ditches, over a crumbling adobe wall, and up the steep slopes of the Cerro de Guadalupe. But their drive petered out before reaching its objective, and over one thousand Frenchmen were left sprawled on the field, dead or dying. Laurencez paid for his contempt. The Mexican army held, and then Zaragoza led a counter-attack that drove Laurencez back to Orizaba and, after a short reprieve, attacked him again and drove the remnants of his army to the coast. This was the first time French troops had met defeat in nearly half a century, and it was handed them not by a major power of Europe but by the penniless, war-torn republic of Mexico. This battle for Puebla, fought on May 5, is yearly commemorated in Mexico by a national holiday, and there is hardly a Mexican village, town, or city that does not call its main street Cinco de Mayo.

While French troops were suffering this humiliating rout, Archduke Maximilian directed gardeners in landscaping the grounds of his fairy-tale castle at Miramar (near Trieste on the Adriatic Sea). But his seemingly idyllic life was, in fact, fraught with discontent arising from the endless, and sometimes violent, arguments between himself and his brother, Emperor Franz Josef, over affairs of state. And his wife Carlotta nagged at him constantly that the court of Vienna was not treating her as it should. He therefore entered into preliminary discussions with two Mexican diplomats, Gutiérrez Estrada (who had written the sensational pamphlet) and Manuel José Hidalgo (no relation to Miguel Hidalgo of Dolores), both of whom claimed to represent not the constitutional government of Juárez but the Catholic government of General Miramón. Archduke Maximilian found their offer to ascend the throne of Mexico flattering and almost irresistible. Carlotta was radiant at the prospect of becoming an empress. And they both knew that Napoleon III was pleased with the idea, although he had expressed his pleasure only in conversations, not in writing.

News of the French defeat at Puebla stunned all Europe and threw Napoleon III into a fit of rage. Now French honor was at stake and had to be vindicated whatever the price. He immediately dispatched an army of two divisions totaling twenty-eight thousand men under the command of General Foray, with generals Bazaine and Douay serving as his division commanders.

1863

On March 16, General Foray began his siege of Puebla, defended this time by thirty thousand Mexicans under the command of General Gonzalez Ortega, who was determined to repeat the previous year's success of Zaragoza (who had since died). But Foray was not so foolhardy as Laurencez. He progressed slowly and with planned strategy, and he so battered and outmaneuvered Ortega's army that by May 16 Puebla capitulated.

Juárez hastily prepared Mexico City for a siege, but when he found that his best generals had been either captured or killed during the siege of Puebla, and that he could muster an army of only four thousand men, he evacuated the capital and moved his government to San Luis Potosí. On June 10, General Foray entered the undefended capital and was welcomed by jubilant church dignitaries and rich Catholic Creoles. In the great cathedral *Te Deums* were sung at solemn high mass celebrating Mexico's deliverance from the hated government of Juárez.

Though Foray was a creditable soldier, as a statesman he could do nothing right. First he unwittingly outraged the clergy by refusing to restore confiscated church lands; he then insulted Mexican officials by making himself a dictator; and finally he provoked the wrath of Napoleon III by requesting he send out Maximilian immediately. This last was such a gross blunder—the Mexican people, *not* a French general, were supposed to ask for Maximilian—that Napoleon promptly replaced him with General Bazaine.

1864

When the high tide of Confederate hopes had been reached and turned back at Gettysburg in July, 1863 foretelling a northern victory, Napoleon realized the urgent need to resolve his affairs in Mexico quickly. He could not withdraw, for that would be admitting to the world that he had made a mistake and might possibly provoke an uprising in his own country. Opposition to his government was strong and was still rising. He was, in fact, a victim of his own cunning and saw no honorable way out but to carry on with a plan he knew perfectly well was doomed to failure. So in March of this year he lavishly entertained Maximilian and Carlotta in Paris with rounds of parties and balls, ceremoniously toasting them as the emperor and empress of Mexico. During a lull in the festivities he drew Maximilian aside and in the manner of a hard-driving businessman exacted from the young prince a pledge to pay 260,000,000 francs for the use of the French army for three years, during which time —or by 1867—Maximilian should have established his monarchy and should have trained a Mexican militia loyal to his crown. To these terms Maximilian foolishly agreed and a pact was signed March 12.

Apparently the young archduke never fully realized what a serious step he had taken until he returned to Austria where his brother, Emperor Franz Josef, asked him to renounce in writing all pretensions to the Austrian crown. Maximilian was outraged. Renounce his divine right to rule Austria! It was like asking him to renounce his blood. But his brother was adamant. An emperor could not rule one country while his loyalties and vested interests were in another. The break with Austria had to be complete and final. In the emotional argument that followed, accusations and counter-accusations were hurled back and forth, the brothers tore their hair and they wept; in the end Maximilian, shaken with sobs, signed the paper prepared by his brother renouncing his right to the throne of Austria. This agreement, called the "Family Pact," Maximilian tried later, unsuccessfully, to break.

1864

On April 14 the emperor and empress of Mexico boarded the frigate *Novaro* docked at the private pier of his seaside palace, Miramar. A large crowd of friends and relatives had gathered there to bid them a last farewell. The young couple stood on the quarterdeck in a steady sea breeze and were seen still waving as the ship, under full sail, became but a speck in the distance. According to the ship's passengers, the emperor remained at the rail gazing in the direction of Miramar long after his beloved palace had faded from view. And when he turned away, his face was streaked with tears.

Maximilian's optimistic attitude toward Mexico endeared him to his Mexican friends, but it was the worst possible attitude he could have had in those troubled times. He had the notion that all problems tearing at Mexico would be somehow resolved quickly as soon as he ascended the throne, and that his imperial duties would be, therefore, mainly social rather than political. And so during his six-week ocean voyage he prepared himself for the trials ahead by rewriting his six-hundred-page manuscript on court etiquette! When his Mexican friends gave him reproachful looks for being thus employed, he explained that his book would be the most authoritative one on the subject (which it was).

The *Novaro* docked at Veracruz on May 28 without an official on hand to welcome her. General Almonte, assigned to meet the emperor, badly misjudged his time and arrived five hours late. It was dark when he bustled them through the empty streets of Veracruz which was, he said, a city strongly opposed to being ruled by a foreign monarch. This news stunned the emperor and caused him to doubt seriously, and for the first time, the words of Napoleon III, who had assured him that Mexico was unanimously in favor of a monarch. A better welcome, however, was given them at Orizaba, Puebla, Cholula, and, of course, Mexico City—all towns under French military occupation and French martial law. In each, the royal carriage rumbled past thousands of silent but inquisitive Indians straining for a glimpse of the royal pair. Maximilian's long, flowing, red beard and his white skin fascinated them and reminded them, perhaps, of the legend of Quetzalcoatl's return. In any case, the Indians preferred to be subjects of Maximilian rather than citizens of Juárez, as they proved later in the wars that followed. When the emperor finally reached Mexico City, exhausted by the long, grueling journey, both he and Carlotta were dismayed to find that their rooms in the National Palace were unswept, beds were unmade, and cockroaches were everywhere. Though the emperor spent his first night on a pool table, he was bursting with enthusiasm the next day and made plans to move into Chapultepec Castle (built 1783–86), which formerly had been the summer house of the Spanish viceroys. He completely renovated it, and it remains to this day a monument to his taste as a decorator.

Maximilian was too quixotic to make a good emperor. He built his government on democratic principles much to the chagrin of the clergy and the rich Creoles who since 1823 had been longing for a centralized monarchy modeled after the governments of the viceroys. As he showed no inclination to repeal the hateful laws of Juárez, nor to restore church land, the conservatives, only six months after he arrived, denounced him as a liberal in royal trappings, no better, basically, than their archenemy Juárez. The archbishop of Mexico, Labastida, sent an appeal to the Vatican imploring the Holy Father to bring pressure upon his wayward son Maximilian. When a nuncio arrived—the Pope's special envoy—Maximilian, with Carlotta at his side, stoutly refused to change a letter of the law and, what was more, announced his intention to confiscate more church land in order to finance his government. To Maximilian, these remarks perhaps

sounded like a herald of trumpets from the side of righteous-
ness, but to the rich Mexicans and the clergy they sounded
like a hackneyed version of an old liberal tune. His policies
not only alienated him from his Catholic sponsors (the clergy
even circulated vile stories about his sterility), but they also
won ridicule from the liberals. When Juárez received from
him an invitation to join his imperial cabinet as his personal
adviser, the offer was considered, by Juárez, too ludicrous to
warrant an answer.

But as the author of the most authoritative book on court
etiquette, his conduct and manners were impeccable and
Mexican society lionized him. In six months he gave 16 balls,
20 banquets, and 70 luncheons. In one year his wine bill
alone exceeded 100,000 pesos.

While the emperor was engaged with entertaining Mexico's elite, the commander of the French army, General
Bazaine, with a force thirty thousand strong, occupied one
Mexican town after another without ever coming to a showdown battle with the Juárists. At first he went in pursuit of
Juárez himself, the wandering symbol of the constitutional
government, who fled northward in the plain black carriage
which he used as his office, from San Luis Potosí, to Chihuahua and to Paso del Norte (now Ciudad Juárez) on the
American frontier. At length, Bazaine despaired of ever catching him and turned south to concentrate on Oaxaca, held by
Porfirio Díaz. Oaxaca fell after a short siege and Díaz was
captured but later escaped with the aid of liberal sympathizers. Bazaine was beginning to weary of his task. Every
town he "captured" would, upon being evacuated by the
French army, immediately revert to being liberal. By the end
of 1864 he had "captured" most major towns in Mexico, but,
being a hard realist, he knew that the country was far from
being loyal to its imported monarch.

1865

In the spring of this year the tide turned and ran against
the French. During the American civil war a trickle of supplies in arms and munitions was crossing the Texas border

and reaching Juárez forces, but when Lee surrendered to
Grant, that trickle became a gushing stream, although it ran
surreptitiously beneath legal channels. Wrote Phil Sheridan
in his papers: ". . . we continued covertly supplying arms
and munitions to the liberals, sending as many as 30,000
muskets from Baton Rouge arsenal alone." The victorious
Union army assembled on the Texas border ready to support
Juárez if required. Wrote Grant to Sheridan: ". . . concentrate at all available points in the States an army strong
enough to move against the invaders of Mexico, if occasion
demanded."

Bazaine's operations were now hopeless. No sooner did he
down one guerrilla band than others would pop up like heads
of a hydra-headed monster; and prisoners, assisted by sympathetic citizens, escaped from his jails in droves. Angered
and frustrated, he insisted that the emperor sign a bill em-
powering him to shoot all captured Juárist soldiers. Maximilian thought this too severe a measure but was irresolute and
allowed the strong-willed Bazaine to override his objections.
So on October 5 he signed the fatal bill which would ultimately be the cause of his own execution two years later.

1866

By this time Napoleon III had too many pots boiling—his
claims in Mexico, the French army under Bazaine, Maximilian, and now Prussia, the most potentially dangerous kettle
of them all, which was requiring more and more of his attention. Bismarck of Prussia was rapidly gaining ascendancy
as the political arbiter of Europe, and Napoleon, wishing to
check his encroaching power, felt the need of a strong army
near him in case Bismarck became unmanageable at a conference table. He therefore sent secret instructions to Bazaine
to begin withdrawals from Mexico in three sections—the first
in November, the second and third in March and December
of the following year. Though relations between Bazaine and
Maximilian had been strained almost to the breaking point,
the general felt obliged to warn the emperor that the French
army had been ordered home and that Maximilian had, then,

no alternative but to abdicate immediately and leave with the troops. Maximilian tended to agree, since he knew quite well that his empire was not strong enough to stand alone without French support. But Carlotta was outraged by his talk of leaving. She was an empress and she would remain an empress. Abdication, she said, was a cowardly retreat from the great obligations inherent in the family name of Hapsburg. Rather than that, she would go herself to the French court and prevail upon Napoleon III to change his orders to Bazaine.

She left July 9, at the height of the rainy season. All the forces of nature, it seems, converged at that moment to play a tempestuous overture to the tragedy before her. Torrential rains opened deep ruts in the road to Veracruz; and she had twice, in terrific downpours, to abandon carriages sunk to the axle in mud. And on the high seas her ship was lashed by perilous storms whose fury kept the ship's crew in constant alarm. The moment she landed at St.-Nazaire, she telegraphed Napoleon III advising him of her intention to see him before the week was out.

Napoleon III, by this time, was a sick and tired man. A lifetime of indulging in excesses of rich foods, wines, and women had left him, in his fifty-eighth year, bedridden with agonizing pains. Carlotta's cable, when read to him, noticeably worsened his condition. When Carlotta arrived, Empress Eugénie tried to dissuade her from seeing the emperor, but Carlotta would not be put off. An interview was finally arranged for her on August 11, at the Château de St.-Cloud, in the sumptuous bedchamber of the emperor. After an exchange of polite formalities, Carlotta gave vent to the wrath raging inside her and delivered an impassioned diatribe against the sick man; but a servant bearing a glass of orange juice on a large tray clumsily banged open a door of the room and so frightened Carlotta that she faltered in her speech and finally could not go on. Eugénie, baffled by Carlotta's sudden silence, entreated her to drink the orange juice, which the young empress did tensely, sip by sip, but she seemed quite unable to collect her wits. Napoleon, grateful for this unexpected reprieve, begged to be left alone. Carlotta, pale and trembling, was returned to her suite of rooms in the Grand Hotel, her chosen home while in Paris, since she was too proud to accept hospitality from the French government.

Three days later, against the advice of her friends who were concerned for her health, she was back in the emperor's chamber, this time armed with letters written in Napoleon's own hand and containing promises to aid Maximilian whenever his empire was in need. By withdrawing French troops from Mexico, cried Carlotta in a quavering voice, he was killing her husband just as surely as if he put a gun to his head and pulled the trigger. Napoleon, writhing with embarrassment, promised to speak to his ministers about rescinding the orders to Bazaine. This somewhat placated Carlotta, and she returned to her hotel looking calm and composed.

Napoleon's council of ministers had never been in favor of the Mexican venture and considered further aid to Maximilian an extravagance which the French treasury could then ill afford. They came to a quick and unanimous decision: Maximilian was to be abandoned.

Napoleon decided to deliver this heavy news himself to Carlotta. Aching and wheezing and attended by a nurse, he rode in a special carriage to the Grand Hotel and hobbled upstairs to Carlotta's apartment. Though he spoke gently and judiciously, his message threw Carlotta into raving hysterics. His efforts to comfort her aggravated her still more. Even the sight of him filled her with loathing. And so he left, feeling considerably worse for having done what he considered to be only his duty.

1866

Carlotta traveled first to Miramar and then to Rome, arriving there September 24. The once-proud beauty of Europe was, by then, reduced to a pale, haggard, nerve-taut woman who at twenty-six looked twice her age. Cardinal Antonelli at the Vatican received her with cool formality and expressed his deep disappointment at the way Maximilian had handled church affairs in Mexico. She had not the strength to argue with him but pleaded for a private audience with the Holy

Father. When admitted to the Pontiff's presence three days later, she fell on her knees, sobbing hysterically, and begged His Holiness to save her from poisoning. She was babbling incoherently about poisoned orange juice and agents of Napoleon sprinkling poison on her food. When Vatican guards came to take her away, she shrieked and attacked them, screaming they were assassins in the pay of Napoleon III. Nothing would calm her but the promise that she might stay the night in the Vatican. She remained there all the next day writing letters of farewell to her friends, stating in each that murderers would soon destroy her. On October 9 her brother, the count of Flanders, arrived to take her away to Miramar. She was declared insane by the doctors of the day, although on several occasions after that her mind was perfectly sound. She died at the age of eighty-seven, January 19, 1927, on her family's large ancestral estate, the castle of Bouchout, near Brussels.

1866

On October 18, Maximilian received a cable telling him Carlotta was under special treatment by Dr. Reidel. On asking his staff physician if he knew a Dr. Reidel, he was told, "Oh yes, of course. He's the head of the insane asylum." That was how the emperor learned of his wife's insanity. The news, naturally, depressed him terribly and resolved him to leave Mexico with the next detachment of troops. He drafted a speech of abdication, lovingly packed all his most cherished belongings into crates ready for shipment to Veracruz, and retired to the town of Orizaba, beneath the snow-capped volcano of Orizaba and within sight of the gulf coast. To keep from falling into morose thoughts about Carlotta, he made studies of the flora and fauna, going daily on field trips into the luxuriant countryside. In the evening he would spend long hours conversing with a certain Father Fischer, who was a kind of free-lance Catholic priest. This Father Fischer was like a picaresque character of fiction. Born in Germany, he migrated to the States when a young man and became a settler in Texas; but he was soon lured away by rumors of gold in California and was for a few years a luckless prospector. He apparently despaired of ever achieving any earthly success and so entered a monastery. After being ordained a priest, he drifted through Mexico, settled in Orizaba, and took for himself a wife who bore him many children. The emperor was spellbound by his effusive personality, his nimble wit, and his great self-confidence. "Why leave?" asked Fischer. Carlotta's great sacrifice, he argued, would be totally lost. And life in Europe as a dethroned monarch would be unbearably dull. But most important of all, the illustrious name of Hapsburg would be forever stained by his abdication. A Hapsburg, he reminded the emperor, never retreats. Maximilian could offer no rebuttal. Indeed, he felt so inspired by Fischer's remarks that he reversed his decision and returned to the capital to resume, once again, his duties as emperor. He avoided, however, Chapultepec Castle—living there alone with memories of Carlotta would have been too painful—and he took up residence in Tacubaya in the large house of a Swiss friend.

1867

General Bazaine pleaded with him to leave, claiming it was madness to remain in Mexico a moment longer. Liberal troops were already in Guadalajara, Oaxaca, Monterrey, and Tampico; and they were steadily closing in on the capital. The emperor, then under the sway of Father Fischer, drew himself up to his full, towering height and replied that he had complete faith in his Mexican army of twenty thousand which was stiffened by Belgian and Austrian volunteers.

So on February 5, Maximilian stood with friends at his window watching the last detachment of French troops file out of their garrison and begin their march to Veracruz, with General Bazaine at their head. When the last soldier had passed from view, he dropped the curtain and said, "Now, gentlemen, at long last I am free!"

Commanding the armies of Juárez were five seasoned generals: Díaz, Escobedo, Corona, Regules, and Palacio. The imperial forces of Maximilian were commanded by only three: Márquez, Mejía, and Miramón. They were, however, better trained and more experienced than the Juárists. The day Bazaine left Mexico City, Miramón made a brilliant raid on Zacatecas, routing Juárist troops and coming within an ace of capturing Juárez himself. Two days later, however, Escobedo counter-attacked and retook Zacatecas, capturing 101 French troops who had elected to remain in Mexico with Maximilian. By orders of Juárez, all were shot. Miramón re-assembled his retreating troops in Querétaro where he was joined by General Márquez and his straggling army which had been badly defeated at Monte de las Cruces, in the pass above Mexico City. Since their combined strength represented the bulk of imperial forces, Maximilian was urged by his council to join them and take command of their armies. So on February 13 he rode out from Mexico City toward the imperial redoubt of Querétaro.

Querétaro is a picturesque colonial town 174 miles north of Mexico City. It is situated in a relatively flat part of an undulating valley and divided by a tiny stream called the Querétaro River which winds through the town. Its main water supply, however, is a large communal basin in the main plaza into which gushes water from the ancient Spanish aqueduct whose long length runs to springs far away in the hills. At the east end overlooking the town is the Franciscan convent, Convento de la Cruz; on the west, outside of town, is the Cerro de las Campanas—the Hill of the Bells.

As the town was open on all sides, virtually impossible to defend, Maximilian chose to build his defenses on the Hill of the Bells; but as the battle progressed, he occupied the convent, which subsequently became his imperial headquarters. He had roughly nine or ten thousand men; General Escobedo, commander in chief of the Juárist army, had forty thousand. A few Juárist soldiers were armed with American guns, but the rest were poorly equipped and were physically unfit for sustaining a long, grueling siege.

1867

Notwithstanding their vast superiority, the Juárist army, at the start, took a terrible beating, mainly because communications between Escobedo's headquarters and his front-line troops were deplorably bad and often lacking altogether. General Márquez of the royalists terrorized his enemy with lightning raids on isolated camps, leaving hundreds of Juárist soldiers dead and capturing vitally needed supplies of food and munitions. Also, these raids kept General Escobedo continually off balance and incapable of launching a full-scale offensive. Once Márquez went as far as San Miguel, some fifty miles away, and might have held it if Miramón had rushed forward reserves to support him. Maximilian highly praised these daring raids, but he well knew they won only battles but had little chance of winning the war. He therefore called a temporary cease-fire in order to let the enemy take up fixed positions. When it was known where Escobedo had concentrated his main force, an all-out attack would be hurled against it. If the imperial army emerged victorious, as the emperor firmly believed it would, the siege would be broken and the imperialists would thereafter be on the offensive. The emperor elected General Márquez to lead a body of twelve hundred dragoons through the enemy's lines in a dash for Mexico City, where he was to raise another army that would attack the Juárists from the rear. To distract the enemy's attention, a small battle was fought near the Hill of the Bells while Márquez and his dragoons galloped away unnoticed in the opposite direction. He reached Mexico City on March 26 without a casualty.

1867

On that day General Noriega, commander of the imperial army defending Puebla, was being heavily bombarded by a sieging Juárist army under Porfirio Díaz. Márquez, on an impulse, decided to help Noriega and led his army to Puebla to raise the siege. But Noriega, not knowing relief was on its way, capitulated to Díaz on April 4 and Díaz and his army swept into Puebla. Almost at once Márquez attacked but was defeated and was hotly pursued through the mountain pass and up to the very gates of Mexico City. Liberal orators within the city had won over most of the populace to their cause, and Márquez, fearful of being shot either by a citizen or by a soldier of his then demoralized and mutinous army, went into hiding. Disguised as a peasant, he passed through Juárez-held territory and in Veracruz caught a ship for Cuba, where he spent the rest of his forty years as a pawnbroker in Havana.

News of Márquez' rout considerably dampened the hopes of the imperialists. By the beginning of May conditions within Querétaro were critical, since General Escobedo had not massed his army for an attack, as expected, but had, instead, thrown a tight blockade around the town, hoping to starve it into surrender. Early in the siege the aqueduct had been cut, and the river water, regularly polluted with rotting corpses, was undrinkable. And food was so scarce that everyone, including Maximilian, was eating the barest minimum. At a council of war, called by the emperor to decide on some means of escape, it was agreed that a full-scale attack should be made on the weakest sector of the enemy's encircling ring till a gap was opened through which the entire imperial army could charge. Once free, they would rendezvous in the hills of Sierra Gorda where General Mejía's Indian army was still holding out. Zero hour was set for midnight, May 14.

The plan might have worked if there had not been among them a traitor, a Colonel López, one of Maximilian's confidants who had been at the emperor's side since Maximilian landed in Veracruz three years before. For weeks López had brooded incessantly on the hopelessness of the imperial cause, and he was terrified at the thought of being killed in the confusion of flight. So one night, under cover of darkness, he slipped over to General Escobedo's headquarters and, for a promise that his own life would be spared, conspired with Escobedo to capture the emperor. Then, before dawn, he crept back into Querétaro and, during the day, asked the emperor to put back zero hour from midnight to three in the morning, claiming he needed three extra hours to prepare for battle. The emperor, seeing nothing unusual in his request, changed the hour accordingly.

1867

At midnight, then, on May 14, López led a detachment of Juárist soldiers through the intricate maze of trenches and barricades surrounding Querétaro, and up to the quarters of the emperor. But at that moment López lost his nerve and screamed out frantically for Maximilian to save himself. The emperor, however, was gone. An hour before he had been roused from sleep by a German soldier of fortune, Prince Salm-Salm, who had won distinction in the American civil war as a commander in the Union army and who, as a general under Maximilian, had become the chief strategist for the imperial army. Having somehow anticipated the treason of López, Prince Salm-Salm arranged with General Mejía to make a last stand on the Hill of the Bells, and the emperor, hearing of it, enthusiastically supported them. The Juárist soldiers brought in by López overwhelmed the guards manning the town's principal barricade, and the main body of the Juárist army, waiting outside for their signal, surged into Querétaro. The church tower was scaled and its bells clanged wildly, announcing the fall of the city. After a short skirmish the tiny band defending the Hill of the Bells was overpowered, and as the gray mist of dawn melted away, General Escobedo went forward to meet the emperor. Calmly and ceremoniously Maximilian unbuckled his sword and held it out to him in a traditional gesture of surrender. Even in defeat the Hapsburg prince was observant of decorum.

Of Maximilian it could truly be said:

> . . . nothing in his life,
> Became him like the leaving it; he died
> As one that had been studied in his death . . .
> Macbeth, Act I, scene 4

He seemed indifferent to his own fate but was deeply concerned about the welfare of others. Though he was offered dozens of opportunities to save himself—the last coming during the siege from General Escobedo, who promised him safe passage to Veracruz if he would abdicate—he remained stoutly beside his men, stating that only if his entire army were given the same treatment as himself would he leave. Six young officers and a young lieutenant colonel presided over his court-martial and pronounced him guilty of treason for having signed the law by which hundreds of Juárist prisoners were shot. Three voted for his banishment, three voted for execution, and the lieutenant colonel, after some deliberation, cast his vote for execution. Miramón and Mejía were also found guilty of treason and were given the same sentence. It was decreed that all would be shot on June 16.

Supplications for clemency poured into the office of Juárez —letters from each of the crowned heads of Europe and one from William H. Seward, then the United States Secretary of State. But Juárez was a lawyer, grimly determined to enforce the last letter of the law. For him, mercy was weakness and he detested weakness. Princess Salm-Salm (who before marrying Prince Salm-Salm had been a stunt rider in a circus) was supposed to have offered herself to Juárez if he would give Maximilian his freedom. On being refused she fell to her knees before him, sobbing. Said the unemotional Juárez, "I am sorry, lady, to see you on your knees at my feet. But if all the kings and queens of Europe were in your place, I could not spare his life."

On June 16, Father Soria came to administer to the doomed trio the last rites. He heard their confession, said mass, and gave them Holy Communion. But at three o'clock in the afternoon, the hour of their scheduled execution, nothing happened. An hour later they were informed that Juárez had granted them a three-day reprieve. Hope again flared that the sentence would be changed or at least modified. Maximilian courageously offered to stand alone before the firing squad if his two generals were released. His offer had no effect, nor, indeed, was it even told them why the stay of execution had been granted.

So on June 19, long before dawn, they were awakened, taken to high mass (again said by Father Soria), put into carriages, and taken to the Hill of the Bells where they were placed against a wall—the emperor between his two generals. Before the rifles were raised, Maximilian turned to Miramón and said, "General, a brave man should be honored by his sovereign even in the hour of death. Permit me to give you the place of honor." And he stepped aside and let Miramón have the center position. When the riflemen were ready, waiting the command to fire, he cried out, "I pardon all and pray they will also pardon me. Would that my blood might help save this country. Long live Mexico!" Three volleys rang out and reverberated through the city and the valley, waking the people to a new day which promised to be bright and warm. And the soldiers with their long muskets went forward to inspect the lifeless body of the man who had been the emperor of Mexico and who, by assuming that role, became a legend.

CHAPTER TEN

1867–1910

1867

The famous black carriage of Benito Juárez rolled toward the capital, followed in line by the elegant coach of his minister of state, Sebastian Lerdo de Tejada. Juárez sat alone, grim and unsmiling. He had been informed that Porfirio Díaz had spent twenty thousand pesos—nearly all his money—on decorating the city for the president's triumphal entrance. But Juárez disliked and distrusted generals; they were useful, certainly, in winning wars, but in times of peace, they were a menace. General Díaz, resplendent in gold braid and highly polished boots, rode out on a prancing white horse to greet the president at Tlalnepantla. Juárez grudgingly nodded to him and signaled his coachman to drive on. Díaz was stunned. The president had snubbed him—he who had risked his life in dozens of battles for the Juárez government. Lerdo de Tejada, in the second carriage, who witnessed the incident and who was quick to realize what horrible consequences could result from a rift between these two men, directed his carriage over to Díaz and urged him to get in. They would ride into town together. Díaz accepted, hardly able to speak and when he did it was to swear on his life to avenge this insult of Juárez.

The first act of Juárez was to discharge two thirds of his army. He simply sent away sixty thousand men with a few words of thanks and nothing else—not a pension or even the promise of one. Many protested loudly and some went back to their old trade of guerrilla warfare, vowing to overthrow the government. But Juárez had retained an energetic watchdog named General Sostenes Rocha who gloried in beating down each rebellion as it cropped up. Porfirio Díaz resigned his commission as general, since his army had been taken away from him anyhow, and retired to his native state of Oaxaca where the citizens, in token of their gratitude for his wartime services, gave him the large hacienda, La Noria. There he settled down ostensibly to raise sugar cane, but in a shed at the back he set up a foundry for casting cannons.

Mexico had never been in a more deplorable condition. The treasury was empty, the roads were infested with bandits, the internal debt—growing steadily since the days of Hidalgo —had reached the staggering sum of three hundred million pesos, disgruntled bureaucrats worked listlessly at their jobs, and remnants of loyal imperialists were still rattling their sabers in provincial towns. That Juárez could win the election that year by a wide majority clearly demonstrates that the people had faith in him however bad conditions were.

1869

Even the weather added to his woes. A terrible drought that year scorched the earth and caused widespread famine. Without funds, he could do nothing to relieve the suffering. This year, indeed, marks the nadir of Mexico's decline, but it also marks the beginning of her long arduous climb upward, a climb which began then but goes on to this day.

Methodically and meticulously Juárez dealt with each problem as it arose. With the aid of his prudent Secretary of Treasury, Don Matías Romero, he somehow staved off financial ruin. He called in British engineers to resume construction on the Veracruz—Mexico City railroad, begun in 1850 but abandoned during the war. He appointed Gabino Barredo secretary of education to work out a school system that conformed with the soundest principles of the day. And he encouraged the development of industry.

The budding talent in literature, retarded by the war, now burst forth full blown. Ignacio Altamirano wrote classical novels, and Orozco y Berra and José Fernández Ramírez wrote scholarly books on Mexican history.

For the first time Mexico was showing unmistakable signs of a unified, national consciousness.

1871

The big test came in this election year. Three candidates were running: Díaz, who was popular for his outspoken criticism of the government and was a particular favorite with the army; Lerdo de Tejada, who, by splitting with Juárez, was drawing votes away from the government; and Juárez, who was being accused of wanting to monopolize the presidency. The election results proved a three-way tie, and it devolved on congress to decide the winner. Their decision: Juárez president, Lerdo de Tejada vice-president. At this announcement the country did not fall into anarchy, as many disaffected generals had predicted it would, but kept its peace, except for a revolution in Oaxaca led by Díaz, who claimed, as was expected, the election was a fraud.

Juárez unleashed his bad-tempered, hard-drinking general, Sostenes Rocha, who flew savagely at a *Porfirista* rally held in the capital and before his bloody work was done two hundred people were dead. He then gathered his army and marched on Oaxaca. Felix Díaz, brother of Porfirio, attempted to defend the city but was no match for the fierce fighting of Rocha and after a short battle surrendered. In his flight to escape he was captured by Indians of the village of Juchitán who denounced him as a heretic because his rebel troops had knocked over and smashed the statue of their patron saint. They therefore had him stoned to death. Porfirio Díaz, disguised as a priest, escaped into the hills and sought refuge with an Indian chieftain named Lozada who commanded a rebel army of Indians in the jungles of Nayarit.

1872

On the morning of July 18, in this year, Juárez climbed the stairs to his humble office in the National Palace, sat down to a deskful of work and . . . slumped forward, the victim of a fatal heart attack. In his sixty-six years he had endured battles, long flights, periods of near-starvation, and calamities that would have broken the spirit of any ordinary man; yet in the quiet of his office and in the company of his beloved books he met his end. He died later that night, and the nation went into deep mourning for several weeks.

It fell to Vice-President Lerdo de Tejada to take over the presidency.

Lerdo was an immaculate dresser, and he had a talent for rhetoric which he punctuated with grandiose gestures; he also had an unhealthy hunger for flattery. Society lionized him and, because he was a bachelor, women vied for the honor of his presence at their parties. To demonstrate the confidence he had in his government, he published a decree granting full amnesty to all political outlaws if they would lay down arms within fifteen days. Díaz, who had not been able to get along with the haughty Indian chieftain Lozada (he was actually half-English), accepted the olive branch and went to the capital to pay his respects to the president. Lerdo apologized to Díaz for having ruined his hacienda (which Sostenes Rocha demolished after the fall of Oaxaca) and offered him, by way of compensation, a helping hand to start life anew in Veracruz. Díaz took his offer and opened a furniture shop in the tiny village of La Candelaria.

1873

By this time the sound planning of Juárez was beginning to bear fruit. The Veracruz–Mexico City railroad line was completed and, because of its many curves and uphill gradients, was hailed as one of the greatest engineering feats of its day.

1874

Eight thousand schools had been opened with a total enrollment of 350,000. Though this was undeniably a giant step forward, Mexico was yet a long way from educating her young. There were still 2,000,000 children of school age not attending school.

1876

After three years the arrogance of Lerdo was beginning to pall on his public, especially the army, which he treated with indifference or else with downright contempt. His announcement to run for a second term was not popular, neither in Mexico nor in the United States where he had incurred the disapprobation of the State Department. Not one petition from American companies to build railroads connecting Texas with Mexico City had he honored. "Between weakness and strength there should lie a desert," he exclaimed, parroting, more or less, the ideas of Juárez. Díaz, watching events from his furniture shop in La Candelaria, saw the dawn of his career breaking and decided it was time to act. In January his party, the *Porfiristas*, raised the Plan of Tuxtepec calling for "effective suffrage" and "no re-election," while he slipped into the United States to solicit financial aid for his revolution.

Ex-soldiers in a dozen states harkened to the call of their old commander, cleaned up their guns, and went off to join local revolutionaries. In March, Díaz re-entered Mexico through the border town of Matamoros which fell without firing a shot. With only twenty-five hundred men he marched on Monterrey, expecting, perhaps, that his very presence would trigger off a nationwide revolt that would carry him into the presidency. If so, his dream was shattered at Icamole where he was soundly defeated by government troops and was sent running ingloriously back into Texas. Undaunted, he went to New York where he boarded an American ship, the *City of Havana*, whose captain, Alexander Coney, an admirer of his, signed him on as a Cuban doctor. His disguise and his acting fooled the port officials at Tampico, but at Veracruz he had to assume the role of a stevedore, and, hoisting a bale of cotton on his shoulder, he marched down the gangplank into a dockside warehouse where he hid until nightfall. Then, in the dark, he crept stealthily to the house of Colonel Enrique, a loyal friend, who gave him a horse. By dawn he was in full gallop toward Oaxaca, the stronghold of his revolution. When Lerdo heard Díaz was in Oaxaca, he was not greatly disturbed—his small army in the north had defeated him once, and he saw no reason why General Escobedo with a larger army guarding the capital could not beat him again. But what did bother him was his vice-president, José María Iglesias, who was a stickler for accuracy in reading the law and who questioned Lerdo's right to the presidency. The July elections, which Lerdo claimed he had won, were, according to Iglesias, not valid since some states, because of the revolution, had failed to vote. Lerdo, incensed by this obvious aspersion on his honesty, ordered Iglesias to be banished from the country. Iglesias, however, collected some soldiers and fled to Guanajuato where he proclaimed himself president until a new election was held. With the government thus divided, Díaz could hardly fail in his *coup d'état*. He and his army moved into Orizaba.

Another of Lerdo's misfortunes was that General Escobedo chose that moment to become temperamental. Escobedo wanted no active part in a war against Díaz, though he refused to relinquish command of the army. He did, however, dispatch General Alatorre to check the advance of Díaz, but handled Alatorre like a puppet, moving him this way and that according to instructions sent by runners. Despite this absurd arrangement, Alatorre fought Díaz to a standstill at Tecoac on November 16; but the battle was not decisive. Both sides awaited the arrival of reinforcements. Soldiers of the rebel Manuel González arrived first, swelling the ranks of Porfirio Díaz, who immediately attacked and overran the outnumbered troops of Alatorre. The path to Mexico City was then clear, and Don Porfirio occupied the capital on November 21.

Two days before, Lerdo had sacked the treasury and had left for Acapulco where a boat was waiting to take him to the States. Iglesias, after a long interview with Díaz, realized the futility of opposing the strong man and voluntarily went into exile.

1877

Díaz called for a new election which, with his popular banner—"Effective Suffrage" and "No Re-election"—he won by a landslide. On February 17 he took office as interim president for Lerdo's unexpired term—or until November 1880.

Porfirio Díaz was not then the drawing-room idol that Lerdo was, but he was infinitely more astute as a politician. He quickly buried grudges, he ignored prejudices, and he accepted everybody as his friend. Supporters of ex-President Lerdo and Iglesias were taken back into the government and even long-outlawed imperialists were forgiven.

One of his first decrees, hailed by all honest citizens, called for the organization of a rural police force, known later as the *rurales*. Recruits were acquired by capturing a few bandits, giving them felt hats, smart gray uniforms, and the promise of regular pay if they would bring in more bandits, either as volunteers for the *rurales* or as prisoners. In this way (using thieves to catch thieves) a sharp decline in banditry was immediately noted, and for the first time in living memory the roads in Mexico were safe for travel.

But peasants were soon to learn that one evil had been merely replaced by another. The *rurales* were, after all, still bandits in fancy uniforms who were committing crimes of rape and robbery with perfect impunity. And the *Ley Fuga* (the right to fire on escaping prisoners) exonerated them from cold-blooded murder. Each year, on an average, they reported that three hundred peasants had foolishly tried to escape from them. The *rurales* were therefore a terror to the peasants who looked anxiously for some means of fighting them.

Díaz was not inclined to follow the Juárez policy that favored European capital over American. In his first term of office he began negotiating with American firms for contracts to build railroads in Mexico.

1879

The only blot on his otherwise stainless first three years of
rule came in June of this year. It was discovered that partisans of Lerdo were holding meetings in Veracruz at which
ways to overthrow the government were being discussed. Díaz
ordered the governor of the state, Mier y Teran, to round up
all suspects and have them shot. Nine men were immediately
arrested and, without trial, stood up before the firing squad.
Later it was discovered that none of the nine had been even
remotely connected with the conspiracy. This incident is usually held up by critics of Díaz as an example of his brutality.
But when it is compared with the horrific slaughter of several
hundreds perpetrated by Sostenes Rocha and condoned by
Juárez, it becomes merely an unfortunate affair.

1880

Since Díaz had swept into office bearing the banner "Effective Suffrage" and "No Re-election," he could not—at least not
then—mock his own slogan by nominating himself again for
president, so he chose a stooge to take his place: Manuel
González, an army man who had fought at the side of Díaz
in overthrowing Lerdo.

Unfortunately, González was vain to an almost psycho-
pathic degree. Those who realized this covered him with flattery and became his closest "friends." They were given gifts of
land, haciendas, coveted contracts, and loans. It was a harmless enough game to begin with, but eventually the cost of
González' vanity ate into the treasury and finally into the
country itself.

To raise money for his "friends" he sold off great tracts of
land to foreigners, and he increased his margins of profit
(graft) on every government contract. He pushed forward at
a reckless pace the policy introduced by Díaz of using American capital. And he gave away gratis to American surveyors
one third of all land they surveyed. The rest was sold at a

pittance and on easy terms to Americans who knew how to lay on the flattery. But Americans and other foreign land-holders complained that the old Spanish mining laws—which gave the state (not the landholder) subsoil rights, or owner-ship of all metals and oil contained in the ground—were im-peding progress. No foreigner, they claimed, would spend his good money on mining in Mexico so long as those antiquated laws were in effect. So they plied González with great lashings of flattery, and he, intoxicated by their attention, committed the greatest folly of his four-year term by changing the law. Not only had he sold away his country's land, but by giving subsoil rights to foreigners he sold away her mineral wealth as well. Some twenty-five years later Mexico would be ravaged by a terrible revolution fought primarily to correct this gigan-tic blunder of González. When it was known abroad what González had done, it caused a stampede of foreign mining engineers to Mexico. Soon exportation of precious and in-dustrial metals skyrocketed, and Mexico produced more gold and silver in the following twenty years than she had in the four preceding centuries combined. By the end of 1884, when González left office, Mexico had been perniciously bled and the treasury teetered on the brink of ruin.

While González was squandering away his country, Porfi-rio Díaz at first went to Oaxaca where he was made governor. He cut down state spending, initiated a campaign for honesty and efficiency in municipal offices, and within two years bal-anced the state budget, no mean task considering the sorry state of Oaxacan economy after the war. But he grew restless with provincial life and longed for the hurly-burly of the capital again. So when González offered him a seat on the court of justice, he accepted with alacrity.

The deposed President Lerdo had, in his four-year term, made his best decisions when he took advice from his erudite and crafty cabinet minister, Don Manuel Romero Rubio. Rubio, after the fall of Lerdo, left for Cuba, stating that he strongly disagreed with Don Porfirio and could not associate with his government. But his beautiful nineteen-year-old daughter, Carmen, chose to remain behind in Mexico City. Though her father had been a staunch anti-Catholic, she had been provided with a good education in an exclusive Catholic convent in the States. Left on her own to support herself, Carmen opened a school for teaching English and felt honored when her first pupil turned out to be none other than Don Porfirio Díaz himself. Another pupil, Dr. Eduardo Liceaga, joined the class, but when he realized that Don Porfirio was more interested in the teacher than the teaching, he tactfully withdrew. In the spring of 1883, Díaz, then fifty-three, made the young and lovely Carmelita his wife.

From that day forward Díaz was a changed man. Carmelita improved his table manners, his speech, his deportment at parties, and under her tutelage the blustering, swaggering ex-guerrilla fighter became a clothes-conscious, courteous diplomat. He discovered the delights of presenting his radiantly beautiful Carmelita at state balls, and he was soon accepting all invitations to parties where white tie and tails were required, for he loved dressing up. In fact the whole country underwent a subtle transformation—at least in the upper classes—and an era began which was characterized by women in large feathery hats and long sweeping gowns and men in derby hats smoking long Havana cigars and wearing tight-fitting striped suits. It was the beginning of the Golden Era of Don Porfirio.

From his small corner in the government—a seat on the court of justice—Díaz railed incessantly at his own stooge, González, blaming him entirely for bringing the country into a financial crisis. His speeches, cogent and full of fire, caused senators and deputies to conclude that the only man capable of saving the country was Don Porfirio himself, and so they elected him president once again. Obviously Díaz was by then the political arbiter of Mexico and his slogan "No Re-election" had been discreetly forgotten.

Working in close consultation with his minister of finance, the able Don Manuel Dublán, he used drastic means to avert a depression. He ruthlessly cut salaries of bureaucrats, he refused to honor any mortgages made by González, and he consolidated the national debt. He also pledged his government to fulfill the promise made by González to pay off a long-outstanding debt to England totaling ninety-one million pesos. He well realized that foreign debts had to be paid if Mexico was to establish her credit abroad. But the newspapers saw this as utter folly and wrote scathing editorials criticizing his irresponsible use of government funds. Their articles so rankled him that he ordered a heavy censorship to be put on the press. From then on, the press became an organ of the government. And it was tacitly understood that any voice raised in protest against the government would be quickly silenced by the police. His dictatorship was taking shape.

It must be said that Díaz, as a dictator, was no bully. He resorted to violence only when other methods failed and that was seldom. The game he excelled at was pitting one political opponent against the other, thereby gaining control of both. For example, two generals, Treviño and Naranjo, governors of northeastern states by appointment of former President González, threatened to revolt if Díaz attempted to remove them. But Díaz had no intention of removing them. He used them as a foil against the ambitious young general, Bernardo Reyes, whom he made commander of the army in that area. Díaz first supported Reyes against Treviño and Naranjo until Reyes became too popular and powerful, then he switched sides and backed Treviño and Naranjo against Reyes. In this way neither side could gain an ascendancy and Díaz, by merely adding a touch now and then, kept the scales in balance.

1888

Don Manuel Romero Rubio, father of Carmelita, came out of exile in Cuba and begged forgiveness for his stupid mistake of having backed Lerdo against the man destined to be his own son-in-law. To redeem himself, he promised to work wholeheartedly and unstintingly for the Díaz government. His talent for intrigue was just what a thoroughgoing dictatorship needed, and so Díaz let bygones be bygones and made Romero Rubio *Jefe de governación* (boss of the interior government), gave him control of congress, and made him director of the *bravi*, the Mexican secret police who eliminated any political opponents that were beyond the reach of the law.

The policy of selling land at bargain prices to foreigners,

inaugurated by González, was stepped up by Díaz. During his dictatorship 125,000,000 acres of land were sold—approximately one fourth of the republic—which contained the richest oil deposits and mineral veins in the country. Indian tribes such as the Yaquis of Sonora drove back every government expedition sent out to take possession of their land. Ramon Corral, governor of the state, called the Yaqui resistance an intolerable crime against progress and gave orders to have them starved into submission. In time the Indians surrendered, and their chieftain, an Indian named Cajeme, was brought before the governor. Corral was struck by Cajeme's intelligence, his eloquent use of Spanish, and his great knowledge of tactical warfare. Nevertheless it did not mitigate the sentence he passed on the Indian: execution by the firing squad. Corral then committed a truly great crime, not against progress, but against humanity, by selling the Yaqui Indians like cattle, at 75 pesos a head, to rich plantation owners in Quintana Roo, where the Indians were worked like slaves, under a tropical sun, until they dropped. Meanwhile, rich Creole landowners grew richer and fatter with the territory they had extorted from the Indians . . . and called their profits "progress."

Up to this time Doña Carmen Díaz had but one great gnawing problem: how to bring her husband back into the Church. After endless entreaties and naggings, she finally persuaded him to meet the archbishop of Mexico, Labastida. The first interview of Díaz with the Church's high dignitary led to a second and a third, and the final outcome of their long series of talks was that Díaz agreed not to enforce any of the anti-church legislation written into the constitution if, in exchange, the priests would preach from the pulpits loyalty to the Díaz regime. The Church was allowed to buy back some of her land and her ecclesiastical ranks swelled from 500 priests (at the time of Juárez) to about 5000 in 1900. The increase, however, was made up mostly of French, Spanish, and Italian missionaries sent out from Rome. By 1910 the Church was very close to the same high place she held during the reign of the viceroys.

1892

Though Díaz would tolerate no serious opposition to his dictatorship, he nevertheless insisted on the formalities of an election. But as most self-respecting citizens indignantly refused to take part in the farce, ballots were distributed in the penitentiaries and each prisoner filled out hundreds of forms. In this way Díaz "won" every election by a landslide.

This was a crucial year for the Díaz regime. Because of a drought which damaged the harvest, along with a drop in the world's silver prices, Mexico went through a mild depression. It was nothing very serious and would certainly have worked itself out in time, but it badly frightened Díaz and resolved him to find a more vigorous minister of finance. His choice was José Limantour.

Limantour was the son of a French adventurer who had gone to California to dig for gold but later made a fortune buying and selling confiscated church land in Mexico. Young José was sent to France to be educated and, as a young man, was launched on a career in banking for which he showed an amazing aptitude. While José, as a banker, added millions to the family's already large fortune, a group of talented young men—all rich Creoles like himself and all products of an English or European education—met in the study of his large mansion to discuss "ideas." They decided that in view of the great progress made by science, the best political philosophy for Mexico was that of the early nineteenth-century French writer August Comte, who held that the individual stood higher in matters of politics than did ethics. They also gave the emotions secondary importance. They made a kind of religion of science and laid before its cold Euclidean altars all their problems—social, economic, and even racial. The trouble was that this rational religion of weights and measures had only one guiding principle: profit! With a clear, untroubled conscience they could exploit the lower classes, amass fortunes, and adapt the law to suit their own financial interests. The only "good" they were likely to acknowledge was a black figure on a balance sheet. By making Limantour minister of finance, Díaz lost what roots he had among the common people and his government identified itself with the rich. After that, the poor got poorer and the rich got richer.

1893

In his first report to congress Limantour announced that the country's expenditure had been 41,000,000 pesos and its revenues 43,000,000. A thunderous applause swept the assembly. For the first time in her eighty-three years of independence Mexico had, at long last, balanced her budget. Now, claimed the *politicos* surrounding the dictator, revolution in Mexico was impossible for, with a reserve in the treasury, the government could buy off its enemies. The reserves steadily rose and by 1910, Mexico's revenues were bringing in 110,-000,000 pesos, half of which stayed in the treasury. State treasuries also prospered and by 1910 they were collecting 64,000,000 pesos from revenues.

Wags referred to Limantour and his erudite clique as the *científicos* (the scientists), a name by which they were ever after known. Díaz, who did not like them personally (they were rich Creoles and he was a lowly Mixteca Indian) but who tolerated them because they served his purpose, referred to them as *mi caballada* (my stable of tame horses). As financiers, they made millions by knowing in advance, through their exclusive grapevine, what the government needed and was going to buy. When, for example, José Limantour nationalized the railroads, his brother, a partner in the banking firm of Scherer-Limantour, bought up stocks in railroads and within a few days resold them to the government at nearly twice the price. Nevertheless, the statistics of the Díaz regime under the guidance of the *científicos* looked good. By 1900 more than 9000 miles of railroad were in use; harbors had been dredged and improved; large plantations were producing an abundance of sugar, coffee, henequen, cotton, rubber, and tropical fruit. Steel mills and textile factories were rapidly expanding and foreign trade at 200,000,000 pesos had quadrupled since 1870.

Even the intellectuals, once the vanguard of liberalism,

were lured to the side of the dictator. They conceded that he, at least, was better than anarchy. Justo Sierra, the celebrated historian and essayist, gave classes in literature at the national preparatory school in the mornings when he expounded radical and exciting ideas in philosophy, and then in the afternoons he would wearily take his seat on the supreme court where a dictator's notion of justice prevailed. In the evenings, alone in his study, he would sort out his thoughts and put them to paper. These writings won him recognition as the dean of Mexican philosophers. The iconoclast Francisco Bulnes—also a historian—took a morbid delight in running down his country's heroes. His books on Morelos, Hidalgo, and Juárez were like brilliant diatribes which the rich Creoles and *científicos* read avidly and with great pleasure.

And the capital was beautified. Journalists were referring to Mexico City as "the Paris of America." Broad boulevards were opened and palatial homes were constructed. The Juárez monument in the Alameda Park was designed, carved, and erected by Italian sculptors. French artists were commissioned to build the monument to Cuauhtémoc (now standing on Paseo de la Reforma) and a whole team of artists were put to work on the monument to the Mexican independence (farther down the Reforma). Its tall triumphal column is topped with a golden angel, and its base is arrayed with statues of principal figures in the wars of independence—Hidalgo, Morelos, Allende, and others. Perhaps the most imposing edifice built at this time was the Palacio de Bellas Artes (the Palace of Fine Arts). It is so designed that one cannot remain indifferent to it. It has been called everything from "the most magnificent flower of Mexican architecture" to "that hideous example of bastard architecture." Huge, in white marble, it apes all styles, from the slender roman columns on its porches and the rococo sculpture adorning its front, to the golden cathedral-like dome on its roof.

1904

Before the elections of this year, intimates of Díaz advised him to choose a successor. They agreed that he was incredibly robust for a man of seventy-four, but something could happen to him and if there was no one prepared to take his place the country would surely fall into anarchy. The army urged him to make the highly efficient general, Bernardo Reyes, vice-president; the *científicos* were clamoring for Limantour. At a crowded session of congress Díaz announced his choice: Ramon Corral. Gasps of surprise and even guffaws broke out. The corrupt, Indian-baiter Corral, despised by many and liked by none. Why had Díaz chosen such a nonentity? He confessed to friends later on that if he had made a more popular man vice-president, he would have been inviting assassination. With the disreputable Corral he felt safe. He even contributed stories of his own to add more discredit to the character of Corral, for the worse Corral appeared, the safer Díaz felt.

What statisticians would call the "hard facts" of Mexican prosperity were, in fact, only an assessment of improvements enjoyed by the privileged few—the rich. Of the 10,000,000 inhabitants in Mexico, 9,500,000 owned no land whatsoever and worked in virtual serfdom for those who did. More than half the country was owned by only 3000 families (roughly 100 square miles per family) and seven American companies owned three fourths of all the mines and over half the oil fields. American capital in Mexico was then $1,250,000,000! No wonder Mexico was then being called "the mother of foreigners and the stepmother of her own children." And while rich people broke laws with perfect impunity, 9,500,000 Mexicans were being treated to the *Ley Fuga* by the *rurales*. Except for the bureaucrats (whose salaries during the Díaz dictatorship increased 900 per cent) Mexico had no middle class. The nation Juárez had knitted together fell apart into two unequal extremes—the ubiquitous poor and the few ivory-towered rich.

The first stirrings of serious dissension began in the industrial areas where the Magón brothers, Ricardo and Enrique, members of the Industrial Workers of the World, preached socialism and tried to organize unions. Their efforts were brutally suppressed. Workers at the copper mines of Cananea in Sonora and at the textile mills in Veracruz who dared to dispute the authority of their employers were fired on by government troops.

But deep cracks in the dictatorship were caused by Díaz himself in his sixth term, when he tampered with Mexico's foreign policy. For several years he had been concerned over the growing strength of American capital in Mexico and decided finally to throw favors to the British. His favorite game of pitting one power against another could be played, he assumed, internationally as well as nationally. The English bankers, Pearson and Sons, then in Mexico to contract for the draining of Lake Texcoco, were surprised to hear that special concessions had been granted their oil fields, concessions which had been denied those owned by the Americans, Rockefeller and Doheny. Also Díaz flouted the American State Department by giving political asylum to Nicaragua's former president, Zelaya, whose government had been overthrown by a revolution backed by the United States. Later in 1907, when the United States was disputing with Japan over immigration quotas and segregation of orientals in San Francisco, Díaz invited a corps of Japanese marines to Mexico City and feted them with a gala ball. Despite these intentional taunts, United States diplomats maintained an outward show of friendliness, and as late as 1908, Elihu Root, then Secretary of State, paying a courtesy call on Díaz, delivered a bombastic speech in praise of the dictator, calling him "one of the greatest men to be held up for the hero worship of mankind." But officials in Washington were tending to aid and abet political exiles of the "great man." They announced that their agreement to close the frontier to escaping political refugees was no longer in effect.

1907

Díaz, at seventy-seven, was not as nimble-witted as before, and his once-keen political sight was definitely failing. An American journalist, James Creelman of *Pearson's* magazine, New York, inadvertently tripped him up during an interview, and when Creelman's interview was published, the dictator never quite regained his balance. Díaz enjoyed being interviewed, especially by correspondents of important newspapers and journals, for it gave him opportunity to advertise to the world Mexico's great progress under his rule. Magazine readers on two continents were well familiar with portraits of the solemn-faced, venerated Mixteca Indian, with his bushy mustache and his magnificent uniform crowded with medals. Creelman sincerely wanted to eulogize the dictator and began his article with a long string of flattering phrases, but he, in fact, started a revolution when he quoted the "hero of modern Mexico" as saying, "No matter what my friends and supporters say, I retire when my present term of office ends, and I shall not serve again." Apparently Díaz meant this information to stay in New York and Washington where it belonged as a propaganda piece, but copies, naturally, filtered through to Mexico where they were read with popeyed disbelief. Newspapermen besieged the president's office clamoring for confirmation of the article, but Díaz haughtily closed the doors and assumed an inscrutable silence.

A furor of excitement spread through the country. Did the great man seriously mean to step down in 1910? General Bernardo Reyes, the efficient and popular administrator of Nuevo León, seemed to think so, for he backed a new political party, *Los Democraticos*, and paid for the publication of a controversial book, *Grandes Problemas Nacionales*, which assailed the corrupt agrarian program of Díaz and attracted nationwide attention. Another political party, called the *Anti-reeleccionistas*, sprang up right in the heart of the capital, actively supported by several brilliant young men—José Vasconcelos, Palavicine, and Luis Cabrera—and financed by a political dark horse named Francisco Indalecio Madero.

Of all the extraordinary twists and turns in Mexican history, none is more extraordinary than the rise of Francisco I. Madero. He, opposing Díaz, was like David stepping forward to slay Goliath. His story borders on the fantastic and reads like the kind of novel that provokes wonder and sympathy.

He was born the second son of a rich Portuguese-Jewish family, Catholic for generations, proprietors of vast estates in the north, and owners of large cotton mills, breweries, and smelting plants. As a boy, Francisco with his elder brother, Gustavo, attended a Jesuit school in Saltillo where he drove the headmaster, Father Spina, to weeping despair with his hypersensitive nature and his regular breakdowns of screaming tantrums. The good priest undoubtedly sighed with relief when Francisco was taken away to finish his education in the United States and France. Once free from the watchful eye of his stern father, Francisco renounced his Catholic religion and fell in with spiritualists, vegetarians, and teetotalers. During a séance his Ouija board spelled out that he was to be the next president of Mexico. That startling message regenerated the pint-sized, shrill-voiced, beady-eyed millionaire and he threw himself into politics pell-mell.

1908

He first attracted national attention by publishing a book in this year called *La Sucesión Presidencial en 1910*. It was a bland rehash of politics that came to the not-very-original conclusion that Díaz should be, after all, re-elected but that someone else beside Corral should be elected vice-president. Mild as this sounds today, it caused a sensation in 1908, for it expressed boldly what most men hesitated to say even in private. The rich Maderos, who had always regarded Francisco as a loose end of the family, sent frantic messages advising him to get out of politics at once, but when they saw what success his book was having, they humored him and even offered him help. Mercedes and Angela, his two sisters, took up posts in Mexico City at his *Anti-reeleccionista* headquarters, and brother Gustavo took over the party's finances. Díaz watched these developments with amusement.

1909

By November it was perfectly clear that the Creelman article was not to be taken seriously. Bernardo Reyes, the most formidable threat to Díaz, was sent to Europe on a diplomatic mission, it was said. But the policy of Díaz, as everyone knew, was to get rid of troublesome opponents (too popular to be eliminated by the *bravi*) by sending them abroad as diplomats. Fellow party members of Reyes, *Los Democratistas*, then threw their support behind Madero, making the latter the symbol of Díaz opposition.

In December, Madero began campaigning seriously, touring towns in the northern states where he spoke in the open air to large crowds of peasants. The deafening roars of "Viva Madero!" that nearly drowned his speech were so full of fiery passion that they frightened his party members who realized they were tampering with the emotions of the masses, something more dangerous than dynamite. Díaz was also frightened, but for a different reason: Madero was gaining strength.

1910

Early in this year Madero was granted an interview with Díaz at the National Palace. Madero opened the historic discussion by proposing that Díaz make him vice-president in the next election. Díaz replied gravely that such a thing was impossible, whereupon Madero vowed to use every means at his disposal to defeat him at the polls; and he warned Díaz to respect the law and to count the votes honestly. Díaz commended his civic spirit and on this friendly note the interview ended. Later, however, Díaz remarked to friends that Madero would make a better candidate for an insane asylum.

After that, Madero resumed campaigning with renewed vigor and his appearance took on the pinched expression of a man obsessed with a mission. His plump, complacent wife traveled with him, sitting sedately on the speaker's platform while he ranted and raved about the injustices of the Díaz government. So popular were his speeches that in Alamos, Sonora, club-swinging police, by orders of Vice-President Corral, waded into the crowds and broke up his rally.

On April 15, the *Anti-reeleccionistas* officially announced Francisco Madero their candidate for president and made Dr. Vásquez Gómez his running mate for vice-president.

Dr. Vásquez Gómez had been for years the family physician and personal friend of Don Porfirio but had, in those months before elections, argued bitterly with the dictator over the deplorable state of the nation's agriculture. This is indeed the most serious objection that can be made against

the entire thirty-five year dictatorship of Díaz: that he did
next to nothing to help the farmer or to forestall soil erosion,
Mexico's relentless enemy. Since the doctor's arguments fell
on deaf ears, he, in a fit of anger, broke all ties with Díaz and
gave his wholehearted support to the *Anti-reeleccionistas*.
After being nominated vice-president, Vásquez Gómez returned to Chapultepec Castle on June 24 to attempt to clarify
for his old friend, Don Porfirio, some of the problems gnawing at the country. Gómez, outspoken as usual, called Limantour a crook whose nefarious dealings in finance were causing
widespread poverty in Mexico that shocked the sensibilities
of any normal man. And to have such a man as Corral as
vice-president was a disgrace to the nation. The first step toward cleaning up the government, said Gómez, was to get
rid of Corral. But, wailed the dictator, Corral was Limantour's choice. If Corral went Limantour would go too,
". . . and what," he asked, "am I going to do without Limantour?"

Vásquez Gómez summed up the situation succinctly. "General, your dilemma is this: either you sacrifice Limantour
and prevent a revolution or you keep Limantour and let the
country go up in flames."

Obviously the old man was but the figurehead of a dictatorship that was actually controlled by the ambitious and brilliant Limantour. Moreover, Díaz at eighty was crotchety and
intolerant of advice. He gruffly announced he would run for a
seventh term and that Corral would again be his vice-
president. A month before elections he had Madero jailed in
San Luis Potosí on a charge of inciting people to riot. In July
he published the election results: Madero (who was still in
jail) 196 votes, Díaz several million. September 16, the annual commemoration of the "Cry of Dolores," was in 1910 the
biggest, gayest jubilee Mexico had ever known. Three mo-
mentous events were being celebrated at once: first, the cen-
tenary of Hidalgo's "Cry"; second, the president's eightieth
birthday; and third, the president's "victory" at the polls for
the seventh time. Streets were festooned with bright-colored
banners, military bands played in the parks or marched on
parade, and at night palatial homes were ablaze with candled
chandeliers beneath which whirled fashionable couples to the

waltzes of stringed orchestras. At Chapultepec Castle twenty carloads of champagne were consumed by ambassadors and envoys from every nation in the world who toasted the dictator as "the hero of modern Mexico!" This happy occasion has been aptly compared to the last glorious bloom of a flowering tree whose roots have been cut.

Through the intercession of Bishop Montes de Oca, Madero was released from prison on October 7. He went to Texas where he denounced the presidential election as an outrageous fraud and published his plan—*Plan de San Luis Potosí*—which called for a revolt on November 20. On that day Madero supporters all over the country were asked to rise up against local authorities while Madero, at the head of a large army then forming in the north, would march on the capital. The day, however, was a fiasco. Madero crossed the border into Mexico, lost his way in the hills, and after creeping stealthily through miles of woods, found twenty men, only half of them armed, who knew nothing about a large army. Crestfallen, Madero returned to the States and seriously considered giving up politics altogether.

At the same time, government troops at Pedernales, in the state of Chihuahua, had been attacked and soundly defeated by a group of armed peasants commanded by a village storekeeper named Pasqual Orozco and a free-wheeling cattle thief named Doroteo Arango, better known as Pancho Villa. Villa organized a rip-roaring cavalry of cowboys with broadbrimmed sombreros, who continued raiding government garrisons throughout the state as far north as the American border. News of their successes revived the spirits of Madero, who rushed to join them and to take his place at the head of their movement.

By then the wind of revolution blew over smoldering coals and hotter ones burst into flames. Emiliano Zapata, in Cuautla, outraged since birth by the unjust code of landownership, taught his army of Indians and lowly Mestizos to take what land they wanted and to shoot the first person to stop them. Guerrilla bands were active in six states, terrorizing their local caciques, most of whom had been appointed by Díaz and, like Díaz, had been in office for thirty years or more.

1911

Before the July elections Díaz sent Limantour on a diplomatic mission to France, probably to get rid of him (while elections were on) but also to negotiate for a loan. But with revolutions exploding all around him, he cabled Limantour to drop whatever he was doing and race for home. Limantour arrived in New York on March 11 and conferred with Gustavo Madero and Dr. Vásquez Gómez, who were there collecting funds for the revolution. Dr. Gómez blamed Limantour outright for starting the revolution by forcing the despised Corral on Díaz. Limantour, according to the doctor, sank back in his chair, holding his head and murmuring, "Yes, that was my sin!"

He arrived in Mexico City on March 19 and, like a whirlwind, sailed through the National Palace barking out orders and sending congressmen into a flurry of activity. He threw Corral out of office, dismissed the cabinet and formed a new one without *científicos*, and he cabled Bernardo Reyes in Europe to return immediately. In April he was ready to make peace with Madero.

But by this time Madero, with the army of Orozco and Villa, was laying siege to Ciudad Juárez (on the American frontier), held by federal troops under the command of Colonel Navarro. Well aware that he was greatly outnumbered, Navarro called for a truce of indefinite period during which many mediating talks were held between himself and Madero. Villa's soldiers, bored with the proceedings, went swimming in the Rio Grande and while splashing around were sniped at by trigger-happy sentinels of Navarro. The enraged bathers scurried for their guns to return the fire, and the long-postponed battle was on. Villa led a cavalry charge down the main street of the city, and his infantry, following close behind, overwhelmed the defenders. Navarro was caught and would most certainly have been shot if Madero hadn't interceded. Madero assisted him to escape at night to the American side of the river.

This victory swelled the heads of the insurgents and filled

them with confidence that they could topple the dictator. They rejected Limantour's offer for peace and wrote their own terms, which were signed at 10:30 P.M. on May 21 by the light of candles and car headlights because no one had a key to the customs house nearby. They demanded the immediate resignation of both Porfirio Díaz and José Limantour.

When these terms were read to Díaz on May 23, the old man was in a near coma of agony with an abscessed tooth and could concentrate on nothing but this throbbing, excruciating pain.

On May 24 a large crowd of Madero supporters demonstrated outside the National Palace, shouting for Díaz to resign. Soldiers on the ramparts (some were in the cathedral tower) panicked, thinking a new revolution was starting, and stupidly fired on the crowd. More senseless bloodshed. By midnight the plaza was empty except for two hundred corpses.

At four o'clock that morning Díaz, feeling a bit better, sat down at his desk and penned a long, self-adulatory resignation. Friends, waiting anxiously in the antechamber for this announcement, sighed with relief and informed the crowds outside the presidential house of this news. A cheer went up and people swarmed through the streets shouting "Victory!" The bells in the cathedral were rung continuously till daylight.

On May 26, Díaz and Carmelita boarded a special train in the St. Nazaire station where a handful of faithful friends tearfully bade them farewell. A boat was waiting at Veracruz to take them to France. A week later Limantour followed them into exile.

Porfirio Díaz died July 2, 1915, in Paris while Mexico was being torn apart by Villa, Obregón, Zapata, and Carranza. On his deathbed when told of these events, he shook his head sadly and said, "You see? I know my Mexico!"

CHAPTER ELEVEN

1911–1928

1911

No man in Mexican history ever enjoyed such tremendous popularity as did Don Francisco I. Madero when he entered Mexico City on June 7, 1911. Surrounding him were dense crowds of wildy cheering *campesinos* (country people) carrying banners that hailed him as the "Apostle of Freedom." Celebrations in the capital went on continuously for three days and nights. But at each banquet it was noted that some member of the Madero family was always hovering over him and that he would answer all questions concerning the future with, "I'll ask my papa about that," or, "I'll see what my brother Gustavo has to say." Clearly, his family were keeping him under their sway.

True to his Plan of San Luis Potosí, calling for honest elections, his first act was to ask each political party to select its candidate for a general presidential election to be held in October. His own party dropped Dr. Vásquez Gómez, whose speeches had become too scathingly critical of the Madero family, particularly of Gustavo, and they elected Pino Suárez, a clever but obscure journalist from Yucatán, to be their vice-presidential candidate.

Before elections, Madero visited Zapata in the sugar-cane country near Cuernavaca to convince him that further hostility was unnecessary. Zapata agreed to lay down arms if Madero would immediately rewrite the laws of landownership. The two men made a pact to this effect, and Madero, to prove his sincerity, called off federal troops that had been hunting down, unsuccessfully, Zapata's army.

In October, Madero was elected president in what was perhaps the most honest election ever held in Mexico. He immediately gave freedom to the press, encouraged labor unions to organize, and opened, in Mexico City, the Casa del Obrero Mundial (House of the World Worker). But he was slow to tackle the land problem and so Zapata resumed his revolution and published his *Plan de Ayala* (written by a country schoolteacher, Otilio Montano), calling for the restoration of lands stolen from the Indians by the government of Porfirio Díaz. That was the first note of discord to be heard in Mexico under the new government of Madero.

The second was sounded by Bernardo Reyes, who, it will be remembered, was brought back from Paris by José Limantour during the collapse of the Díaz regime. Reyes at first enthusiastically supported the Madero revolution, but he argued constantly with Gustavo Madero and at length slipped off to the north where he hoped to collect an army. But by then his name had lost its magic and former friends avoided him. He was arrested for inciting a revolution by government troops in December and was taken to the Santiago Tlaltelolco prison in Mexico City.

1912

In February the most serious uprising occurred. The rich cattle barons of the north, the Terrazas family, furious over Madero's reform bills limiting land holdings to 5000 hectares (roughly 20 square miles) bribed the ex-storekeeper Pasqual Orozco (whose army had played an important part in overthrowing Díaz) into raising a new revolt against Madero. The first federal army sent to smash Orozco was defeated and its commander committed suicide. The man most qualified to fill the vacancy was General Victoriano Huerta, but Madero (a teetotaler) disapproved of Huerta's heavy drinking and would not appoint him. When friends of Huerta informed Madero that General Grant, Lincoln's commander, also drank, the president grudgingly accepted Huerta with all his sins and sent him off after Orozco. With savage fury Huerta flew at the rebel army and drove it over the border into Arizona, and then returned expecting to be hailed as the savior of Mexico. Instead he was asked to give a full account of the million pesos the government had allowed him for the campaign. He refused to do so, grumbling that a soldier's honor and honesty should never be questioned by his government. At that, Madero demoted him.

In October, Felix Díaz, nephew of Porfirio, started a revolution in Veracruz, but he was captured within ten days and would have been shot if Madero had not interceded and had him brought to Mexico City to be confined in the penitentiary. Both Felix Díaz and the other political prisoner, Bernardo Reyes, were treated like hotel guests—their cells were large and well furnished, their meals ran to several courses, and they daily received dozens of friends. It was not long before the prisons became a breeding place for revolutions.

José Vasconcelos, Mexico's talented writer and a loyal supporter of Madero, wrote that the principal mistake of Madero had been in not purging the government of grafting politicians left over from the *Porfirista* era. Madero's tolerance of these thieving bureaucrats came naturally from his childlike belief that all people were good—a commendable belief, certainly, but one which no politician, for his own good, can afford to keep too long. Madero was convinced that his positive attitude would infect everybody and that all would work together like one big happy family. Notwithstanding this possible flaw in his character, Madero was a good man whose efforts to turn Mexico into a democracy were absolutely sincere.

His land and labor reforms, however, did not at all suit the big oil companies—Standard Oil, Shell Oil, and Aguila (the English company)—all of whom had made millions during the Díaz dictatorship. For the first time, they banded together to meet their common enemy: the tiny, intense Madero. The English-language newspaper in Mexico City, the old *Mexican Herald*, denounced Madero in editorials which were read with pleasure by Americans living in Mexico City. The United States ambassador in Mexico, Henry Lane Wilson, was a vigorous practitioner of America's new foreign policy which President William Howard Taft called the "dollar diplomacy." As early as January 1912, Wilson informed Washington that Mexico was "seething with discontent." That was a gross exaggeration. There were rumblings of discontent which would have undoubtedly subsided in time, but that discontent was nothing compared to the destructive revolution precipitated by the unauthorized acts of Henry Lane Wilson. For many years he had been the fawning friend of the Guggenheims, owners of rich mines and oil fields in Mexico. He, like most Americans in Mexico, stood with his back to the future and gazed at the past, proclaiming that Mexico's only hope was to regress to a Díaz kind of dictatorship. Though Madero brought back justice to Mexican tribunals, and allowed thirteen million pesos of the national budget for education (Díaz had never given more than eight), the oil companies and Henry Lane Wilson decided that he must go.

In February a hundred thousand American troops were massed along the Texas border as a result of Wilson's fantastic reports to Washington. The embassy was receiving shipments of arms and munitions in preparation for a siege, and embassy workers were telling Americans to leave Mexico before the revolution started. But Mexico, in fact, was then at peace, although the warlike attitude of the embassy was certainly causing panic and alarm that spread like a contagion throughout the city. By the end of 1912 it was common knowledge that Miguel Mondragón, a grafting general of Porfirio Díaz whom Madero had made commander of the garrison at Tacubaya, was conspiring with Bernardo Reyes in the penitentiary to overthrow the government. It was brought to Madero's attention that Henry Lane Wilson was implicated in the plot, but the little man did nothing. Woodrow Wilson had just been elected president of the United States and he would certainly recall the meddling ambassador before a revolution started.

1913

Throughout January everyone in the capital trembled in anticipation of war—everyone, that is, except Don Francisco, who went about smiling and nodding, blithely oblivious of the trouble brewing.

On Sunday, February 9, the shooting started and lasted

ten days. This period was called *La Decena Trágica* (The Ten Tragic Days). Mondragón's troops at Tacubaya were joined by the military cadets of Tlalpan and marched first on the prison of Santiago Tlaltelolco, to release Bernardo Reyes, then on to the penitentiary to release Felix Díaz. Bernardo Reyes, by arrangement, took command of the troops and led an assault on the National Palace, which, he was told, would capitulate without firing a shot. All this happened before eight in the morning.

But at daybreak Gustavo Madero had been awakened by a gardener of Chapultepec Castle who in the dark hours before dawn had heard the tramping of marching feet passing through Tacubaya. Gustavo, sensing what was up, quickly dressed and raced to the National Palace to alert the palace guards. General Villar, a staunch supporter of Don Francisco, took command of the situation and deployed guards along the roof. When finally Bernardo Reyes appeared in the plaza at the head of his army, Villar, well prepared for a fight, shouted for him to surrender. Reyes appeared not to have heard, but continued his advance on the palace. Villar then gave orders to fire, and the whole front wall of the palace exploded with cannon fire and rattling machine guns. Bernardo Reyes fell dead on the spot. Felix Díaz, taking command, returned a volley of rifle fire and then led a retreat through the streets of Mexico to the *ciudadela*, a military arsenal and garrison a mile or so away.

When Francisco Madero arrived at nine o'clock, the main square was the scene of appalling tragedy. The dead numbered five hundred, many of whom had been hapless churchgoers on their way to Sunday mass. General Villar himself had been gravely wounded, and the only man to take his place was—again—Victoriano Huerta. Excited by the explosions of battle, Huerta, in full public view, embraced Madero and swore by the Virgin of Guadalupe (whose medal he always wore) to defend the government with his life. At that, Huerta was made commander general of the army. A better choice would have been General Felipe Angeles, who was then in Cuernavaca fighting Zapata. Madero ordered him to return to the capital at once.

1913

Felix Díaz, defending the *ciudadela*, should have been crushed easily within a matter of days, but Victoriano Huerta, personally directing the assault troops, fought halfheartedly and even negotiated with his enemy. It could be said that Huerta's character was as black as Madero's was white. Huerta challenged Díaz to an artillery duel, and soon shells were screaming over the city, falling into crowded streets, on office buildings and into shops, killing untold hundreds of people while only two shots hit the National Palace and one, the *ciudadela*. Putrefying corpses were so numerous they were heaped on funeral pyres in the *zócalo* (main square), drenched in gasoline, and set afire. Conflicting rumors spread that the real enemy of the government was not Felix Díaz, as was supposed, but Victoriano Huerta himself. And indeed Huerta and Díaz during the *Decena Trágica* had reached an agreement which was drawn up and signed on February 17 at midnight *in the office of the American Ambassador Henry Lane Wilson!* This was called the *Plan de la Ciudadela* (sometimes derisively called the "Plan of the Embassy") which demanded the immediate resignation of Francisco Madero and the installation of Huerta as interim president, and Felix Díaz as his cabinet minister.

Henry Lane Wilson's behavior in this business is truly to be deplored. Even the great exponent of the "dollar diplomacy," President Taft, thought Wilson had gone too far and wired him to stay out of Mexican affairs. But Wilson was one of those incorrigible, self-righteous meddlers who simply could not leave well enough alone. When Felipe Angeles set up his artillery battery near the American embassy, Wilson complained to Huerta that the noise and sulphureous smoke would disturb his embassy staff. And so Angeles, at Wilson's request, was removed along with his guns.

1913

On February 18, Colonel Riveroll and a handful of soldiers pushed their way through to the Sala de Los Consejos de Ministros (Chamber of Ministers) and seized the president. While struggling to drag him off, a palace guard, trying to rescue the president, shot Riveroll dead. The soldiers panicked and fired wildly into the group of startled ministers and deputies, killing one outright. After wrenching himself free, Madero, Pino Suárez, and Felipe Angeles headed for the grand staircase intending to escape, but they were met by General Blanquet, who, brandishing a pistol, forced them back to the guard's quarters and there locked them into a small room. While this was taking place, Huerta was having drinks and lunch with Gustavo Madero in a downtown restaurant. By arrangement thugs burst into the restaurant—while Huerta "happened" to be away answering a phone call—and carried Gustavo off to the *ciudadela* where the soldiers of Felix Díaz tortured him to death.

When Huerta heard that Francisco Madero had been placed under guard, he ordered the bells of the cathedral to be rung, then drove to the National Palace in his long limousine. From the central balcony he made a speech to the few people gathered there, announcing that Madero had been deposed for the convenience of the government, and that prices, from that day forward, would go steadily down. Those who heard his speech testified that he was reeling drunk. That evening Felix Díaz, at the head of his motley army, marched out of the *ciudadela* and through the streets to the National Palace, applauded by old-guard *Porfiristas* who hoped to see the country put under a dictatorship again.

Later that night congress was convened for an extraordinary session (reluctant congressmen were forced at bayonet point to attend), at which Huerta held up to them the resignation of Don Francisco I. Madero, president of Mexico, and asked them to vote, by a show of hands, on its acceptance. (Madero had written it in the belief that, by doing so, he and his family would be given safe conduct out of the country. He didn't know his brother Gustavo had already been murdered.) Considering that menacing guards armed with swords and pistols counted the hands, it is remarkable that even six men had the temerity to vote "no" both to Madero's resignation and to Huerta's move to be made president.

On the following day President Huerta asked Henry Lane Wilson what he should do with Madero—banish him or put him in a lunatic asylum. Wilson, wishing to wash his hands of the whole sordid affair, replied that he "ought to do that which was best for the peace of the country." This pompous remark could mean but one thing to the villainous Huerta. On February 22, at eleven o'clock at night, while Madero and Pino Suárez were being transferred from one prison to another, a policeman named Cárdenaz carried out his orders to kill them. Huerta announced that a gang of fanatics had attacked the escort of the deposed president in an attempt to abduct him, and in the scuffle Madero was accidently shot. Wilson urged Washington and other embassies to accept this tale as the official story, but it was such a blatant lie that Wilson by using it added still more discredit to his name. Even Secretary of State Philander Knox detected the stench of crime behind the story and wired to Wilson: "Huerta's consulting you as to the treatment of Madero tends to give you a certain responsibility in matter." Because Wilson allowed his personal interests to override ethics, Mexico lost an idealist, a humanitarian, and a potentially great president. Of Madero, Vasconcelos wrote: "He was one of the few Mexicans on whom the Mexican race can base its pride."

1913

Huerta, as president, was so addicted to alcohol that he usually conducted the nation's affairs from a table in a saloon. His senators often toured the city in limousines looking for the particular *cantina* (saloon) he had chosen to honor with his patronage. It was not long before ministers and deputies were resigning; and as they left, their places were taken by bovine thugs from Huerta's army. One of the more astute members of congress, Dr. Belisario Dominguez, who preferred to fight Huerta rather than resign, delivered from the senate floor one of the most vitriolic diatribes ever heard against Huerta, and then sadly predicted his own assassination. He was right. Two weeks later the corpse of Dr. Dominguez was found in a ditch in Coyoacán. Horrified members of the senate walked out in protest and Huerta had a hundred and ten of them jailed for insubordination. More soldiers were rushed in to take their places. As Lesley Byrd Simpson states: "Popular revulsion against the shame of Victoriano Huerta was the real beginning of the [Mexican] revolution."

Three states in the north announced their opposition to Huerta's government: Sonora, dominated by an ex-factory hand named Alvaro Obregón; Chihuahua, under the military dictatorship of Pancho Villa; and Coahuila, governed by the dignified and distinguished-looking Venustiano Carranza. Carranza's rimless glasses and long flowing beard gave him the look of a humble scholar; but these looks were deceiving. He was a rugged horseman, an excellent shot, and could be, on occasion, stubborn as a mule. His *Plan de Guadalupe* united the opposition against Huerta by demanding that Huerta resign immediately. But as to who or what should replace him, it said not a word, though it made Carranza the "First Chief of the Constitutionalist Army," a grand title sufficiently vague to be meaningless, yet meaningful enough to be anything. Carranza's army, commanded by a loyal but not too bright general named Pablo González, was smashed by federal troops and the "First Chief" was pursued into the hills. But he escaped capture, crossed the mountains of Durango and Sinaloa, and emerged at Nogales, on the American frontier, where he set up his revolutionary government. He then sent out agents to exhort Obregón and Villa to join him.

Pancho Villa at that time was fighting his own private war of revenge against Huerta and wanted no interference from outsiders, particularly from Carranza, whom he instinctively disliked. Two years before, Villa had fought at the side of Huerta in putting down the second Orozco rebellion, and, indeed, his gun-blazing cavalry charges had accounted for most of Huerta's victories. But the coolly courageous, boisterous Villa had always irritated Huerta (who was hypersensitive about his short size anyway) and Villa gave him a hateful feeling of inferiority, as though he, Huerta, were losing his command. In an effort to assert his authority he arrested Villa and tried him for insubordination. Found guilty, he was sentenced to be shot. Villa was before the wall facing a row of rifles when a telegram from Madero arrived granting a stay of execution. By orders of Madero, Villa was to be sent to Mexico City where he would be retried. For that lifesaving intervention of Madero, Villa proclaimed him his dearest friend, and for a friend Pancho Villa would walk through fire. At the penitentiary in Mexico City, Villa bribed a guard and effected his escape and two weeks later boarded a boat in Veracruz bound for the States. When, in Texas, he heard of Madero's murder, he swore to avenge that crime even at the cost of his life. On March 13, 1913, he, with eight companions, rode and swam horses across the turgid waters of the Rio Grande and headed south on a wild conquest of Mexico. He had already reached Chihuahua when Carranza published his Plan of Guadalupe.

Agents of Carranza prevailed upon him to give up his personal hatred of Huerta and join the big revolutionary movement which was fighting to establish a society free of plutocracy, praetorianism, and clericalism. Perhaps Villa did not understand these words, but he liked the gist of their meaning and joined up, though he still found Carranza unbearable.

In March, Woodrow Wilson took office. When the State Department briefed him on recent events in Mexico, his strict, Scottish sense of propriety was shocked by their accounts of Huerta. Surely, the United States wasn't backing a drunkard? Immediately he recalled Henry Lane Wilson and sent down Mr. John Lind from Minnesota with instructions to sound out different rebel leaders as a potential benefactor of American aid. Unfortunately, Lind was a blond northerner with no sympathy for Latins, with little knowledge of Mexico, and with no understanding of Spanish. Wilson sent him not as an ambassador, but as an emissary on a "mission of peace," though his documents were addressed "To Whom It May Concern" and he arrived on a battleship. Lind confirmed Wilson's poor opinion of Huerta and after a few interviews found Carranza less repugnant than either Villa or Obregón. At once an arms embargo was slapped on Huerta, while Carranza continued to receive munitions which were paid for by driving herds of cattle (supplied by the Terrazas family) over the border into Texas. But Wilson was impatient with Carranza's progress and wished to hasten Huerta's fall. He therefore ordered a fleet of American warships to patrol Mexican waters and to seize any foreign boat shipping arms to the Mexican federal government. Thus, by preparing for trouble, he got trouble.

1914

On April 10, nine uniformed American sailors scrambled up the docks at Tampico and unwittingly entered a prohibited zone which was under bombardment by Carranza forces laying siege to the city. A Mexican colonel arrested the sailors and took them to General Zaragoza, commander of federal forces defending the city. On learning the sailors were Americans, Zaragoza released them immediately with profuse apologies, and even escorted them to their boat. The whole incident lasted not more than thirty minutes.

But Admiral Mayo, commander of the American fleet, felt the American flag had been insulted and demanded from Zaragoza a twenty-one gun salute as an apology. President Wilson stoutly supported Mayo in his demand. Huerta, showing more spunk than was expected, refused to humble himself so basely and would not allow Zaragoza to give such a salute without first putting the matter before the Hague Tribunal. Wilson, hell-bent on ruining Huerta, rejected this offer for mediation and became louder in his demand for the salute.

Then, on April 21, at two o'clock in the morning, Wilson was awakened and handed a telegram stating that a German vessel, the *Ypiranga*, carrying seventeen million rounds of ammunition to Huerta's army, was due to dock at Veracruz in the morning. Wilson gave orders for marines to occupy Veracruz at once and then returned to bed to regain his deep, untroubled sleep.

The *Ypiranga*, somehow, intercepted his orders and steered

off to Tampico where it safely unloaded all the ammunition to Huerta's forces. In the meantime, squadrons of American marines swarmed over the docks at Veracruz and took up firing positions. Huerta's federal army, frightened at the sight of so many marines, did an about-face and marched off into the jungles. But infuriated citizens formed a partisan army, which cadets from the naval academy joined. Using revolvers, old muskets, and a 25-mm. cannon, they fought ferociously in defense of their city and when the battle ended at sundown, 19 Americans were dead and 70 were wounded. The Mexican losses: 193 dead and an estimated 600 wounded. Damage done to Veracruz by bombardment: not officially stated but it was undoubtedly considerable.

The Veracruz massacre (which is how the Mexicans refer to this invasion) is a perfect example of how armed intervention gives exactly the opposite effect to that desired. Huerta suddenly became a national hero and his popularity soared almost higher than that of Carranza, who, as everyone knew, was receiving aid from Wilson. Carranza, therefore, at the risk of jeopardizing his good standing in Washington, joined Huerta in denouncing the American invasion as a violation of the Treaty of Guadalupe Hidalgo (which it was). Mobs assaulted American business houses in the capital, and Huerta, when coherent, vowed to invade Texas.

For Wilson the battle of Veracruz had been a terrible disillusionment. He truly believed that Mexico was waiting for American intervention and would welcome American marines with gratitude. (Lind was responsible for that absurd notion.) To heal the wound to Mexican-American relations, Wilson agreed to submit the whole affair to a mediation board of three nations—Argentina, Brazil, and Chile—who, observing strict impartiality, convened on the Canadian side of Niagara Falls. Representatives of Huerta's government (Carranza also sent representatives, but only as observers) and those of the United States haggled for many long and dreary sessions over international law without reaching any resolution. The time they used for arbitration, however, afforded Wilson an opportunity to withdraw his marines gracefully from Veracruz and his huge fleet of nearly eighty American warships from Mexican waters.

During this period Pancho Villa and Alvaro Obregón were rapidly converging on Mexico City. Obregón swept down the Pacific coast, and Villa, with troops clustered on the tops of trains (his *Dorados*) boisterously singing the song of the revolution, "*La Cucaracha*," steamed down the center plateau. Huerta, powerless to stop them, ransacked the treasury and on July 15 fled to Europe where he could peacefully drink himself to ruin. Carranza, fearful that Villa would reach the capital first (the two men mutually detested each other), held up a shipment of coal destined for Villa's trains temporarily stranded in Zacatecas. When Alvaro Obregón entered the capital in triumph on August 15, Carranza released Villa's coal, but by then Villa was so incensed by Carranza's spiteful treachery that he split from the main revolutionary movement and went to Chihuahua where he declared open war on Carranza. The "First Chief of the Constitutionalist Army" entered the capital five days after Obregón and took over the role of president.

After that, anarchy spread like a rampaging prairie fire. Thousands died when brigands posing as revolutionaries murdered, plundered, and raped without fear of reprisals, except from families who were banding together to protect themselves and their possessions. Nearly every Mexican who lived through that period can tell a hair-raising tale or two about his personal experiences during those years.

Venustiano Carranza, it could be argued, actually brought on anarchy by nullifying the constitution of 1857 and declaring Mexico to be in a "Preconstitutional State"—another vague term implying that a new constitution would be written somehow at some future date. Until then, however, Carranza's word was law, and that changed erratically.

Honest citizens could no longer abide the situation and beseeched revolutionary leaders to resolve their differences with cogent arguments instead of guns. Villa, Obregón, and Zapata agreed and a convention was held on October 10, 1914, at Aguascalientes. Carranza, in one of his stubborn moods, refused to attend, denouncing the convention as a political maneuver of Villa aimed at driving him, Carranza, out of power.

At the convention it was agreed that the chief cause of the

nation's disorder was the Villa-Carranza rivalry, which would exist so long as one or the other was president. The delegates, therefore, tactfully eliminated both Villa and Carranza from being presidential candidates by passing a motion that no general could be president. Villa went further still by proposing that both he and Carranza commit suicide! By refusing to be a party to such a pact, Carranza was blamed by Villa for being the sole reason for Mexico's disorder. The convention elected Eulalio Gutiérrez, a man of integrity and ability, to be interim president of the republic until general elections could be held. The convention ended November 18.

Carranza packed his bag and sped to Veracruz where he was soon joined by Alvaro Obregón, who had reached the conclusion that Carranza was, after all, a better bet than Pancho Villa. Something at Aguascalientes had turned Obregón against Villa, and the consequence of the rift would be horrific.

1915

Pancho Villa was then "cock of the walk." He put Gutiérrez in the president's chair and surrounded him with two thousand honor guards to ensure that he stayed there. Strait-laced American businessmen and Secretary of State William J. Bryan began to respect Villa for not smoking or drinking, two vices which Villa always considered more revolting than killing or raping. Moreover, on his staff Villa had General Felipe Angeles, the best artilleryman in Mexico. Indeed, it was the genius of Angeles that made Villa invincible.

Recently, Angeles has been made out to be the most noble figure of the Mexican revolution, and well he might have been. Tall and quiet, he was described in *Tempest over Mexico*, by Rosa King, who knew him, as having "delicate features, and the kindest eyes I think I have seen on any man. He called himself an Indian, laughingly, but he was decidedly the type the Mexicans call *indio triste* (sad Indian)." A top student at his military academy, Angeles won a scholarship to study artillery tactics in Europe. In time he became an artillery expert and even invented a new kind of cannon.

Returning from Europe, he supported Madero against Díaz and was given the post of director of the Colegio Militar. He fought briefly against Zapata in Cuernavaca before Madero recalled him during the *Decena Trágica* to put down Felix Díaz. Huerta in his *coup d'état* arrested him but instead of shooting him sent him abroad to France on a "diplomatic mission." When Huerta fell, Angeles returned to Mexico and offered his services to Carranza, then forming his government in Nogales. But Carranza felt uneasy with the elegant and aristocratic Angeles and used him sparingly and then for menial tasks—filing, typing, and running errands. When Villa split with Carranza, Angeles joined the former and proved immediately how valuable a first-class artilleryman could be. With Angeles, Villa never lost a battle.

Villa knew Zapata only by reputation until December 4, 1914, when Zapata, at Villa's request, came to Mexico City with his Indian army. Slender, saturnine, lithe as a cat, somber as death, neatly dressed in a trim, silver-embroidered *charro* costume, Zapata was Villa's opposite in every way; but the two men saw and respected in each other great physical courage, which was the basis of their fast friendship and camaraderie. Zapata's Indian army, reputed to be cruel and barbarous, astonished the capital's populace with their gentle, mannerly deportment. Humbly they begged their food at the doors of the rich, while Villa's army of the north, the *Dorados*, disgraced themselves with drunken orgies and riotous shootings.

1915

All this while Carranza had maintained in Washington energetic lobbyists who finally convinced a few members of the State Department that by aiding Villa they were backing a losing horse. Secretary of State Bryan was in time persuaded to switch sides and assist Carranza, and after that the fortunes of Villa went into a decline. On January 29, Obregón chased him out of the capital and on April 6 challenged him to a showdown battle at Celaya.

Obregón then had 22,000 men and had dug trenches and

laid barbed wire in preparation for the big battle. Villa had
15,000 men but was missing his most indispensable officer,
Angeles, who was up on the border. Angeles, informed in de-
tail about the impending battle, wired Villa to stay away from
Obregón at all costs. But Villa's volatile temper, goaded by
Obregón's very calculated taunts, exploded, and, angry as a
bull, he led a foolhardy cavalry charge on Obregón's defenses.
What followed was the most terrible battle ever fought on
Mexican soil. It lasted three days and claimed 12,000 lives!
At one point, flying shrapnel tore off the right arm of Obregón, and he, wild with pain, yanked a pistol from his belt,
held the muzzle to his temple, and pulled the trigger. Luckily for him the gun wasn't loaded. By April 15, Villa was running away northward on trains, pulling up rails behind him as
he went. At Agua Prieta he was defeated again, this time by
an up-and-coming general named Plutarco Calles. The once
invincible army of Villa dwindled rapidly, and he, with a few
faithful followers, crept into the hills surrounding Chihuahua (he knew every nook and cranny of those hills) where he
could elude his pursuers indefinitely. Zapata also suffered a
series of setbacks and withdrew into his lair in the jungles.

1916

Villa blamed President Woodrow Wilson for his defeat,
claiming that Wilson, by backing Carranza, had double-
crossed him. To get even, Villa vowed to terrorize every
American in Mexico and those in border towns as well. In
January he held up a train standing beside the station at
Santa Isabel and had eighteen of its passengers shot—all
American mining engineers. In March he made a night raid
on Columbus, New Mexico, burning the army barracks, robbing stores, and killing eighteen townspeople. He and his
men escaped by dragging branches of trees behind their
horses which raised clouds of dust that screened their galloping retreat.

With the presidential election approaching, Wilson could
not afford to let this incident pass without reprisals. He therefore sent General "Black Jack" Pershing on a "punitive expe-

dition" to capture Villa. Again armed intervention boomer anged and hurt Wilson more than it did his antagonist. Wilson was criticized by the Senate and the American press (who were finding Villa more exciting than the New York Yankees) for meddling in Mexican affairs. On the other hand, Pershing was criticized for failing to win anything but inconsequential battles. And Carranza lost face for allowing the United States troops to invade Mexico once again. Villa, however, became a Mexican idol, hailed as the first Mexican to raid the United States and claim some restitution, however small, for the two American invasions of Mexico. By February 1917 the ineffectualness of the "punitive expedition" was painfully clear to everyone, and Wilson, having won the election, ordered Pershing to withdraw.

But the "punitive expedition" had toughened up the American army with its long marches over Mexico's rugged terrain and had prepared them for trench warfare in France.

1917

Venustiano Carranza's fame is based, primarily, on the Mexican constitution of 1917, not because he wrote it, nor because he presided over the constituents that wrote it, nor because he enforced it, but because he was in power when it was accepted by the Mexican government. He was chiefly concerned with only one article: that giving dictatorial powers to the president. When that was passed, he turned away from the proceedings and allowed Alvaro Obregón and his friends to do what they liked. Fortunately for Mexico, they liked very idealistic and high-principled things. Meeting in the theater at Querétaro, the hand-picked delegates used the Juárez constitution of 1857 as their guide but added, at the suggestion of General Múgica, two articles which completely changed the character of Mexico's constitution.

One, Article 27, written by Andres Molina Enrique (Mexico's most prolific writer on agrarian problems), states that "property is not a right but a social function." From this it follows that the government has the right to confiscate any land it considers is not serving a "general good for the country." (This was aimed at rich Mexicans who lived luxuriously in Europe while their vast estates in Mexico ran to seed.) The second, Article 123 (after which a street in the heart of Mexico City has been named), guarantees rights for the workingman: an eight-hour day, a minimum wage, a yearly vacation of at least fifteen days, dismissal with compensation; it abolishes child labor and it grants the worker the right to strike.

The oil companies and most big businesses were in an uproar over these two articles, and they were joined by the Church, which also could not tolerate Article 3, outlawing parochial and private schools and making primary education (in secular schools) compulsory. Even Carranza felt these articles were too strong and assured the Church and the oil companies that they would never be enforced so long as he was president. Still, Carranza's name is forever linked with this rather remarkable constitution simply because he was president when it was ratified by congress on February 5, 1917.

Carranza remained president so long as his army eliminated those popular enough to overthrow him. Felipe Angeles, having renounced all political affiliations, had gone to live in a cave in the hills of Chihuahua where he was captured by government troops led by a reward-seeking informant. Refusing legal counsel, he defended himself at his trial for treason which, to accommodate the crowds, was held in a theater in Chihuahua. Found guilty by a pro-Carranza judge, he was executed by a firing squad November 26, 1917. Emiliano Zapata was trapped by a traitor, and his bullet-riddled corpse was borne like a trophy by federal troops who had been hunting him unsuccessfully for so many years.

1918

That Carranza was unpopular was proved in 1918 when workers demonstrated against the worthless script Carranza had issued for money. And in Saltillo, workers, in defiance of Carranza's troops, met to form a union. Luis Morones, sent by Carranza to dominate the proceedings, denounced the president and formed Mexico's first nationwide union, *Confederación Regional de Obrera Mexicana*, better known as simply CROM.

1920

The end of Carranza came early in this presidential-election year when a railroad strike broke out in Sonora, a northern state governed by a big, barrel-chested man who, when not in politics, was a powerfully loud opera singer and who, even in politics, enjoyed singing arias in his rich baritone. His name was Adolfo de la Huerta (no relation to Victoriano Huerta). Carranza sent troops into Sonora to break up strike demonstrations, but de la Huerta declared Carranza's act a violation of states' rights and seceded Sonora from the republic. General Plutarco Calles backed him, and together they published their Plan of Agua Prieta calling for Carranza's immediate resignation. Carranza became frightened and ordered his guards to arrest anyone speaking against the government. Alvaro Obregón, then noisily campaigning in the capital for his own election, was nearly arrested or shot, but escaped to the state of Guerrero disguised as a mechanic and there joined the army of Calles, who was marching against Carranza. Ministers, deputies, congressmen, and generals flocked to the side of Calles, leaving Carranza practically friendless.

In May he quit. He literally gutted the treasury by stuffing five million pesos worth of gold and silver bullion into trunks and dragging them aboard a special train bound for Veracruz. His flight was accompanied by a heavily armed escort of guards, but as the miles rolled by they singly or in groups deserted him, till finally there remained only a few soldiers and General Rudolfo Herrera, who, when news arrived that Veracruz was waiting to arrest the president, persuaded Carranza to abandon the train and strike off through the jungles for Tampico. Herrera led him to an Indian village called Talxcalantongo where they spent the night in bamboo huts. That was May 21, 1920. The next morning Carranza's hut was found sprayed with bullets, and Herrera coolly reported that Carranza had committed suicide.

Adolfo de la Huerta reigned as interim president (and a good one) until November when Obregón was elected president by an overwhelming majority.

The ex-factory hand and farm laborer Alvaro Obregón, though an outstanding military leader, was too realistic, too uncompromisingly practical to make a brilliant president. It is said that his family had actually been O'Briens, Irish emigrants who entered Mexico through Texas, but as the name was practically impossible for Mexicans to pronounce, O'Brien became Obregón. The flowery speeches of his utopian-minded politicians, declaiming the noble objectives of the revolution, left him unmoved. Without compunction he trimmed the constitution to suit his purpose. His talk was punctuated with a kind of tough and rather witty jargon which, however, failed to amuse American senators who heard in it overtones of communism. They therefore prevailed upon President Harding to withhold American recognition of Obregón's government. It was during this time, however, that Obregón was, in fact, deporting communists by the dozens, most of whom had illegally entered Mexico from the United States. He was not particularly disturbed by Washington's attitude until 1923 when the presidential elections drew near and he realized the danger of the American State Department's backing some ambitious revolutionary leader against him. So he negotiated with the firm of J. P. Morgan, whose two representatives, Charles B. Warren and John B. Payne, met with Mexico's minister of finance (then Adolfo de la Huerta) at Bucareli 85, a house near Mexico's foreign relations office, where the Treaty of Bucareli was drawn up and signed. This stated, in effect, that Article 27 of the Mexican constitution was not retroactive—lands acquired before 1917 were not touched by it—and that Mexico would not expropriate lands without first paying for them *in cash*. This pleased the oil companies enormously, for they felt certain the Mexican government would never have enough cash on hand to pay for their lands. Washington by approving the treaty, *ipso facto*, gave recognition to Obregón's government, and that was what Obregón wanted.

1924

Obregón's announcement that Calles would be the nex
president of Mexico set off a string of explosions in the state
of Yucatán, Tabasco, Veracruz, and Jalisco, where renegade
army units, to show their contempt for the government, ter
rorized the populace. Adolfo de la Huerta, after some delib
eration, heeded the advice of friends, broke with the govern
ment, and went to Sonora where he announced his intention
of opposing the Obregón-Calles succession. Most rebel bands
rallied behind him and clashed with federal troops in several
skirmishes and in one decisive battle outside Mexico City,
when they nearly stormed the capital. But in losing, the rebels
also lost their most inspired leaders, who were captured and
imprisoned. De la Huerta, hounded by federal agents, was
forced to take refuge in Los Angeles, where he resumed his
music career by giving singing lessons to young ladies. Calles
was sworn into office amidst the rattle of machine-gun fire
while political prisoners were being executed.

As a country schoolteacher, at the start of the revolution,
Plutarco Elías Calles had been strongly attracted to socialism. He organized the citizens of his town into an army and
fought beside Pancho Villa and then Obregón and showed
such amazing aptitude for warfare that he soon rose to the
rank of general. But his greatest talent was revealed in politics. He had an uncanny sixth sense that told him which man
to back and for exactly how long. And so he had been the
"staunch" ally of Villa, Carranza, de la Huerta, and finally
Obregón, abandoning each in turn as they fell from power.
As he himself rose in importance, he lost his taste for socialism and, indeed, ended on the extreme right—a dictator with
strong fascist sympathies.

His hatred of the Catholic Church bordered on the path-
ological. When in February 1926, *El Universal*, Mexico's
morning daily newspaper, published Archbishop Moya y del
Rio's stinging criticism of the Mexican government and its
constitution of 1917, Calles, incensed by the article, vented
his wrath by enforcing with full rigor all the anticlerical laws

of the constitution which his predecessors had, for political reasons, ignored. One law required that only native-born Mexicans could be ministers of a religion in Mexico. Calles ordered a raid on Carmelite and Redemptorist convents from which two hundred Spanish priests were seized and promptly deported.

On June 14 congress ratified his *Ley Calles* (laws of Calles) which gave him still more lethal weapons with which to fight the Church. They said: no priest could teach primary school, no priest could speak a word against the constitution or the government, no priest could appear in public in a distinctive garb (Roman collars were prohibited), and the government could close any church on short notice for failing to conform with the above laws. (These laws are still on the statute books, though they are rarely enforced.) The Church was driven to play its highest trump card: either Calles changed the law or the Catholic Church would abandon Mexico. Calles refused, whereupon all churches in Mexico closed July 31, and nuns and priests left for Guatemala or Texas.

Almost immediately a kind of mass madness swept over the country. In January 1927, Catholic laymen calling themselves *Cristeros* raised a revolution that drove federal troops from rural areas where Catholic priests were still giving the sacraments. Caciques throughout the republic used the *Cristero* rebellion as an excuse to persecute the upper classes. Women were publicly whipped, their daughters were ravaged by soldiers, and rich men were mutilated in horrible ways. Calles in the meantime picked a fight with the oil companies by requiring that they exchange their land titles for fifty-year leases.

1927

Throughout the first half of this year, Mexico and the United States indulged in a lot of childish name-calling over the handling of land titles of oil fields, but the Teapot Dome scandals suddenly shamed Washington into silence (the American ambassador to Mexico himself was implicated in illicit oil deals) and the State Department, to repair its damaged reputation, made one of its more brilliant moves by appointing Dwight Morrow, formerly a partner in the firm of J. P. Morgan, ambassador to Mexico. He was one of the best American ambassadors Mexico had ever seen. Intelligent, with easy manners, a subtle wit, and an abundance of Yankee charm, Morrow fascinated Calles the moment he presented his diplomatic credentials on October 29 at the National Palace. Unlike most of his predecessors, Morrow was genuinely in love with Mexico and everything Mexican. He bought a big house in Cuernavaca, furnished it with Mexican handmade furniture, and his guests were always treated to Mexican music strummed and crooned by strolling *mariachis*. But most important of all, Morrow was not tainted with that professional sin of diplomats—the superiority complex.

Notwithstanding his many good attributes, Morrow got off to a bad start by accepting too hastily an invitation by Calles to make a tour of several states of the republic. A day before this tour began, on November 23, a Catholic priest, a Jesuit named Father Pro, was arrested as a potential assassin of Calles. Father Pro had been traveling through Mexico disguised as a mechanic, giving last rites to the dying, hearing confessions, saying mass in private houses, when agents of Calles finally tracked him down. Without a trial he was executed behind police headquarters which then stood where now stands the National Lottery building. Newsmen with flashing cameras photographed the gory event from all angles, and pictures of the dead priest appeared on the front pages of all Mexican newspapers (at the request of Calles) publicizing the vengeance being wreaked on clerical enemies of the government. Catholics (almost 90 per cent of the population) were horrified by this murder of an innocent priest and bitterly accused the American ambassador of giving countenance to Calles by accompanying him on a tour only one day after the crime was committed. The truth was that Morrow knew nothing about Father Pro until the tour was under way. The story, of course, deeply disturbed him, particularly the news that Catholics were discrediting him for his association with Calles. Even in Washington, before going to Mexico, Morrow, though no Catholic himself, had resolved to side with the Church whenever the religious question arose. The dreadful killing of Father Pro seemed to fire his determination to work openly and unremittingly until Catholic mass was again being celebrated in all the thousands of churches in Mexico. This, Morrow well realized, could not be accomplished with a conference or two. A carefully planned diplomatic campaign was required, and he was just the man for the job.

At a large reception held in Washington, Morrow had been introduced to Colonel Charles Lindbergh, then at the height of his fame for having made the first solo flight across the Atlantic. On the basis of this brief encounter, Morrow wrote to Lindbergh asking him to make a good-will flight to Mexico. It was arranged and on December 14, 1927, the *Spirit of St. Louis* dropped into a smooth landing at Mexico City's airport and taxied up to the large, sprawling crowd of cheering Mexicans. Heading the welcoming committee was Plutarco Calles, smiling affably—a happy change certainly from his usual grim, somber expression. The tough revolutionary was at last beginning to show signs of mellowing. The romantic sequel to this good-will flight of Lindbergh was that he later married Morrow's gifted daughter Anne—the celebrated poetess.

Will Rogers, with his keen wit and cowboy drawl, also helped Mexican-American relations by appearing frequently as Morrow's guest at diplomatic social functions in Mexico City.

In May of 1928, Morrow arranged for Father John Burke of New York to meet and talk with Calles. Not wishing to attract public attention, Calles interviewed the priest and his party at the island fort of San Juan de Ulúa in the harbor of Veracruz. But Calles so ranted and raved in a fit of bad temper that nothing could be accomplished except to arrange another meeting at Chapultepec Castle a week later. At the second interview, and particularly at the third, held a week after that, Calles behaved better and even granted concessions to the Church that led ultimately to the reopening of the churches in June 1929, when Portes Gil was president.

For the part Morrow played in settling the conflict between the Catholic Church and the Mexican government, he won the admiration of British historian Arnold Toynbee, who called it "the greatest diplomatic triumph Mr. Morrow achieved . . . an extraordinarily delicate enterprise for a citizen of the United States, who did not happen to be a Catholic himself, to undertake in a country where he was his own Government's official representative."

1928

One law in Mexican politics which has remained sacred and inviolable since the fall of Porfirio Díaz states that no man shall be president for more than one term. Alvaro Obregón, heady with success (his supremacy in Mexican politics was then unchallenged), thought he could romp over this law, as he had so many others, without fear of reprisal from anyone. When Calles retired, he would, he announced, again be president.

Civic-minded citizens were by then nauseated by the travesty made of so-called "popular" elections, and mutterings of another revolution were heard. The boyishly handsome and dashing General Francisco Serrano, a quondam friend of Obregón (Serrano's losses at the gambling tables each night were being covered by the national treasury), broke from the government and began campaigning as a presidential candidate to oppose the Calles-Obregón succession. His large and enthusiastic following so frightened Obregón and Calles that they had him arrested while he was delivering a speech in Cuernavaca. That evening army trucks supposedly transporting Serrano and thirteen of his companions to a jail in Mexico City stopped on the highway and the escorting guards assassinated them all. That cluster of crosses motorists see when driving the "old road" to Cuernavaca mark the spot where Serrano and his companions were killed.

In an attempt to make his election more palatable to the people, Obregón delivered a series of bombastic campaign speeches in several states, calling his re-election "the will of the people" and alluding to his supporters as "the bulwark of the Mexican revolution." In July he returned to the capital after a two-month speaking tour, to oversee the workings of the political machine that would re-elect him.

But on July 17 an extraordinary thing happened that struck

terror in the hearts of all politicians, and completely changed the drift of Mexican politics.

Obregón was attending a gala banquet given in his honor at the Bombilla restaurant in San Angel—it was situated where the Obregón monument now stands—when a young cartoonist named José de León Toral timidly approached his place of honor to show him sketches he had made. While Obregón, smiling benignly, looked them over, Toral pulled out a gun and shot him dead. The loud report caused pandemonium and the assassin, caught by bodyguards of Obregón, was nearly beaten to death on the spot. But he was spared for questioning, and was dragged off to jail.

Rumors circulated that Toral was the paid gunman of some political enemy of Obregón—perhaps of Calles himself, or of Luis Morones, the head of CROM. Calles, to clear his name (of that crime) personally conducted the case against Toral. Though the wretched youth was subjected to the most horrible tortures, he could not be made to admit that anyone had hired him. (Many politicians trembled while he was interrogated for fear their names might be linked to Toral's.) A thorough investigation proved conclusively that Toral was nothing more than a religious fanatic unbalanced by a persecution complex.

But for politicians this news was more terrifying than if Toral had been a paid *pistolero*, for *pistoleros* were at least influenced by money. Religious fanatics were beyond their control. Toral was proof that a breaking point had been reached. The normally tolerant and courteous Mexican people had been driven to distraction and to desperation. Even the highest government official was at the mercy of a desperate person, and lesser officials were even more vulnerable.

Calles convened congress in the chamber of deputies for an extraordinary session, and from the tall, imposing speaker's platform delivered the most remarkable speech ever heard by the august assembly. It was practically an admission of guilt. Mexico, he said, had been dominated too long by military men. He himself was stepping down from the presidency and wanted congress to elect some man of integrity to replace him, someone who had no military background. At first there was a stunned silence. Then a thunderous roar of approval rent the air. On the side, in the diplomat's box, Dwight Morrow applauded loudly, and might even have jumped to his feet and cheered if the British minister, Mr. Ovey, sitting beside him had not restrained him. Whispered Morrow, slightly abashed, "I suppose I ought not to have done that." "No," replied the dignified Englishman. "You ought not."

CHAPTER TWELVE

1928–1970

1928

The governor of the state of Tamaulipas, a lawyer named Emilio Portes Gil (pronounced Hill) was chosen by congress to be the interim president of the republic for the rest of the unexpired term of Calles, or until June of 1929 when new elections would be held.

1929

Portes Gil had the polished manners of a veteran diplomat —he had held many posts in revolutionary governments—but unlike Calles, he still maintained some of his early convictions that socialism was best for Mexico. In contrast to the rightish tenor of Calles, he favored unions rather than management in labor disputes and gave new life to the land-distribution program which, under Calles, had been allowed to languish. Calles, still the arbiter of Mexican politics (though officially retired into private life), affected not to notice the leftish policies of Gil because, apparently, his mind was still too full of brooding thoughts about Toral who, shortly before, had been executed. To prove conclusively (as much to himself as to the nation) that his desire to reform Mexican politics was sincere, he planned and organized a national political party called *Partido Nacional Revolucionario*, known later as PRN, and invited various lawyers, professors, writers and scholars—regardless of their political background—to be delegates to the first PRN convention held at Querétaro in March 1929. The purpose of the party was

MAP of MEXICO

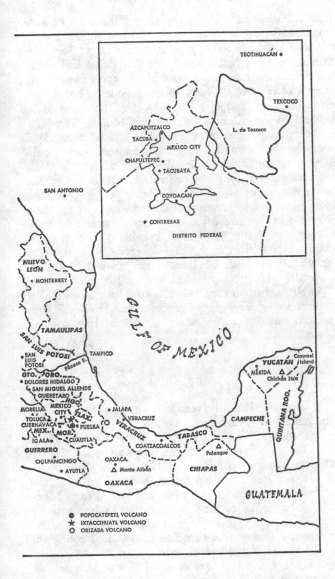

to eliminate, once and for all, the stifling influence of gun-carrying *caudillos* (military men) on Mexican politics and to give Mexico some semblance of a true democracy. That was the purpose, but in effect it was found that Calles had no intention of relinquishing his control of the government. The assembly wanted Aarón Sáenz to be president, but Calles passed the word around that Pascual Ortiz Rubio was to be elected and, to the chagrin of high-principled men, he was.

Mexico's illustrious writer, philosopher, and educator, Don José Vasconcelos, who had tirelessly and vehemently criticized every revolutionary president since Francisco Madero, formed his own political party, called the *Anti-reeleccionistas*, and made himself its presidential candidate to oppose Calles, his PRN party, and its unimpressive candidate, Pascual Ortiz Rubio. Vasconcelos, like Madero (whom he meant to emulate), campaigned the length and breadth of the country, fearlessly exposing scandals of the Obregón-Calles oligarchy and drawing the public's attention to the colossal wealth accumulated by revolutionary leaders, particularly military men who "blasphemed when they used the word 'patriotism.'" His crowds were so large, henchmen of Calles came to heckle him and even to menace individuals who cheered him too enthusiastically.

1930

The general elections this year were such an obvious "fix" that the published results meant nothing except to show officially that the brilliant and popular Vasconcelos had been defeated by an overwhelming majority—20,000 votes as against 1,000,000 for the PRN candidate, Rubio. Vasconcelos retired to the States (to escape arrest, some claimed) where he denounced the elections as a fraud and retired from Mexican politics. Later, during his self-imposed exile, he wrote his most celebrated book, *Estética*, a philosophical treatise on beauty which is now required reading in advanced courses of philosophy at the National University.

A quick wit and a delicious sense of humor is innate in most Mexicans; indeed, humor in their hands can be an insidious weapon capable of damaging irreparably the reputation of anyone, no matter how powerful or important he be. Calles, the dictator, and his puppet president Rubio were so mercilessly bombarded with jokes and quips that the government was in danger of becoming so ridiculous as to have no meaning whatever. Every imaginable pun was made on the name of "Calles," which in Spanish means "streets." Once Ortiz Rubio was wounded by a would-be assassin and was whisked away by a Red Cross ambulance. While being jolted along over badly pitted streets, Rubio is said to have wailed, "*Qué Calles! Qué Calles!*" And if someone was so naïve as to ask who was behind the crime, he was told to "Calles'e y Pórtes'e bién!" (Be quiet and behave yourself!), implying that both Calles and Portes Gil were involved. At the time an underpass was being dug near San Juan de Letran (a main street in the downtown area) and a popular riddle was: why is the San Juan de Letran underpass like Ortiz Rubio? Answer: because they're both under Calles (streets). The street of Cuernavaca on which Calles and his large satrapy of henchmen lived in gaudy splendor was tagged "the street of the forty thieves." In Mexico City, Calles took a house facing Chapultepec Castle from which he could watch the comings and goings of Ortiz Rubio. One morning a large hand-painted banner was found strung across the castle gates, reading:

> *Aquí vive el presidente.*
> *El que mande vive enfrente.*
> (In this castle lives the president.
> In the house opposite, his boss is a resident).

After the long nightmarish horrors of the revolution, people were once again able to laugh at the absurdities of Mexican politics.

By 1931 the worst of the revolution had spent itself, but its storms had brought to the surface odd species of millionaires. They obtruded in the then new and exclusive residential district of Mexico City, the Lomas de Chapultepec, and at their command dozens of large, pretentious mansions of pseudo-Spanish style went up. Long, shiny limousines—Packards and Pierce Arrows—drew up their driveways and from them stepped highly scented, richly bejeweled matrons in

furs. The lord and master of the grandiose pile was apt to b
a beefy, thick-necked, cigar-chewing ex-general of the revolu
tion who was having his hour to strut on the stage.

The worst of this vulgar display of wealth was the crim
that went on behind the scenes. All ex-generals kept *pisto
leros* on their payroll to eliminate tiresome people, and tire
some people, it was agreed, were mostly Catholics. This wa
merely a convenience. So long as the Catholic-baiter Calle
was the strong man in Mexico, ex-generals found it good pol:
tics to demonstrate their "patriotism" by sending their un:
formed *pistoleros* to harass Catholic services. The vogue i
Nazi Germany and Fascist Italy was then "black shirts" an
"brown shirts," and Mexico, always quick to ape a fashion
broke out with an epidemic of "red shirts" and "gold shirts.
The "gold shirts" were a gang of thoroughgoing fascists aide
and abetted by Calles and his clique of millionaire friends
On several occasions the "gold shirts" loitered outside cathe
drals maliciously jibing churchgoers until a fist fight was pro
voked. Immediately guns flashed and several people wer
killed. In Coyoacán angry Catholics overwhelmed the "gol
shirts" and lynched one from a tree in the main square.

The "red shirts" were mainly in the state of Tabasco, a re
gion of dense, tropical jungles and numerous rivers whicl
was the setting for Graham Greene's superb novel on Mexico
The Power and the Glory. Tomás Garrido Canabal, the so
of a rich plantation owner, was made governor of the state i
1920 by Alvaro Obregón. Lazy, sensuous, ill-mannered, quick
tempered, and rather stupid, Garrido Canabal saw the revolu
tion as a kind of willful perversion (which, in some cases, i
probably was), and for him, a good pervert meant a goo
revolutionist. Judged in this way, Canabal made an excellen
revolutionist. He named his two sons Lucifer and Lenin an
his daughter Zoyla Libertad, which, when pronounced, be
comes *Soy la libertad,* meaning "I am freedom." He decree
that only married Catholic priests could reside in his state
He hired illiterate prostitutes and *pistoleros* for schoolteach
ers, and, as a consequence, school children learned nothing
but popular songs and swimming in some nearby river. Hi
gang of "red shirts" tore down every Catholic church in the
state, and when a group of peasants was found huddled to

gether praying in the ruins the same "red shirts" sprayed them with machine guns. Wrote Graham Greene: "I have never been in a country where you are more aware all the time of hate. There has always been hate, I suppose, but now it is the official teaching: it has superseded love in the school curriculum."

1932

The Catholic Church (to which 90 per cent of the population belonged) was then the favorite whipping boy for these rich, cruel, unprincipled politicians. In these years persecution of priests and nuns and religious laymen reached an all-time high, and Catholics responded by holding massive demonstrations of protest before the National Palace. The utterly ineffectual president, Ortiz Rubio, terrified that a revolution might explode, submitted his resignation, not to congress (which would normally receive a president's resignation) but to Plutarco Calles in Cuernavaca! Could there be any doubt as to who ruled the roost? Calles promptly made the astute and prudent businessman Abelardo Rodríguez president (he was a banker and owner of several gambling houses) to fill out the rest of Rubio's term.

By this time Calles was one of the richest men in Mexico. As Lesley Byrd Simpson says, "When he spoke, no dog barked." He went to France and came back with a startling new message which in effect said: Socialism doesn't work; we must now help the rich to become richer. After that announcement land distribution to the peasants practically stopped and a small but potent group of right-wing extremists rose to dominate the government.

But the most brilliant scholars and writers were still in a preponderance on the left—from the extreme radical to the moderate liberals. Among them was Vicente Lombardo Toledano, an ex-university professor who organized the CTM (Confederation of Workers and Peasants) as an alternative to the graft-ridden union of Luis Morones, the CROM, which had by then become nothing but a racket. Morones had learned early on that industrialists were willing to pay handsomely for a promise that their factories would not be shut down by strikes. Thereafter workers' protests were "settled" in favor of management, and Morones became a millionaire several times over while the wretched members of his union were paying him stiff monthly dues, only to see their conditions steadily deteriorate.

1934

For several years a noisy group of young idealists clamoring for honest government had given Calles a great deal of worry. They were, in this presidential-election year, far too popular and influential for him to ignore. So he made what his advisers considered a smart political move by going among them to choose his next president. This certainly appeased and silenced his critics, but he precipitated his own end by choosing a man too determined, too devoted to his ideals to be held in bond by the strings of Calles. He was Lázaro Cárdenas.

For sure, Cárdenas had not been picked for his outstanding beauty—he had the strong, rugged features of a guileless *campesino*. His eyes, particularly, had that frank, unwavering stare of a sincere, fearless man—a penetrating look that many politicians found quite disturbing. When they warned Calles that Cárdenas might prove to be unmanageable, Calles replied, "Nonsense! I know him well. All he is, he owes to me." To the surprise of those not familiar with his integrity, Cárdenas went on a sixteen-thousand-mile speaking tour, seriously campaigning as though his election depended on it. Of course it did not, but because of his personal appearance before millions of his countrymen, his popularity, when he was sworn in as president in November 1934, was solid throughout the country.

Calles, however, was unmoved by all this pro-Cárdenas sentiment, or, if he felt anything, found it rather irritating. He strongly criticized the way Cárdenas handled strikes; workers were being given their full rights as written in Article 123 of the constitution (Calles, even as a socialist, had never done that), and, as a consequence, strikes broke out everywhere and were nearly paralyzing the country. When a fairly critical condition had been reached, Calles called several senators down to his house in Cuernavaca to discuss methods of removing Cárdenas. While they talked, Cárdenas acted and dealt two staggering blows to the Calles dictatorship.

He dismissed those senators conspiring with Calles, and he threw out of his presidential cabinet pro-Calles men and replaced them with young men noted for their outspoken remarks against Calles. This bold act drew unashamed admiration from many senators and deputies, some of whom had the temerity to make public their avowals to back Cárdenas against all his enemies—meaning, of course, Calles. Spontaneous pro-Cárdenas demonstrations took place before many municipal buildings in state capitals where governors (most of whom were appointees of Calles or Obregón) were made to swear their allegiance to Cárdenas. Only the demoniacal Canabal in Tabasco refused to be so intimidated by the masses, and he ordered his "red shirts" to fire on the demonstrators. Several people were killed and scores were wounded. Cárdenas, unlike his predecessors, could not stomach Canabal's barbarities and for this crime had him banished from the country and his "red shirts" disbanded.

1936

Calles, feeling the reins of control slipping from his hands, left his Cuernavaca mansion and moved into the big city where he could keep a closer watch on developments. He was naturally highly indignant to find grim detectives wearing dark glasses trailing him wherever he went; even when he went golfing, they would slink along the fairways behind him. Luis Morones, the deposed labor leader, was also being closely watched.

Rumors spread through cafés and restaurants that Calles and Morones were plotting a *coup d'état*. Tension mounted as the populace prepared itself for yet another appalling scene of rioting, shooting, and senseless bloodshed. But one morning in April, Cárdenas stunned the nation by making what many analysts of Mexican affairs consider the boldest of all his many bold moves. Calles, Luis Morones, and some twenty of their cronies were rounded up by special agents of Cárdenas; roaring with rage, they were shoved onto planes, flown to Texas, and there unceremoniously dumped, with an edict by Cárdenas never to return to Mexico unless specifically invited. Screaming headlines announcing the event brought looks of bewilderment from the Mexican public—they had been led to believe, by a government-controlled press, that Calles was a great man—but in the chamber of deputies, many broad, satisfied smiles were seen.

After that, the authority of Cárdenas was uncontested. Senators and ministers were ungrudging in their support of him, for they respected him, his integrity, and his unswerving resolve not to be influenced by any coalition group no matter how strong. He was a dictator, to be sure, but he was a benevolent one. Unlike Hitler and Mussolini and the strong men of Latin America, he did not identify himself with the rich or use secret police to prey on his enemies; nor did he suppress the freedom of the press—indeed, he encouraged it to voice the public's true opinion. The picture most Mexicans preserve of President Cárdenas is that of him in shirt sleeves wearing a broad-brimmed sombrero, standing on a train platform either going to or coming from some rural district in the interior. He was an inveterate traveler and visited—without guns or bodyguards—remote Indian villages that had never before seen a president. There he would sit for hours with the village elders, patiently listening to their litany of woes.

A pet project of Cárdenas was the Laguna community farm in the north of Mexico. This had been a rich cotton-producing area of some 3,000,000 acres, owned, in the days of Porfirio Díaz, by a handful of *hacendados*. These lands were cut up and given to 38,101 individuals and the *ejido* bank was founded to give loans at reasonable rates to the small farmer. The project was a controversial issue for many years, and even to this day opinion is divided as to whether or not the project was, or is, a success. It was supported by so many subsidies that experts are confounded by props and project and cannot yet determine where one ends and the other begins. Laguna's population of over 200,000 looks prosperous enough—healthy, well dressed, some have cars, radios, and television—but whether this reflects the industriousness of the people or the large sums of money loaned to them by Cárdenas is a question for debate.

In this year President Franklin D. Roosevelt turned his charm on Latin America with his "Good Neighbor Policy" and to cement friendly relations of this hemisphere signed a pact at the Pan-American Convention in Buenos Aires pledging non-interference in the internal affairs of any Latin-American republic. Within less than a year that pledge was strained to its utmost when Cárdenas expropriated American-owned oil fields in Mexico. That event gave Roosevelt an opportunity to prove that the promises implicit in his "Good Neighbor Policy" were indeed sincere.

1938

Of all the foreign-owned industries in Mexico, the oil companies were the most disliked. Shell, Standard Oil, Hearst and Doheny were held in scorn by the people for having backed Victoriano Huerta against Madero and for having consistently opposed every government effort to ameliorate conditions for the working class. Mexican newspapers had often deplored the fact that irreplaceable wealth was daily being drained away from the country and that Mexico was paying more for its own oil than any country she exported to, simply because the oil companies, being monopolists, had fixed the prices that way.

Since early 1936, when the pro-labor policies of Cárdenas took effect, the threat of a major strike loomed like a specter over the oil companies. Company executives distrusted Cárdenas and labeled him a communist for sending arms to the Loyalists in Spain's civil war—the side backed by Russia—and for giving political asylum to writers, artists, and professors who were on Franco's blacklist. The workers, laboring in oppressive jungle heat and living in shanties or hovels, had submitted to the oil companies a 175-page report demanding many improvements including, among other things, wage increases and a guarantee that Mexicans would be allowed to hold executive positions. (Top spots were then filled exclu-

sively by Americans.) The companies turned down their demands, whereupon the workers struck.

A government mediating board was called in to review the
case and after a careful study ordered the companies to meet
the workers' demands. It should be borne in mind that the
battle building up then was not one over who owned the oil
fields; it was all the primary offices of the Mexican government—the executive, the legislative, and the judicial—lining
up against a very few rich Americans. For Mexico, it was an
emotional problem of national honor. For the oil companies,
it was purely a legal problem, and so long as it remained one,
they, with a stableful of crafty lawyers, could easily win a
settlement to their own advantage. They therefore refused,
tactlessly and ill-advisedly, to accept the mediation board's
decision and threw their suit before the Mexican supreme
court.

This was tantamount to a slap at the Mexican government,
and Cárdenas, after consulting with expert lawyers, responded
by issuing a warrant, on March 18, 1938, for the seizure of
seventeen companies engaged in the production and the distribution of oil. If he wanted to be dramatic, he could not
possibly have done a better thing. Five days later a mammoth
demonstration was held in the *zócalo* of Mexico City. From
a balcony in the National Palace, Cárdenas, surrounded by
admirers, smiled and waved to the seething, roaring mass of
Mexicans packed in the square below holding aloft tall banners that proclaimed him a new liberator of Mexico. Some
hailed March 18 as a new day of independence, and in a
sense they were right. For the first time since the fall of
Tenochtitlán in 1521 Mexico was again in the hands of
Mexicans.

Wrote Silva Herzog, a Mexican economist: "News of the
expropriation was enthusiastically received, not only by citizens of Mexico but also by the better men of Latin-American
countries and other continents who for decades had been victims of unheard-of exploitations by the international vam-
pires (oil companies)."

To his everlasting credit, President Roosevelt stood by his
word and promised that ". . . the United States would show
no sympathy to rich individual Americans who [had] ob-

tained large land holdings in Mexico for virtually nothing
. . . and [who] claimed damages for seized property . . ."

When the full price of expropriation was known, however,
the cheering ended in a dying wail. The bottom dropped out
of the Mexican oil industry for several good reasons. First,
Mexican engineers were then not capable of handling the
complicated machinery used for oil production and refining.
The newly formed national oil company, Pemex, had, therefore, the added expense of importing foreign engineers. And
it was noted, with exasperation, that politicians who had assumed executive positions in Pemex were rapidly becoming
millionaires while the company they headed floundered near
bankruptcy. (Yet while they amassed fortunes the workers
whose strike had provoked the expropriation received not a
cent in wage increase; some in fact were laid off.) At the same
time, markets for Mexican oil simply disappeared. The
United States, England, and Holland, grimly determined to
ruin Mexico for her audacity, agreed on a boycott. Wrote
Josephus Daniels, United States ambassador to Mexico: "Out
of resentment for the expropriation, and the hope that Mexican operations would fail, markets for Mexican oil in the
United States and Britain suddenly dried up. Without markets the Mexicans would be drowned in their own oil, and
the expropriation would fail."

1939

At that time the mechanized armies of Mussolini in Ethi-
opia and those of Hitler on the Polish frontier desperately
needed oil and Cárdenas confounded those critics who had
labeled him a communist by supplying Axis needs. He was,
in fact, compelled to, since Mexico was, as Ambassador Daniels had so aptly put it, drowning in her own oil. As war
spread throughout the world, England and the United States
lifted their boycott and became voracious consumers of Mexican oil. The Second World War, then, saved the Mexican
National oil industry from being stillborn.

By far the most serious and far-reaching consequence of
the Cárdenas expropriation was the price paid to the oil com-

panies. After much haggling a settlement was reached in 1942 and the Mexican government found itself saddled with a debt of $130,339,000. This colossal debt (for Mexico) caused the country much financial grief and accounted, indirectly, for two devaluations. Ironically, the government's darling, Pemex, though nearly forty years old, is still being weaned on subsidies, and as late as May 1960, President Lopez Mateos had to write off its back taxes amounting to 1,700,000,000 pesos, since Pemex was hopelessly beyond ever paying them. Considering that Rockefeller, Doheny, and Lord Cowdray made millions in half the time, using the same wells, and charging the public less, the heavy losses of Pemex can mean only one thing: maladministration. Fortunately for Mexico, the future of Pemex is cheering. Under President Lopez Mateos many internal troubles were corrected and its finances were put on a firm footing through the negotiation of large loans from American, British, and Belgian banks. Large oil refineries in Salamanca are now capable of producing many of the highly profitable chemical by-products of petroleum, and within a few years Mexico hopes to fill not only her own national needs for such products, but to enter the world market in competition with other chemical-producing countries.

As "*anarquía*", means disorder, so "*sinarquía*" means order or orderly, and the coined word *Sinarquistas* became the name of a secret society founded in the city of León in 1937. Its two leaders, José Antonio Urquiza and Salvador Abascal, preached a doctrine not unlike that of the Spanish *falange*: God, church, and family. Their followers were Catholic, agrarian Mestizos with more Spanish than Indian blood. They denounced not only the government of Cárdenas but the entire succession of Mexican governments since the rise of Santa Anna. They claimed (not without cause) that the Mexican government had never been anything more than a sorry imitation of some imported form of government—either from France, the United States, Russia, and (to some extent) Nazi Germany. For this reason they acknowledged no Mexican government as being, or as ever having been, truly Mexican, since none of them had been founded on the Christian principles as taught and practiced by the early Spanish friars— Pedro de Gante, Vasco de Quiroga, Archbishop Zumarrago,

Sahagún, and others. These time-honored principles had maintained peace and order in Mexico for over three hundred years, and chaos resulted when Mexico abandoned them and accepted ideas from abroad. The *Sinarquistas* preached nationalism and Catholicism, two isms close to the emotional heart of the lowly *campesino,* and also passivism, something truly revolutionary in Mexican revolutionary movements. Each of their unarmed demonstrations was broken up by gun-brandishing police. In three years there were eight hundred thousand *Sinarquistas,* most of them rural people, in the region around Guanajuato and León.

1940

By 1940 the PRN political party was operating smoothly, and its rather bland candidate, Avila Camacho, swept to victory without a disturbance. He had been a general who reputedly fought well in putting down the minor rebellion of Escobar in 1929. But why he, out of all the many brilliant and experienced men surrounding Cárdenas, was chosen to be president, no one quite knew, except confidants of Cárdenas, and they never told. In any case, Camacho appeared suddenly on the scene of Mexican politics with such an undistinguished record that wits referred to him as the "unknown soldier."

The multimillionaire Juan Andreu Almazán formed the opposition party which was joined by that political freak, the renowned painter Diego Rivera. Catholics, capitalists, and fascists who backed Almazán must have found the famous painter an odd bedfellow, since Rivera had been, up till then, one of the leading lights of the Communist party. As PRN controlled the voting, Almazán never had a chance, no matter who backed him or how many voted for him.

In 1942 the *Sinarquistas* launched what is perhaps the most fantastic adventure of modern Mexico. Having pledged themselves to a life of poverty, loyalty, and obedience, they chose two of the most arid and discouraging areas of Mexico to found *Sinarquista* colonies—one called, hopefully, Maria Auxiliadora (Mary the Bountiful) in Lower California near the Magdalena Bay area, and another called Villa Kino (after the famous sixteenth-century Jesuit priest and explorer), set in the desert of Sonora. After two torturous years the first camp folded, but the second continues to this day.

Following the sinking of two Mexican oil tankers, Camacho in 1942 declared war on the Axis powers. Mexico's only military contribution to the Allied armies was an air group of Mexican pilots that assisted General MacArthur in his conquest of the Philippines. Its contribution in raw materials, however, for war plants in the United States was invaluable.

Under Camacho, who was a devout Catholic, Mexico lost much of its communist and socialist leanings. The ministry of education, for instance, was advised to throw out scores of textbooks that smacked of Marxism, and books free of all isms were chosen to replace them. Practically all church persecution disappeared, and for the first time in over a generation priests and nuns were again seen on the streets in their civilian black garb—their religious mufti.

The war gave Mexican economy a terrific thrust forward. British, American, and European investors, impressed by the growing prosperity of Mexico—a country relatively safe from the vicissitudes of the New York stock market—deposited small fortunes in Mexican banks for speculation; and Mexico, for the first time since the *Porfiriano* era, was again accumulating capital.

About this time Mexico's intelligentsia fell into step with world trends to industrialize so-called "backward" countries and agreed to change Mexico from an essentially agrarian country to an industrial one. Strong arguments by farmers and cattle raisers deprecating the change were either ignored or talked down, and money that could have been used on agriculture was poured into steel mills, chemical plants, mammoth generators for producing light and power, and factories making household accessories or tubing. Once on the road to industrialization, there was no turning back, even though crop production lagged far behind the people's needs. Corn and beans, vital to every Mexican's diet, still had to be imported, and in 1943–44, a drought year for Mexico, President Camacho spent over a million dollars in the United States buying food for hordes of starving people in famine areas.

However far Mexico advances along industrial lines, the shadowy specter of a possible famine dogs her footsteps until and unless the land problem is given more study.

Indeed, land—its use and possession—has been at the root of all Mexico's troubles since the beginning of time. The revolution of 1910 was, it could be said, primarily a radical change in systems of landownership, from the *hacendado* system of Porfirio Díaz to the *ejido* system as perfected by Cárdenas. Every revolutionary president from Madero to Cárdenas won the people's acclaim by cutting up large *haciendas* and giving them piecemeal to the peasants. This new system undoubtedly regenerated the ego of the lowly *campesino* who was the proud owner of a piece of land; but whether it improved the productivity of the soil is another matter altogether.

The land problem for Camacho was not so much who owned it, but how much could it produce, a problem which will plague every president for decades to come, so long as Mexico's birth rate climbs. In Camacho's time it was found that only 48,000,000 acres out of the country's entire 490,000,000 could be cultivated—only one tenth of the country, or an area roughly the size of Illinois and Indiana combined. Of this area only one sixth, or a scant 7,000,000 acres, was adequately watered by rainfall while the rest needed irrigation. But the most distressing discovery was that erosion, Mexico's sleepless enemy, had eaten into the cultivable land, leaving only half—or about 25,000,000 acres—with top-grade soil.

For centuries the soil in Mexico has been shamelessly mistreated; like the spindly legged burro, it is overworked, underfed, and punished for not performing better. The Spaniards committed the worst crimes when, in fits of homesickness, they chopped down entire forests to make Mexico look like the barren plains of Spain. They also allowed their imported sheep and goats to chomp on the grass roots so necessary for the bedding down of top soil. And they were diabolically successful in draining away many sorely needed lakes at high altitudes. The consequences we see about us today. Many river beds are, except in the rainy season, bone dry; lakes have become, or are becoming, deserts of cracking clay; and dust rises in the wind from hills and plains once covered with lush forests. The denuded soil, then, is beaten unmercifully by the torrential rains and is washed down the craggy *barrancas* (ravines) and thence to the sea. What remains is a powdery, de-energized soil with one of the lowest yields in the world. An average acre of cultivated land in Mexico yields only 7.8 bushels of corn annually, while Canada, an average corn-growing country, produces annually 38.4 bushels of corn per acre.

On discussing the Mexican revolution of 1910, most writers fail to emphasize how Mexican soil had been relentlessly deteriorating for hundreds of years. All during the nineteenth century its agricultural supply went down and prices and demand went up, while in the rest of the world agricultural prices were actually falling off. By the end of the Díaz regime the food shortage was acute and village squares everywhere in Mexico were teeming with hungry men ready—indeed, eager— to revolt. The reader may remember that Dr. Vásquez Gómez argued hotly with Porfirio Díaz in 1910 over Mexico's desperate agricultural problem, but the old dictator was unable to see the growing danger of the situation and did nothing to help land or farmer. His opportunity to act quickly passed, and soon mass suffering passed its tolerance and a revolution ravaged the country. If only something had been done, then, Mexico would have been spared so much grief, but history (we must constantly remind ourselves) has no if's; like ol' man river, it just keeps rolling along.

Because of the war, Mexico's trade balance took a favorable turn and in 1942 exports exceeded imports by 80,000,000 pesos; in 1943 this rose to 127,000,000. On September 30, 1943, the first payment was made to the oil companies, and in 1944, 284,000,000 pesos was paid on the government's public debt.

But Mexico's war prosperity was lopsided. Prices during the war rose 300 per cent while salaries remained almost the same. The margin of profit for tradesmen, industrialists, retailers, and doctors became unnaturally, almost indecently, high and a new crop of millionaires sprang up. Many of them were foreigners whose European tastes created a demand for elegant restaurants and night clubs. In a few years Mexico City was transformed into a sprawling metropolis replete with congested crowds and honking traffic. In fact the capital lost its Mexican character and became the most cosmopolitan city in Latin America. Its beautiful old colonial mansions were pulled down to make room for tall, modern buildings—functional certainly, but in no way Mexican.

1946

Camacho's secretary of *gobernación*, Miguel Alemán, was chosen to succeed him. His election went off with unprecedented calm and order.

In January of this year the *Sinarquistas* staged another of their unarmed demonstrations in León. The quick-tempered commandant of the militia, Colonel Luis Overa Barrón, flustered by jeerings and taunts from the crowd, foolishly gave orders to fire. The result: the *Sinarquistas* had 274 martyrs —27 killed and 247 wounded. The "León massacre" caused such excitement that President Alemán, to mollify boiling tempers, allowed the *Sinarquistas'* candidate to win the gubernatorial election in Guanajuato, making Guanajuato the first anti-revolutionary government in the republic.

The building program begun somewhat timidly by Camacho went forward at a terrific speed under Alemán. Paved roads, in his six-year term, increased from 2328 miles to over 10,000. Dams for generating electricity increased electrical-power usage from 957,000 K.W.H. in 1947 to 1,500,000 in 1952. The University City was begun and finished during his term of office.

In 1947 a survey showed that a million *ejidarios* (peasant farmers) using more than 16,000,000 acres of land were producing only 30 per cent of the nation's crop, while 200,000 private farmers (sort of legalized *hacendados*) using half that acreage were producing the balance, or 70 per cent. Apologists for the *ejido* system hastened to point out that the peasants lacked modern equipment and were working inferior land. They were probably right, but their excuses could not alter the glaring fact that the *ejido* system was falling far short of expectations. Giving land away to peasant farmers was, regardless of what leaders of the revolution claimed, no great boon to the nation. The *campesino* with his small plot of ground could not be trusted to produce food enough for himself *and* the city. Alemán, in an attempt to vitalize the *ejidarios*, initiated a program of loans, subsidies, and price stabilization on farm produce, and he allocated a large part of his budget to the construction of dams and of intricate irrigation systems. One of his prize projects was the Papaloápan commission. An area south of Veracruz inundated with heavy rain was cleared of rank growth, drained, covered with a network of irrigation canals, and then sown with rice, corn, and beans. The Papaloápan commission increased Mexico's cultivable farm land by more than a million acres. Other projects added six million acres more to the aggregate total and during the administration of President Lopez Mateos still more were added.

In 1946 the Catholic National Action Party, better known as PAN (which in Spanish spells "bread") was founded by two leaders of the *Sinarquistas*. Thereafter PAN acted as the opposition party to the powerful PRI (Institutional Revolutionary Party) which, since its inauguration in 1929, (then the PRN) has had a stranglehold on the nation's politics. PAN, like the *Sinarquistas*, is Catholic and is, therefore, the party of provincial and rural Mexico. Though PAN has never won a presidential election, nor is it likely to until and unless votes are counted by some disinterested party, such as a machine, it is living proof that Mexico is groping toward a true democracy. There can be no question that PAN or some derivation of it will one day, and perhaps soon, seriously challenge the political supremacy of PRI.

The war's end reversed Mexico's trade balance and by 1947 money was pouring out of the country at an alarming rate. Alemán, to staunch the flow, clamped heavy duties on most imports—from 100 to 200 per cent—and prohibited outright the importation of 120 items which had up to then accounted for 20 per cent of all imported goods. The pinch was soon felt throughout the country, and angry protests from consumer and retailer alike brought about a slight revision. The 120 items were again allowed into the country, but stiff taxes made them almost prohibitive to buy. For this reason,

American-made automobiles, refrigerators, electric heaters, cooking utensils, etc., cost twice as much in Mexico as they do in the States.

1952

The modest Don Adolfo Ruíz Cortines, a conscientious and scrupulously honest government administrator and former governor of Veracruz, was PRI's choice for president this year. His rigorous campaign to weed out graft and corruption in the government was so effective that even traffic cops refused to take bribes. It was Cortines who first sounded the alarm that Mexico City was becoming overpopulated. He urged people to move to the coast, to the tropics, and offered land to settlers at a pittance. He set his engineers in SCOP (the Ministry of Public Works and Communications) to paving roads through jungles, thereby opening up vast new areas for development. And he launched a whole army of jeep-borne medical men with DDT paraphernalia for stamping out malaria, the scourge of the tropics.

1958

The change-over in presidents this year, from Ruíz Cortines to Don Adolfo Lopez Mateos, was marred by a wave of strikes and rioting. The railroad workers and the workers in the oil fields were demanding a pay increase and the removal of certain union leaders who had been appointed by Alemán's government. Angry mobs of workers outside the Pemex offices near Avenida Juárez in Mexico City were dispersed with tear-gas bombs and club-swinging police. Added to this was a demonstration of university students protesting against a proposed five-centavo hike in bus fares. Scores of buses were crowded off the road by souped-up convertibles jammed with students; bus drivers and passengers were ejected and the buses were driven by students to the university and there confined while the government restudied the bus company's proposal. Employees of downtown shops and offices, stranded on street corners of the city, cursed the whole business, and newspapers lashed out at the government's lenient treatment of student rioters. Within a week some kind of face-saving compromise had been reached; bus fares were raised, the students released the buses, and the bus companies put into operation a fleet of new buses.

Two members of the Russian embassy were caught carrying instructions from Moscow to the striking railroad workers in Coahuila. They were, of course, deported, and the head of the railroad union was jailed for conspiring to overthrow the government.

1959

The ragtag army of Cuban rebels and expatriate liberals, trained secretly on the deserted coast of Mexico's Yucatán peninsula and led by the bearded and bombastic Fidel Castro Ruz, rode triumphantly into Havana, Cuba, atop tanks and gun carriers in January of this year, marking a signal victory for reform-minded, revolutionary leaders all over Latin America. Mexico's president, Don Adolfo Lopez Mateos applied the principles of "self-determination" and non-intervention" in dealing with these events, following a national policy in foreign affairs that is now sacrosanct since it derives from Benito Juárez's much quoted maxim *"El respeto al derecho ajeno es la paz"* ("Peace is the respect for the rights of others").

1960

Nothing in this century (with the possible exception of Mexico's own revolution followed by her bold expropriation of the oil wells) so rocked the structure of Latin American political systems as did Fidel Castro. In Mexico, some prominent members of the PRI, the nation's ruling political party, openly professed their admiration for Castro and his revolution, thereby embarrassing conservative elements of the same party. And two widely discussed magazines in Mexico, *La Política* and *Siempre*, eulogized Castro as much as they damned the United States. But while these sentiments caused some distress in Washington, they were only voices from the moderate left. The extreme left threatened armed revolution against the Mexican government itself. Such fanaticism, of course, could not be countenanced, and so President Lopez Mateos (himself left of center) had a noisy critic of the government and member of this group removed from the Teachers' Union. University students reacted immediately by rioting, and on August 9 David Siqueiros, Mexico's famed muralist and at sixty-four a senior member in the Mexican Communist Party, was jailed for his alleged part in inciting the students to riot.

In November U. S. Ambassador to Mexico Robert Hill, who had worked tirelessly to lure Mexico onto the side of the United States in its breach with Cuba, tendered his resignation to President Eisenhower amid rumors that relations between Mexico and the United States were then severely strained and could very easily deteriorate.

And yet this was the year when Mexico realized the first of several bonanzas to come her way because of Cuba's defection to the Communist camp. Sugar exports from Mexico to the United States jumped from 24,000 tons in 1960 to 191,000 in 1961, in accord with the new quota from Washington that reallocated Cuba's former priority on U.S. sugar imports. And tourism in Mexico expanded steadily 15 per cent each year throughout the sixties. Many Americans, denied access to Cuba, went south to relax on the tropical beaches of Acapulco, Puerto Vallarta, and Mazatlán, or to explore the ruins of Toltec and Mayan civilizations, or to marvel at Mexico's colonial art and architecture in Taxco, Guanajuato, and San Miguel de Allende.

1961

At the very close of 1960 some two thousand demonstrators massed before the Government Palace in Chilpancingo, state of Guerrero, protesting the corrupt administration of Governor Raul Caballero Aburto. Acting on erroneous information that the mob was Communist-inspired, state troopers fired into the crowd. The result: thirteen dead. An investigation of the charges against Aburto convinced President Lopez Mateos that the demonstrators were indeed right in their protest and in January of this year he had the governor thrown out of office. Mexican newspapers cited this as an example of how Mexico's one-party system could deal swiftly and effectively with an explosive situation.

The trouble was that explosive situations this year were cropping up everywhere, and they came in every shade of political color—from blood red to pontifical white.

In March a Latin-American Conference held in Mexico City brought together social reformers with leftish theories from every Latin country of this hemisphere—the large Cuban contingent conspicuous in their beards and battle fatigues. Ex-president Lázaro Cárdenas, up to then so inscrutably silent that newspapers were referring to him as the "Sphinx of Juilquilpan" (his place of retirement in Jalisco), spoke at opening ceremonies and later railed at the press for simultaneously distorting the purpose of the conference and not giving it enough coverage. Meanwhile, in another part of the city, a large anti-Communist meeting drew up a petition asking that the Mexican government outlaw the Communist Party.

And, of course, the Bay of Pigs fiasco in Cuba touched off a wave of anti-American demonstrations all over Mexico, the most violent occurring in Morelia, Michoacán—an area long sympathetic to socialist ideology. There the USIS Binational Center was bombed and burnt and its director was pursued over rooftops by irate students.

But perhaps the most dangerous development, from the government's point of view, was a hardening attitude among Castro supporters and socialist leaders that violence was their only means of wringing concessions from the government. Rival factions of the left were joining forces and on April 21 they marched, fifteen thousand strong, on the National Palace, but squads of police using tear gas and rough treatment dispersed them before the Palace was reached. Interrogation of those arrested revealed that Trotskyites, Stalinists, Marxists, and a wide variety of left-wing thinkers were forming an alliance against the government.

In June the Organization of American States (OAS) sent a team of military experts into the jungles of Chiapas, Mexico's border state with Guatemala, to investigate charges made by Guatemala that a large guerrilla army was being trained there for an invasion of its territory. But according to rumors, this charge was never made—or if made, was intentionally exaggerated. Lopez Mateos, it was said, needed some discreet way of outmaneuvering a popular and very influential Mexican general who was thought to be preparing a Castro-like revolution in Mexico—not in Guatemala. In any case, the city mansion of General Celestino Gasco near Coyoacán was raided early in the morning of September 10 and 224 people gathered there were arrested. A large cache of arms and ammunition discovered in the garage bore damning evidence that the general and his comrades were preparing an explosive celebration on Mexico's Day of Independence —September 15 and 16. On the same day a retired military man, Colonel Coatl Gómez, was overpowered and arrested after leading a band of machete-swinging peasants on an assault of an isolated army barracks in the hinterlands of Veracruz. More arrests were made in the cities of Puebla and Veracruz, and two days later the government announced that a nationwide military-political movement had been smashed before it could develop.

Two new political parties appeared on the scene in 1961— one organized by right-wing ex-president Miguel Alemán, the *Frente Revolucionario de Acción Civil* (FRAC), and the other formed by left-wing ex-president Lázaro Cárdenas and his son Cuauhtémoc, the *Movimiento de Liberación Nacional* (MNL). Neither could meet minimum requirements for official registration that year; nevertheless they posed a real challenge for the PRI. And so Lopez Mateos, in December, made his most brilliant political move by announcing the creation of a Special Committee of Consultants made up of all living ex-presidents of Mexico, then numbering seven. By assigning positions in the government to these men, the President was not only strengthening PRI, but was preserving a national unity in meeting problems that demanded immediate government action.

1962

It was during this year that a dynamic group of Mexican businessmen carried to Germany a magnificently prepared documentary film showing Mexico's sports facilities and spectator accommodations and thereby won for Mexico the honor of playing host to the 1968 Olympic games.

1963

Probably most hurt by the President's round-up of ex-presidents was a new political party of peasants officially born January 7, and called the *Central Campesina Independiente* (CCI). Its left-wing organizers undoubtedly counted heavily on the support of Lázaro Cárdenas, but Cárdenas, now director of the Rio Balzas Project, had only patronizing if not cool words for the CCI. Denounced as "the hand of the Mexican Communist Party" by the dean of Mexican Marxists, Vicente Lombardo Toledano, the CCI made little impact on the government's program for land distribution, despite its flaunted threats to use nationwide demonstrations to break up big land holdings—especially those of foreigners. Nevertheless, the CCI could gain strength by organizing the growing hordes of land squatters who each year make fresh invasions of private property—most often of large, walled-in, empty lots that surround every big Mexican city.

Despite the rising price of silver on world markets, Mexico's silver production was steadily declining, because, claimed mine owners, a scarcity of capital curtailed their prospecting ventures and modernization of the industry. In November the newspaper *Excelsior* published the distressing news that Mexico had fallen to second place among the world's silver-producing nations (surpassed by the United States, whose production was steadily rising). The Mexican government subsequently made a restudy of mining laws and restrictions and is endeavoring to exploit the nation's great untapped wealth of precious metals.

1964

In June of this year, Juana Castro Ruz, Fidel's big sister, made headlines by announcing on a TV show in Mexico City that she was defecting from Cuba and was asking for political asylum in Mexico. Cuba, she said, was "an immense prison surrounded by water," and she accused her brother of instigating subversive activities all over Latin America. She also recalled that Fidel, when a rebellious schoolboy, flew into violent rages whenever something he wanted was denied him.

In the wake of that announcement came one more determined attempt on the part of the OAS to pressure Mexico into breaking ties with Communist Cuba. A proposal, opposed only by Mexico, Bolivia, and Chile, to suspend all trade with Cuba (except for vitally needed foods and medicines) was approved July 26. But on August 3 Mexico's Deputy Foreign Minister, José Gorostiza, speaking on behalf of President Lopez Mateos, challenged members of the OAS to put the Cuban affair before the International Court of Justice. The OAS proposal, he explained, was a blatant violation of Article 96 of the UN Charter, which banned punitive measures against any nation by a regional organization without UN approval. His reasoning, it seems, was sound, since no one accepted his challenge or attempted to refute him.

1965

PRI's presidential candidate, Don Gustavo Díaz Ordaz, formerly Minister of the Interior (PRI's special presidential training grounds), not unexpectedly defeated PAN's candidate José Gonzalez Torres of Chihuahua by an overwhelming majority of votes. In January the new president took up the reins of government.

1966

The United States was to discover this year that Mexico's diplomatic relations with Cuba could be as useful for some as they were embarrassing for others. On December 28 Mexico's new Foreign Secretary, Antonio Carrillo Flores, announced that his Ambassador in Havana had won the release of 169 U.S. citizens. Mexico entered negotiations for freeing these prisoners in 1966 when talks between the Swiss embassy (officially entrusted with U.S. affairs in Cuba) and Castro had broken down.

1967

Acapulco's jet set of beautiful people was rudely disturbed one sunny afternoon in August by the eruption of a monstrous gun battle outside the Cobra Growers Union Headquarters on a back street of town. A union meeting was in progress, claimed union officials, when seven hundred men from a rival faction, headed by César del Angel, deputy from Veracruz, marched on the building and allegedly opened fire. Before order was restored, twenty-three men had been killed and scores injured. César del Angel, himself badly wounded, was arrested and prosecuted (against his protests of innocence) for provoking the fight. The full story has yet to be told, but it is now quite certain that federal authorities, rightly fearing that flocks of tourists would be frightened away by more shoot-ups, have pressured city officials into keeping a closer watch on future union meetings.

After making an impassioned speech in Washington, D.C., to a joint session of Congress, pleading for a more equitable balance of trade between Mexico and the States, President Díaz Ordaz flew to El Paso, Texas, accompanied by Lyndon B. Johnson, where both presidents presided over ceremonies marking the return of "El Chamizal" to Mexico. Ownership of this strip of land between El Paso and Ciudad Juárez had been contested since 1848 when the Rio Grande changed course. John F. Kennedy, in 1962, was the first U.S. President to initiate a settlement of the matter and in 1967 Mexico became the only nation in recent years to broaden its territorial frontiers by legal means.

On November 18 a worldwide run on gold was caused by the devaluation of the English pound, and near panic was created on the following day when the French withdrew their gold reserves from the London Pool. The dollar itself came under attack but rallied when Henry H. Fowler, U. S. Secretary of the Treasury, announced the decision of economists from the seven member nations of the Gold Pool that the official price of gold—$35 an ounce—would be maintained despite recent speculation to the contrary. But implicit in his announcement was a muted cry for help from friendly nations to support the United States in its effort to stabilize currencies. The first nation to come forward was Mexico (soon followed by Japan and Canada), bravely offering the United States all its gold reserves *without limit*. This spontaneous demonstration of good faith and friendship on the part of Mexico endeared her to many a world financier who could see nothing but disaster ahead until the moment Mexico pledged its support of the dollar.

1968

The much publicized student riots of Mexico (probably *over*publicized because of the Olympics, and thereby intensified) started without plan or direction—in fact, they started by accident. On July 24 a savage street fight broke out near the Ciudadela on Avenida Balderas between rival gangs of two nearby prep schools. Police intervened and jailed those students they could catch. Then, two days later, university students massing for their twenty-sixth of July celebration of Castro's revolution formed a protest march demanding that the jailed students be released immediately. Police responded by breaking up the march and jailing more students. The students thereupon stormed the Zócalo, on July 30, rampaging through streets surrounding the National Palace. Five city buses were captured and burnt and around them barricades were raised from which students flung everything available at advancing riot police. Pelted with rocks and bottles thrown by jeering students on the upper floors of an ancient prep school, a block north of the National Palace, federal troops blasted their way into the school with bazooka fire and then made wholesale arrests. By 3 A.M. the main plaza was littered with the debris of battle and the jails were crammed with frightened youths—among them five French students who, in May, had participated in the street riots of Paris.

On August 1 there was a mammoth rally of some eighty-five thousand students at the University City campus. Marching ten and twelve abreast they paraded down Avenida Insurgentes bearing placards and banners scrawled with insults to the President and his chief of police, Luis Cueto. But a battery of army tanks posted near the Insurgentes bull ring discouraged the marchers from going any farther than a large intersection several blocks away.

Because the march ended peacefully, the city's populace hoped that a settlement was being made between the students and the government. But dark rumors flew through the capital that terrible deeds were being done and then hushed up. A run on gasoline was started by an unfounded rumor that students were intending to blow up the Pemex gas tanks in Azcapotzalco. The sight of ubiquitous convoys of army trucks rushing troops back and forth through the city gave some credence to these rumors. In the meantime, students walked out of classes on August 9, signaling a nationwide strike that paralyzed all institutions of higher learning.

President Díaz Ordaz, in his address to the nation on September 1, visibly shaken with emotion when speaking about the recent troubles, solemnly vowed that *nothing* would be allowed to interfere with the opening of the Olympic games on October 12. This implied that Olympic officials had already threatened to cancel the games. Cancellation for Mexico would have meant a loss of approximately $80,000,000—money already spent on spectacular sports palaces and projects to beautify and decorate the city—and probably more if lost tourist dollars were counted. In view of this, the President had no alternative but to use force to suppress any further demonstrations.

Despite these stern warnings, student agitation continued and the government responded by sending troops to occupy University City on September 18—"to protect," as one government spokesman put it, "the autonomy of the university against foreign groups using it for purposes alien to university affairs."

Three attempts, the following day, by students to storm the administration building were repulsed by harmless but terrifying cannon explosions. On September 28 Javier Barros Sierra, rector of the university, deplored the presence of troops on his campus as "an excessive act of force," and then submitted his resignation. But the fifteen-member governing board wisely refused it since the rector had, by then, won the respect of both sides in his extremely difficult role of mediator.

Having lost control of their headquarters at the university, the students turned to the Instituto Politécnico Nacional across town, in the northwest corner of the city. There, on September 24, students for the first time waged tactical warfare employing rifles and automatic weapons. The battle lasted twelve hours, ending with troops silencing snipers in nearby apartment houses and then moving in to occupy the Santo Tomás campus, depriving the students, thereby, of their second headquarters. The day's count of dead was officially set at fifteen.

Despite this death toll, student leaders called for yet another massive meeting on October 2 in the Plaza de Tres Culturas, situated at the eastern end of the Nonoalco-Tlatelolco Housing Development. A tall tower at the western end, resembling an elongated A (designed by Mexico's inspired architect Mario Pani), rises up majestically over the city's skyline. It is interesting to note, briefly, the history of this area. It was here that Cuauhtémoc and the ravaged remnants of his Aztec army retreated during the siege of Tenochtitlán in 1521 and suffered hardships rarely matched in the annals of warfare. Few of the thousands imprisoned there survived the siege, succumbing to starvation, wounds of battle, or just plain exhaustion. After the conquest, Tlatelolco was abandoned and avoided because it was thought that ghosts of the vanquished army haunted and cursed the place. Later it became the city's worst slum and the setting for Luis Buñuel's prize-winning film *Los Olvidados* (*The Forgotten Ones*). On October 2 of this year, amid those impressive blocks of tall, modern buildings (replacing the slums in 1960), the venerated and ancient cathedral of Santiago Tlatelolco, and the recently excavated Aztec temples—each representing one of Mexico's three cultures—Tlatelolco became once again the scene of appalling tragedy, exceeded in this century only by the *Decena Tragica* of 1913—which foreshadowed the fury of the revolution that followed.

On that afternoon six thousand persons, mostly students, assembled there for a march on the Santo Tomás campus about one kilometer away. But news leaked that tanks and riot police were awaiting to intercept them, so the march was called off and student leaders harangued the crowd with political speeches. Suddenly bullets were ripping at the stone pavement around them. Army troops stationed nearby rushed in and poured automatic rifle fire into windows of apartment buildings where snipers had been seen. A cordon of police encircled the plaza, trapping thousands of residents and demonstrators alike, many of whom, finding themselves caught in a cross fire, became hysterical. By eight in the evening, Green Cross and Red Cross workers, undaunted by a heavy downpour of seasonal rain, carried off thirty dead and over two hundred injured. All organized student demonstrations ceased abruptly as of that night.

And so the 1968 Olympic games opened without a blemish; in fact, they were considered to be, by newsmen and regular attendants, the best organized and most spectacular games of any in the long history of this important sports event. Contrary to pre-game opinions expressed by certain doctors, trainers, and aging "experts," the altitude of Mexico City had no adverse effects on the athletes whatever. Dozens of records were broken and some new Olympic records were set that promise to stand for some time to come.

By extending the scope of the Olympic games to include cultural events as well (and thereby setting an Olympic precedent), Mexico offered its many art lovers a cornucopia of symphonies, concerts, ballets, and theater—performed by the world's outstanding orchestras, musical groups, artists, and theatrical companies.

Perhaps the brightest ray of light in this unusually stormy year was a pledge by President Lyndon B. Johnson made February 14 that the United States would uphold the Latin American Atomic Ban Treaty, which forbade the presence of any atomic weapons in Latin America. England had agreed to sign, but France, Russia, and Red China still remained uncommitted. Drawn up and signed by charter members of the Latin American League two years previously, the treaty was first called by the name of the place where it was born: Tlatelolco—where the offices of Mexico's Ministry of Foreign Affairs are located. But the Treaty of Tlatelolco eventually became known as the Latin American Atomic Ban Treaty.

1969

An unexpected advantage of keeping legal ties with Cuba became clear in 1963 when a gunman hijacked a Mexican plane to Cuba. The thug was promptly jailed by Cuban police and then shipped back to Mexico for prosecution. Since then, Mexican planes have been remarkably unbothered by "crackpot" hijackers, except in this year when two former university students, a young man and his girl friend, forced the crew of a Miami-bound Aeronaves jet to fly them to "freedom" in Castro's Cuba. Mexico's request that the pair be returned was ignored by Cuban officials, who claimed the youths were seeking political asylum. Mexico replied with a sharp note indicating that relations between the two countries were growing cool. The temperature dropped even further when Cuban newspapers accused the Mexican embassy in Havana of harboring criminals.

The November presidential election will prove once more that the PRI is still the favorite party of the people. Its candidate, Don Luis Echeverría Alvarez, carefully chosen and well prepared for the job of chief executive, will undoubtedly win over 80 per cent of the popular vote. The problems facing his administration will be overpopulation, thickening smog in big cities, water pollution, illegal exploitation of timberland, colossal smuggling rings, water shortages, agrarian poverty, and—above all—a growing opposition to his own party, the PRI. Actually, opposition channeled through rival political parties could be viable proof that democracy is indeed working in Mexico, but unfortunately the most virulent form of opposition comes from maverick discontents, who invariably provoke the government into militant acts of repression. With luck, Don Luis Echeverría Alvarez might, just possibly, get through the next six years without meeting any worse problems than those that faced his predecessors, Presidents Lopez Mateos and Díaz Ordaz.

BIBLIOGRAPHY

Ancient Mexico, Frederick Peterson, G. P. Putnam's, 1959.

Aztecs of Mexico, George Vaillant, Penguin Books, 1941.

Breve Historia de Mexico, José Vasconcelos, Porrua Hnos. (Mexico), 1944.

History of the Conquest of Mexico, William H. Prescott, Random House, Modern Library, 1939.

History of the Discovery and Conquest of Mexico, Bernal Díaz de Castillo, Doubleday Dolphin Books, 1960.

History of Mexico, Henry B. Parkes, Little, Brown, 1950.

Life in Mexico, Madame Calderón de la Barca, Doubleday Dolphin Books, 1960.

Many Mexicos, Lesley Byrd Simpson, University of California Press, 1959.

Mexico: A Land of Volcanoes, Joseph H. L. Schlarman, Bruce Publishing House, 1951.

Mexico, the Struggle for Peace and Bread, Frank Tannenbaum, Alfred A. Knopf, 1950.

Religion of Ancient Mexico, The, Lewis Spence, C. A. Watts & Co. (London), 1945.

Author's note: The figures in the last chapter pertaining to recent events in Mexico have been taken from *Excelsior*, Mexico's morning newspaper, from *Comercio Exterior*, the monthly bulletin of Mexico's Banco Nacional de Comercio Exterior, S.A. and from "Facts On File" 1959–1969.

INDEX